W9-AVK-275

ON AND OFF
THE AIR

ALSO BY DAVID SCHOENBRUN

America Inside Out
As France Goes
The Three Lives of Charles de Gaulle
Vietnam: How We Got In, How to Get Out
The New Israelis
Triumph in Paris
Soldiers of the Night: The Story of the French Resistance

ON AND OFF THE AIR

An Informal History of CBS News

DAVID SCHOENBRUN

E. P. DUTTON   NEW YORK

Copyright © 1989 by Dorothy Schoenbrun

All rights reserved. Printed in the U.S.A.

No part of this publication may be reproduced or transmitted
in any form or by any means, electronic or mechanical, including
photocopy, recording, or any information storage and retrieval
system now known or to be invented, without permission in writing
from the publisher, except by a reviewer who wishes to quote
brief passages in connection with a review written for inclusion
in a magazine, newspaper, or broadcast.

Published in the United States by E. P. Dutton,
a division of NAL Penguin Inc.,
2 Park Avenue, New York, N.Y. 10016.

Published simultaneously in Canada
by Fitzhenry and Whiteside, Limited, Toronto.

Library of Congress Cataloging-in-Publication Data
Schoenbrun, David.
On and off the air.
1. CBS News—History.   2. Television broadcasting
of news—Political aspects—United States—History.
3. Television broadcasting of news—Social aspects—
United States—History.   4. Journalistic ethics—
United States.   5. Journalists—United States—Biography.
I. Title.
PN4888.T4S36   1989   384.55'4'0973   88-33387
ISBN: 0-525-24765-3

Designed by Margo D. Barooshian

1   3   5   7   9   10   8   6   4   2
First Edition

CONTENTS

FOREWORD

On May 23, 1988, our family and friends suffered a terrible loss in the death of David Schoenbrun. We are deeply grateful for the many, many letters we have received, not only from friends but from the public at large. These letters attest to the great esteem he evoked and to the unique impact he had on audiences here and abroad.

He was by his own definition a "communicator," whether as lecturer, author, teacher, or broadcaster. David Schoenbrun was, above all, a true pioneer in the history of television news. He was part of a small group of men who explored a new vehicle for information, without precedent, and as different from radio and printed journalism as the cinema is from still photography.

They were mainly scholars and innovators in the new media. Their credentials displayed a varied expertise in history, languages, and economics, and no matter what their particular specialty they all shared an acute awareness of the awesome responsibility of this new invention.

Most contemporary broadcasters acknowledge that those early explorers in the new medium created a style and quality that set the standard for TV news that has never been surpassed.

At the time of David's death this manuscript was virtually complete. The only changes that were made are those intended to give an incomplete manuscript its final form. I am especially grateful to editor Paul De Angelis for his guidance and skillful editing which made this possible.

I also wish to thank Scott Meredith, who, for more than a decade, has been a constant source of encouragement to David.

In the course of his long career in broadcasting, which spanned over forty years, David often reflected on how TV news might better live up to its potential. He regretted the lack of time allotted to news analysis, the tendency to picture more and explain less, and finally the treatment of this medium as a craft rather than a profession.

He summed it all up one day in the following thought: "If the medical profession subscribes to a Hippocratic oath as a standard for treating our bodies, might not it be meaningful for journalists to adhere to a similar code of ethics in the molding of public opinion?"

DOROTHY SCHOENBRUN

ON AND OFF THE AIR

1

THE CRISIS
OF TV NEWS

It developed slowly, so gradually that few noticed. Those of us who did see the danger were dismissed as pessimists, doomsayers, or dissidents who had bucked management and were seeking revenge. The entire television world, the networks, the local stations, the advertisers, were like people living on the banks of a river and not noticing that the water was rising to flood levels. A few days of heavy rains and those waters would jump the banks and inundate the town.

The first danger signs were sighted in 1985 when the major shareholders of ABC, veteran broadcasting men who understood broadcasting and had built a national net, sold the company to a non-network conglomerate, Capital Cities Communications, Inc., a holding company of financial manipulators who know little and care less about broadcasting as an art form or a public trust. Their concern is not the public's need and right to know. For them networks, including news, are just a business, and the first law of business is the bottom line: profit.

ABC was not losing money. Conceivably, however, it was not making as much as it might if budgets were more tightly controlled, and waste and extravagance eliminated or at least sharply reduced. There was certainly some waste and a good deal of extravagance in networks that had grown into national dominance, earning hundreds of millions and rewarding their "stars" accordingly. After all, it was an American business principle to pay performers in proportion to the moneys they brought in. That is why some men who dribble and shoot a round ball into a hoop are paid $2 million to $4 million a year.

Television, like sports and movies, developed its own highly paid men and women. The anchormen of the three networks earn from $1 million to more than $2 million a year. The same scale of $1 to $2 million a year is paid to every reporter on "60 Minutes," with $2 million going to its creator, Don Hewitt. Why not? These men and women bring tens of millions of dollars of income to the network in advertising on the programs to which their talents have attracted national audiences.

The new financial operators of ABC were realistic businessmen; they understood the principle of appropriate rewards to those who bring vast income to the company. They did not resent, nor would they alter, the star system. But, if big money was paid to stars, expenses had to be correspondingly reduced in services that did not directly bring in money. The anchors, of course, had to be supported by producers, camera and sound technicians, writers, and the complex infrastructure that produced the pictures, words, and information the anchormen and their fellow reporters need. But a tight rein had to be kept, business controllers felt, on the numbers of bodies and the wages paid to the supporting cast of the news operation.

Capital Cities' efficiency experts and financial comptrollers wasted no time cutting expenses to maximize profits. They dismissed some fifteen hundred employees, including two hundred technicians, writers, and reporters of ABC News. The News Division was used to growing, not shrinking; the firing of two hundred news personnel shook television news out of its complacency and forced it to look at the threat to its operations.

* * *

Then, in October 1987, a seventeen-week-long strike ended at NBC, with a complete victory by management over the striking workers, who got none of their modest demands and crawled back to work. NBC management then rubbed it in, in two ways. First, NBC announced that about two hundred of the striking workers would be instantly fired. Then, to add insult to injury, some five thousand loyal employees, who had filled in for strikers for the seventeen weeks, were each given a bonus of ten shares of General Electric stock.

By 1987, NBC was no longer simply NBC, just as ABC was no longer simply ABC. Both had been taken over by conglomerates operating on rules and principles never before applied to broadcasting networks. NBC had become a very small cog in the giant machinery of one of the world's biggest corporations, General Electric. NBC News had already suffered from the amputation of its radio network, which had been sold off to European investors. "NBC Nightly News with Tom Brokaw," which was riding high as number one in the country, could not escape the corporate ax. It lost two tape producers, key technicians who edit raw tape footage fed to New York by NBC news operations around the world. From four news writers and an editor/writer, the "Nightly News" staff was cut to two writers and an editor who was not permitted to write.

The cuts were a direct consequence of the strike, even more than of the corporate desire to reduce expenses and increase profits. During the full seventeen weeks of the strike, the network was able to put on the air all its programs, including all its newscasts, with one-third of its employees out on strike. Everyone who was not on strike, from secretaries to vice-presidents, was asked to pitch in and learn to do the jobs of the strikers.

A few years earlier that would not have been possible, for cameras and sound equipment were so complex and bulky that only highly trained specialists could use them properly. High technology had simplified and miniaturized much of the equipment, making it possible for unskilled but intelligent personnel to learn quickly how to use the machinery. For more than three months NBC put all its programs on the air without the public noticing anything wrong, without knowing that one-third of the total personnel was out on strike. Management could not fail to read the obvious lessons of the strike: NBC, with eight thousand employees, was overstaffed.

Since being taken over by General Electric in 1986, NBC management had been going through the personnel lists with sharp scalpels. After the strike ended in October 1987, management announced that seven hundred would be dismissed. That was not, by any means, to be the end of the pruning. A corporate spokesman for General Electric asserted that GE policy calls for "streamlining, a corporate task that is never finished." The executive vice-president of NBC, M. S. Rukeyser, Jr., said: "Downsizing is never really done."

But the network hardest hit, the one that generated the most unfavorable public comment and internal dissidence was, not surprisingly, CBS. Just about the time that Capital Cities was taking over ABC, trouble was brewing at "Black Rock," CBS executive headquarters on the Avenue of the Americas in New York City. At first, firings were small; then they grew over a year and a half to the same total of the dismissals at ABC. Fifteen hundred CBS employees were fired, including 215 from the News Division.

Almost from the start of network news in the thirties, CBS News had been the leader, the Cadillac of news. At one point in the forties and fifties, our Murrow team, the "Murrow boys," were not only number one, we were in a class by ourselves. It was CBS News, then the others. NBC producers would come to Paris, drop their things off at their Champs-Elysées office, then walk across the broad boulevard to my CBS terrace office and consult me about their problems. One of them told me he had been having a tough time getting an interview with French Foreign Minister Couve de Murville, and asked if I would be a good fellow and arrange it for him at once!

We all swelled with pride when people began calling us "*The New York Times* of the air." In those days television people were insecure about the validity of our new medium and had an inferiority complex about the experienced, professional newspapers. To be compared with the *Times* was the ultimate accolade. I still recall the day when I broke an important story about General de Gaulle, fiercely nationalistic, always worried about French independence, deciding to pull the French fleet out of the high command of the North Atlantic Treaty Organization (NATO). My New York editor, a bright and able man, Bob Skedgell, first congratulated me and then asked: "David, I haven't seen this story in the *Times* or on the wires. Are you sure you're right?" As television proved itself over the years, editors became less nervous, although they still lean heavily on *The New York Times* and *The Washington Post* even today.

CBS News was preeminent for so many of the fifty years of network broadcasting on radio and then television that, despite occasional successes of its rivals, it kept its crown as the finest news organization, mainly because of two very different but equally effective leaders. For four decades and more, Edward R. Murrow and Walter Cronkite carried the CBS News banner high. Young reporters coming up in local stations all dreamed one day of getting called by CBS News. If they were talented enough and lucky enough to get calls from more than one network, it was CBS News they chose to join, sometimes at lower salaries. That is one of the most valuable dividends of being preeminent—you can recruit the best. When crisis hit CBS News in 1986, as it had already hit NBC and ABC, it somehow seemed far worse.

It began with General William C. Westmoreland's libel suit against CBS News. CBS won the suit but was severely hurt in the process. Its procedures were sharply criticized, its credibility weakened. Then, in September 1986, Laurence Tisch, financial wizard at the head of Loew's theaters and hotels, a non-broadcast capital manipulator, bought his way into the leadership of CBS as its chief executive officer (CEO). Tisch was wise enough to bring back from retirement the founding father of CBS, William S. Paley, the creative genius of broadcasting for more than a half-century. But Paley, in his mid-eighties, was no longer the vigorous, dominant chairman of the board he once had been. And Paley was no longer the principal individual stockholder. His shares had fallen to about 8 percent, whereas Tisch has accumulated about 25 percent.

No one had any doubt who the boss was at CBS. It was not veteran broadcast man Bill Paley, it was financier and non-broadcast man Larry Tisch. CBS had gone the way of ABC and NBC, falling into the hands of men who had never run a broadcast network.

Tisch came in with a good deal of welcome and goodwill. Paley and others on the board had turned to him to save them from a feared predator, Ted Turner, founder of the Cable News Network (CNN). Turner was an ambitious, driven man who had accomplished something like a miracle in setting up a fourth network, though he suffered millions of dollars in losses monthly. His pockets seemed to be bottomless and he courageously was willing to spend hundreds of millions to make his CNN a success. He was admired for his drive and spirit, although feared for what some alleged were his born-again, deeply conservative politics and general air of recklessness.

Leading CBS newsmen, Don Hewitt, producer of "60 Minutes," and Mike Wallace, star reporter of that program, were personal friends of Larry Tisch. They went up and down the windowless, almost prisonlike corridors of CBS News on West 57th Street, singing his praises and predicting great progress under his new leadership. All went well at first. Tisch did start to shake up top news executives, but he appointed a professional CBS newsman, well regarded by the staff, to be president of CBS News: Howard Stringer. Stringer replaced the highly controversial Van Gordon Sauter. All seemed well in the last months of 1986. Then Tisch took over the reins officially at the start of 1987. The crisis began to bubble up and finally burst in March.

It started slowly at first with a strike by CBS and ABC members of the Writers Guild over job security. Television journalists are highly paid, well above their colleagues of the print media. They rarely strike for wages. But most of them work without a contract and are subject to being dismissed at any sudden surge of an austerity wave. Austerity waves were rolling over the entire network world. CBS had fired a few dozen in 1985 and 1986, while ABC and NBC were firing hundreds. The writers were understandably jittery.

Since the board elected him CEO in September 1986, Larry Tisch had been quietly calling in his comptrollers to get their view on CBS staffing. As an efficient executive, Tisch had been appalled to discover that in the last decade before his advent the CBS News annual budget had skyrocketed from $89 million to $300 million. There were some valid reasons for this: the high cost of technology and new expensive equipment; the cost of transmission time on the satellites in the sky, about $3,000 a minute; the emergence of what Marshall McLuhan had predicted would be a "global village" in the television era, with correspondents and technicians everywhere, from Seattle to Warsaw to Bangkok and all places in between and adjacent. No doubt, however, there was fat and waste in a $300 million budget.

Tisch decided that the American public could be well served without bureaus in Seattle, Warsaw, or Bangkok. Other offices could cover them. Above all, Tisch was not going to live with a $300 million news budget. He believed, as many corporate executives did, and often enough with good reason, that you could cut any budget by 10 percent and still get the same or an adequate performance. So he ordered his newly appointed CBS News president, Howard Stringer, to cut his budget by $50 million. Stringer talked him down to $30 million. Translated into human terms this meant Stringer would have to fire about 215 people. This came on top of 200 other cuts in the previous eight months. "60 Minutes" funnyman Andy Rooney was saddened and angered. "It's a disaster," he said. "Tisch put his money in but he doesn't own CBS. Those of us who do the broadcasts, we made CBS. We own CBS. Tisch only owns stocks."

One of the men dismissed was a highly regarded, well-liked, twenty-year veteran of CBS News, Ike Pappas. There was an uproar over his dismissal. Law specialist Fred Graham, a courtly southern gentleman whose Supreme Court reporting was greatly admired, was dismissed, along with a popular, highly competent economic reporter, Jane Bryant Quinn, as well as seventeen out of seventy staffers of the archives. The archives are essential to any thoughtful, well-documented background report. The research files, what newspapers call "the morgue," are so vital that it has long been accepted that "if you kill the morgue, you kill the paper." Many charged that Tisch's cuts, and the way they were done, had killed CBS.

I felt very much the same way when, running down the list of those dismissed, my eye spotted the name Alex Brauer. There was a pang in my heart as I thought of Alex. I had hired him for my Paris bureau near the end of the sixties. My chief cameraman, Georges Markman, sometimes needed temporary help when hell was breaking out all over Paris, which happened often enough. Alex worked well and was finally taken on as a staff cameraman. He gave everything to his job: Alex risked his life on Atlas Mountain peaks in Algeria, sweated in the dunes of the Sahara in Morocco, and was shot at by warring forces. He stood up in riots, stones flying around his head, holding his camera steady to get the best pictures for CBS. We reporters and our camera-sound teams did not punch time clocks or work thirty-five-or forty-hour weeks as the "efficiency experts" back at headquarters in New York did. We felt, as Andy Rooney did, that *we* were CBS News, that *we* had made CBS News.

It was Walter Cronkite who underlined his dislike for the way the firings were done. He denied reports of a shouting match with Tisch, and endorsed the budget cuts. But he told reporters that he deplored the tactics employed. They were, indeed, shabby, and they seriously injured Laurence Tisch's credibility. When the cuts were announced, Tisch asserted that he had not ordered them, but that CBS News President Howard Stringer had come to him and told him that he wanted to cut the budget by $30 million. "All I did was approve the cuts and dismissals, on his recommendation," said Tisch.

In fact, this is what happened: Tisch had toured the CBS News bureaus in Europe and Washington and had come to the correct conclusion that the network had a loose and wasteful operation that needed tightening. After study, he called in Stringer and told him that he had to cut back $50 million of the vast budget. Stringer was shocked, for, when he had been appointed president of CBS News, Tisch had promised him that there would be no more cuts through 1987. Stringer had passed this promise on to the staff and now he was being made to break that promise.

Tisch told Stringer that he would have a report on cuts and new organization made by an outside firm of efficiency experts, Coopers and Lybrand. Stringer protested vigorously, insisting that CBS News could handle its own affairs and he wanted no outsider to do it. Tisch finally agreed and told Stringer to go ahead. Stringer brought in what he told Tisch were the maximum cuts possible, $30 million, not $50 million. Stringer drew up the list of names to be dismissed after Dan Rather refused sharply to have anything to do with it. Technically, then, Stringer did draw up the dismissals list and did propose the cuts to Tisch, as Tisch had stated. What Tisch did *not* state is that Stringer did this only on the demand of Tisch that he do so.

Morale plunged at CBS News. The "Slaughter on 57th Street" became a major news story throughout the nation. The former president of CBS News, Bill Leonard, asserted in the conclusion of his book about CBS, *In the Storm of the Eye*, that "top management appeared to have come to regard CBS news as almost more trouble than it was worth, and that the management of the news division itself began to think of it as just a step up the corporate ladder."

The stars of CBS News were dismayed and wanted to do all they could to stop the cuts and restore morale. Dan Rather, Ed Bradley, and Diane Sawyer, who earn $1 million to more than $2 million a year, volunteered to cut back their own salaries to restore jobs. Tisch rejected their offer, saying that CBS needed permanent reorganization, not stopgap give-backs.

All television was in turmoil and conflict. Over at ABC, President Roone Arledge suspended his most talented senior producer, Av Westin, who ran the highly regarded "20/20" show. Av is one of the very best, most experienced producers in television. He had achieved fame over the years at CBS. I knew Av well, in fact worked with him and helped him as a youngster on his very first assignment in Paris to produce an hour documentary, "The Genesis of an Easter Bonnet." Everyone loved and admired Av, a first-rate man.

The man who suspended him is also a phenomenon. Roone Arledge first achieved prestige as the man who made ABC Sports acclaimed around the world. As director of Sports, Arledge doubled the time, tripled the income of his division. ABC was the innovator of new ways to cover sports events. It triumphed at the Olympics. Its chief reporter and commentator of its extraordinary "Wide World of Sports," Jim McKay, was known and admired everywhere. Sports had truly become a global village under the masterly direction of Roone Arledge. But, when ABC named Arledge as president of ABC News, there were dire predictions that Arledge would impose on the news a corny sports hokum.

The predictions were far off base. Arledge proved himself to be a devoted, responsible director of news. He brought in no hokum, no glitz, none of the half-time hijinks on the football field. ABC News forged ahead under his leadership. It was distressing that an Arledge and a Westin, two of the best in their fields, should have a falling out.

Westin had angered Arledge by sending a memo to top executives complaining about the way the budget crisis was being handled. Westin asserted that twenty years ago he had produced better programs for less money than programs being produced today. Av felt budgets had become bloated, producers pampered and wasteful, but that executives were slashing indiscriminately, not restructuring the system logically. Roone Arledge, as president of ABC News, took this as an attack on him and a Westin bid for his job. Personally, I find this hard to believe. I have known Av Westin for a quarter of a century and he has never been a back-stabber, never tried to walk up the ladder on someone else's shoulders.

The clash between Arledge and Westin was symptomatic of the conflicts and chaos in which television news was writhing. Everyone seemed to be snarling at everyone else, mainly against management, but fights also broke out inside family circles, including the most successful of all CBS News programs, "60 Minutes." One of the men who helped the show win its big audiences with his witty end-piece essays, Andy Rooney, was infuriated by the cuts and the way the company, he felt, was out to crush the writers' union. He wrote critical pieces denouncing CBS management in his syndicated newspaper column. Don Hewitt, producer of "60 Minutes," took offense at Rooney going public about his own company. When queried about Rooney's columns, Hewitt snapped, "Andy cries for the strikers but walks through the picket line and uses the CBS office to type up his newspaper columns and pick up his weekly check." Rooney, apprised of Hewitt's acid comment, snapped, "Don is mean."

The Hewitt-Rooney clash, the Walter Cronkite statements, were nothing compared to the lightning bolt cast by the leader of CBS News, the Captain of the Fleet, anchorman Dan Rather. The anchorman carries the network banner. The network's standing, prestige, and income depend on the success of the flagship show, the "Evening News." Successful beyond compare, as "60 Minutes" is, it is not the keystone of CBS News. CBS News advances or falls back on the strength or weakness of the "Evening News with Dan Rather." When Rather blasted away at management on the op-ed page of *The New York Times*, it was indeed bad news at Black Rock.

Dan Rather went right on the attack. "Let's get one thing straight. CBS Inc. is not a chronically weak company fighting to survive. . . . CBS Inc. is a profitable, valuable Fortune 500 corporation, whose stock is setting new records. But 215 people lost their jobs so that the stockholders would have even more money in their pockets. More profits. That's what business is about."

Rather admitted that "news is business." But, he asserted, it is "something more. It is a light on the horizon." For Dan Rather, news is a "beacon that helps the citizens of a democracy find their way. News is an essential component of a free society." "News," wrote Rather, "is a public trust." So, asked Rather, "Are we a business or a public trust? The answer is both. But, which comes first?"

Everyone at CBS News is struggling with those questions, Rather asserted. Rather agreed that costs must be cut and the operation made more efficient. What he could not accept, however, "is the notion that the bottom line counts more than our responsibility to the public." Then Dan Rather directly challenged CBS management. "We are determined that our new corporate management not lead us into a tragic transformation from Murrow to mediocrity. . . . I have said before that I have no intention of participating in the demise of CBS. But do the owners and officers of the new CBS see news as a trust . . . or only as a business venture?"

Only a man deeply devoted, passionately in love with an ideal, would risk as much as Rather was risking in that searing assault on CBS management. Rather had been awarded a ten-year, $2.5 million annual contract to stay with CBS and turn down a fabulous offer from Roone Arledge that would have made Rather a kind of czar of ABC News. When he warned that he would not participate "in the demise of CBS," he was either threatening to resign or daring management to fire him. Many of us have learned how dangerous that is. Management is prepared to lose its greatest stars, its biggest money-makers, rather than allow the "talent" side to dictate to or harass the corporate bosses. The greatest of all television newsmen, Edward R. Murrow, was driven out of CBS when he trod too heavily and too often on the toes of the then boss, Bill Paley. Howard K. Smith, Fred Friendly, and I were among those who bucked management and ended up leaving the company we loved and to which we had given so much of our lives. Dan Rather is not exempt from the rule that the bottom line is top dog. This fact made his column in the *Times* all the more courageous, proof of his devotion to the highest standards of journalism.

* * *

These public battles in the big networks, combined with technological and sociological changes, have led some doomsayers to predict the future collapse of the networks. I have heard so-called experts in the field or in academia predict that the traditional networks will have disappeared early in the coming century; that networks would become syndicators of programs rather than network broadcasters; that the Rather, Brokaw, Jennings evening news will fade away or become package outfits as they are overtaken by the new cable companies and communications companies.

Veteran newsmen who have gloomily watched the decline of network news accelerate in the mid-eighties have concluded that network news is dying, that, within a decade or so, it will have virtually disappeared. They point to the loss of audience from 1984 through 1988, to the mushrooming of stronger local stations, to news syndicates and communications services, to new networks, to the revolution of high technology, to all kinds of dishes and disks, to video cassettes, to transponders priced even for a single local station, to the loss of advertising revenue, to public saturation with the news. They have more reasons than Nostradamus on his worst day for predicting doom and gloom.

It is certainly true that network news is being challenged as never before in the four decades since regular TV programming began. And there are more difficulties than even the doomsayers have evoked. Today, abroad and at home, newsmen are harassed, pilloried, kidnapped, blindsided by a gaggle of editors, producers, comptrollers, executives who know little and care less about news, and, finally, overwhelmed by floods of government propaganda. Every Cabinet department has dozens of spokesmen and officials ready to call a news conference at the drop or rise of an economic indicator. Congress will hold two dozen committee meetings a day, spouting millions of words, signifying little.

News decisions are being made more and more by executives in ivory towers and not by working newsmen. There has been no decline in the talent of newscasters. Men and women of the highest intelligence and competence are reporting on network news. But power has gradually passed, over the years, away from the correspondents and newscasters into the hands of producers, accountants, lawyers, and management, people who are bottom-liners, budgeteers, legalists, not news people. They are not committed to news as we once were in the great days of the Murrow era. The Murrow years remain the standard of excellence. That is why Rather, in his *New York Times* column, deplored the fall from "Murrow to mediocrity."

In more than forty years as a radio-television reporter and news analyst, I have watched TV news grow from its fumbling, crawling infancy into the most mighty public affairs force in our nation. I have seen it in its golden era, as a member of the Murrow team. After Murrow, I was the news analyst in Washington on the "Evening News with Walter Cronkite." The birth and growth of TV news is one of the most fascinating and important stories of modern history. It was my privilege to live it from the very start.

I did one of the earliest television news broadcasts in history back in 1947, when regular programming had just begun. I feel that I am a survivor of the beginnings of an extraordinary instrument of public service and public trust. This is a rare privilege that carries with it the obligation to examine what has happened to that service and trust, how it happened, and why it happened.

A great many books have addressed themselves to an examination of network news in the past few years. Among the most recent, in the spring of 1988, were two that received intense media scrutiny and comment. One was written by a former president of CBS News, Ed Joyce. It is mainly an apologia for his stewardship and for that of his mentor who named him president, Van Gordon Sauter, when Sauter moved up from the News Division into the higher levels of corporate management. The other was written by the television reporter of *The New York Times*, Peter Boyer, who had himself worked for CBS News as a media critic on the ill-fated "CBS Morning News." Boyer's book is by far the best of the lot. He called it *Who Killed CBS?* and then named the assassin: Van Gordon Sauter. He documents his charges of the decline of CBS News under Sauter and, up to a point, proves his case.

The trouble with all those books and with Boyer's otherwise excellent report is that the authors are like doctors examining a corpse and determining just what disease killed it. They concentrate on what the corpse looks like now, they find the surface symptoms of the diseases that killed it. But they do not know or do not try to discover just how the victim came to contract the disease and what, in its background, was responsible for the decline and death. It certainly gets attention, but it is more than premature. CBS News is in decline but it is far from dead.

None of these reports tells us just how Van Gordon Sauter got to be such a power in CBS News. Who chose him and why? What were the prevailing conditions that led to management changes and power shifts that brought about the crises of TV today? How can you judge the crises of today other than by measuring them against the TV news of yesterday?

Only by exploring the past can we find the seeds of destruction and who planted them and under what conditions. Van Gordon Sauter did not spring full-blown into power in CBS. A great many things happened along the way that led to today's decline. I lived through much of the life of CBS News and saw it weaken. I first went to work for CBS only twelve years after the network had been created in 1928. I watched what happened, why, and who did what to whom.

I invite the reader to join me now in an exploration of this drama—the rise and fall of CBS News, following the actions of the heroes and villains of the plot. In addition to discovering just who has been digging the grave of the network, this exploration has its own rewards. It is a thrilling, colorful story of giants, power, money, fame, and tremendous influence in our society. The story begins more than fifty years ago in another age, in a different America, an America of daring, imaginative entrepreneurs, an America of individual initiative and risk, not manipulative Wall Street wheeler-dealers and corporate managers. It is essentially the drama of changing times in America and in the world, the essence of high drama.

2

HOW IT ALL BEGAN

I first went to work for CBS News in 1941. CBS, owned and operated by majority stockholder, William S. Paley, had gone on the air September 19, 1928, so it was still only thirteen years old when I joined it in a most unusual capacity.

It had come as a shock when the German legions of tanks and Stuka dive-bombers had cut through French ranks and defeated, in a few months, what we had all been told by our "experts" was the finest army in the world.

We Americans were largely cut off from news of Europe. The young networks did not yet have large staffs of foreign correspondents. The editors were hungry for any information they could get. Two of the most brilliant men who truly founded CBS News, Ed Klauber, Bill Paley's right-hand man and adviser, and Paul White, the first and highly innovative director of CBS News, came up with an exciting new idea: the CBS Monitoring Station. It would tune in on all broadcasts from Europe, from Berlin, Paris, Madrid, and so forth. A great deal could be learned or analyzed from the way Hitler's propagandists manipulated the news.

CBS News advertised for men and women who could speak and understand the major tongues of Europe and who could type rapidly enough to get down the essence of a news broadcast, heard, for example, in German, and type it up simultaneously in English. It was a very difficult task. You really had to be a master of the foreign language and a speed typist to do the job.

A German cousin, who had fled Hitler and who had taken his doctorate in history at London University, qualified on all counts. Fortunately, so did I. I was at the time a New York City high school teacher of French and Spanish. My cousin, Reinhold ("Henry") Cassirer, and I rushed over to CBS headquarters, at 485 Madison Avenue, were interviewed, tested, and hired on the spot. That was the beginning of the greatest period of my life working for that still infant news organization. I would watch it grow, and grow with it as CBS became one of the most powerful voices in our nation.

There was no CBS, no radio at all when Bill Paley was born in Chicago in 1901, son of Sam and Goldie Paley, owners of the Congress Cigar Company. In his teens, Bill worked for his father and gained some business experience before entering one of America's most famed business schools, the Wharton School of the University of Pennsylvania. Bill was graduated from Wharton in 1922 and entered his father's business, which was expanding rapidly from six to twelve factories. Bill was being groomed to take over from his father.

For a young man, the twenties were an exciting period of American life, particularly of industrial expansion. The automobile industry was booming, so were aviation and long-distance telephoning, all modern miracles promising a splendid future for all who would dive into the mainstream and swim along with the currents. Bill Paley, much as he loved and respected his father, Sam, was not thrilled by making cigars. There were no modern miracles there. In 1925, the young vice-president of Congress Cigars, Bill Paley, invested the firm's money in an advertising program over radio station WCAU in Philadelphia. He called it the "La Palina Hour," after their biggest-selling cigar brand. And he became hooked on radio as the new millennium.

Many years later, at dinner in Paris, Paley told me that he could take no credit for a grand vision of what network radio and still uninvented television would become when he entered the field. "To tell the truth," said Paley, "my only vision was the thought that this was the most powerful, most effective means of launching a national product, the greatest advertising medium ever devised. That was what attracted me at first. That and the thought that radio was dealing with famous singers, actors, actresses, political leaders, a heady world of celebrities. It was only many years later, during the war, that I sensed the enormous potential, the power of radio to inform the public and, indeed, to shape its thoughts."

Another pioneer genius of those days was David Sarnoff, a Russian immigrant who had worked his way up the ladder to the presidency of RCA, a giant communications firm, and then created NBC, a radio network. He had a partner in NBC, Arthur Judson, a concert master and artists' agency chief. Judson quarreled with him and broke away to form his own small network, the United Independent Broadcasting Company (UIB). He signed up Leon and Ike Levy, owners of WCAU, as an affiliate. He also bought up a small record company, the Columbia Phonograph Company, just as Sarnoff, too, had bought up the Victor Talking Machine as a logical adjunct to broadcasting. UIB gradually dropped its own name and began operating as the Columbia Phonograph Broadcasting System. It made its debut under that long and awkward name in September 1927.

A year later, as they were going broke, they changed the network's name, dropping the word *Phonograph* and calling it the Columbia Broadcasting System. In trouble financially, they turned to their biggest, richest advertiser, the Congress Cigar Company, to bail them out. Sam Paley did not mind using radio to sell his cigars, but he had no desire to own and operate a newfangled network, a world he and his generation could not understand. But his son Bill was ready, willing, and eager.

For years Bill Paley had been waiting for just such an opportunity. With his father's blessing, Bill sold out his shares of cigar company stock and bought up the Columbia Broadcasting System, which went on the air under his sole leadership on September 19, 1928. The deal cost him only $145,000 in cash plus spaced-out notes for another $500,000. Bill was now head of a national network before

his thirtieth birthday. His father had not only given him his blessing, but Sam Paley and Jake Levy had invested $100,000 in Bill's
company to help him meet his first notes.

At that early period in the development of radio, it had not yet
proved itself to be the fabulous advertising medium that it would
become. Few programs were sponsored directly like the "La Palina
Hour." Affiliates were not keen to buy programs without a sponsor
to defray the costs and provide a profit. So young Bill Paley, an
innovator from the start, hit upon the idea of producing his own
shows and giving them to his affiliates without charge, in exchange
for free advertising time on the air. Thanks to that plan, he soon had
ad time right across the nation that he could sell to sponsors who
would not buy an entire expensive program, but would buy five to
ten minutes on a show in selected markets.

CBS grew rapidly and Paley came to the attention of two of the
most powerful men in Hollywood, William Fox, head of Fox Films
and Fox Movietone, and Adolph Zukor, head of Paramount Pictures.
They were mighty moguls of Hollywood, and movies were the
fastest-growing industry in the nation. Both had their eyes on this
new communications system, network radio. Both saw it as a useful
adjunct to movies and newsreels. Both suspected one day it might
even become a dangerous rival. It would be wise, they thought,
quite correctly, to try to merge with it now before it got too big to
handle.

Young Bill Paley was excited and flattered when he received the
call from William Fox to come and discuss a major investment in
CBS. But Paley was shocked and resentful when Fox offered to buy a
half-interest for the same price per share that Paley had originally
put into the company. Fox waved aside what Paley had done to
improve the stock's value, overlooking the rising profits being
earned by CBS. Paley did not even bother to argue the point with
Fox. He was so let down, having been in such anticipation over the
invitation, that he simply stood up, thanked Fox for his interest,
turned and walked out of the office, leaving Fox staring at his back.
People did not do that to William Fox. William Paley did.

His meeting with Adolph Zukor went much better. Zukor, an
immigrant Jew from Eastern Europe like Paley's father, Sam, was a
shrewd and sensitive man. He knew just how much pride moved
Paley and how quick he would be to take umbrage at even the hint of

a slight, something Fox did not understand. Zukor began by prais-ing Paley for his foresight and acumen in sensing the great future for radio. He said that he was growing older, needed an heir to run Paramount when he retired. He offered not only to buy into CBS but to buy Paley himself as his executive vice-president.

Paley was thrilled, deeply flattered, but never lost control of his common sense. He thanked Zukor with great warmth but told him that no man was big enough, strong enough, nor were there enough hours in the day to be operating head of both a major Hollywood studio and a national radio network. He counterproposed an invest-ment by Zukor in CBS.

Zukor agreed and offered to buy 50 percent of CBS for $4 million. This was a most generous offer for a network in which the Paley family and the Levys had put in only $145,000 in cash and $500,000 in notes. But Paley, gritting his teeth, took the gamble of his young life as an industrial tycoon. He said he wanted $5 million in cash.

Zukor realized that he had been right to try to hire this tough, smart young businessman. So he began negotiating in earnest, coming up by quarter-million increments to his "final" offer, "take it or leave it," of $4.5 million. To his astonishment, Paley told him that if he really meant it was a final offer then there was nothing left but to shake hands and exchange regrets that the deal could not be made. The price was $5 million. Paley refrained from adding "take it or leave it." He just stood up, with a sad smile, and offered his hand to Zukor.

Zukor glared at him and said: "Young man, don't you know what a business negotiation is like? You offer a price, I come up a little from my offer, you come down a little from yours and we meet somewhere at a reasonable compromise." Paley grinned and said, "That's not what they taught me at the Wharton School. They told me to put a fair value on my property and, if I did not need money urgently, to hold out for my price. I am happy to say I don't need money urgently and you have heard my true price evaluation."

Zukor threw up his hands in surrender, laughed, and said, "You've got the deal and I wish you'd change your mind and come to work for me. You'll take over Hollywood."

Zukor's offer was a tremendous temptation, but Paley, single-minded in his determination to build the greatest broadcasting company in the nation, could not be seduced. He had that capacity all through the dazzling years of seemingly limitless growth ahead, to take a decision and stick with it even against fearful odds. He succeeded most often, but not even Paley was Superman. For example, in the race with giant RCA to bring out the final color-compatible television system, CBS lost out to its great rival David Sarnoff. Sarnoff had more funds at his disposal and all the retail outlets selling RCA equipment of all kinds. If they wanted to continue to enjoy the profitable RCA franchise, they would, of course, buy RCA color sets.

This defeat for the young CBS manufacturing unit in the 1950s cost Paley and his company hundreds of millions of dollars before he finally admitted he could not compete with RCA in manufacturing. He had to lower his sights and compete with his rival broadcasting network, NBC. That job was quite big enough in itself, for NBC was highly successful.

I lived through that crisis, for Paley had asked me to present the CBS color system to French national TV and to Europe 1, the largest independent station in Europe. It was a quick education in industrial practices and one that convinced me I had been right to choose the career of a reporter rather than a businessman.

Paley had boasted in January 1929 that CBS was already the nation's largest radio network, with almost fifty stations signed on as affiliates. Technically he was correct, but only because NBC had divided itself into two networks, the "Red" and the "Blue." Each, by itself, was smaller than CBS. Together, owned by NBC, they made NBC the largest.

It was this boast of Paley's that had moved Zukor to try to sign him up or to buy into CBS. Their deal was consummated in July 1929. Paley had anticipated the agreement a few weeks before signing it and had committed himself to a new headquarters, six floors in the building at 52nd Street and Madison Avenue, 485 Madison. There CBS would grow and grow like a magic beanstalk, higher and higher, into a multibillion-dollar corporation in the next thirty-five years.

Bill Paley was a wizard in an age of superachievers: Henry Ford in autos; David Sarnoff in communications equipment; Louis B. Mayer, Adolph Zukor, and Samuel Goldwyn (né Goldfish) in Hollywood. When Wall Street digested the Paramount-CBS deal, it immediately readjusted its evaluation of the worth of CBS, boosting it up to $10 million. Bill had bought it for a half-million and it had been valued at a full million in 1928. In nine months, Paley had increased his company's value from $1 million to $10 million. Not even Ford, Mayer, or Goldwyn could top Paley's achievement. It even impressed his father, who was in the process of selling Congress Cigars for $30 million.

No one in those heady days of flappers, red-hot mamas, and an ever rising stock market had an idea what was in store for them. The party was over in the crash of October 1929. Hardly any business escaped the consequences of the reckless policies that had brought on the crash, just as they would never quite understand what happened to them on another Black October in 1987.

One of the businesses most severely hit was Hollywood, including Paramount Pictures. Zukor was caught where it hurt. A few months earlier he had agreed on an exchange of stock with CBS, when Paramount was valued at $65 a share. CBS could buy its stock back at current market prices, or Paramount would have to pay in cash the full $5 million of the purchase price. But Paramount stock had fallen to $6 in the crash. To sell back at $6 instead of $65 would be ruinous. But Zukor did not have the $5 million cash to meet his obligations. Paley, victorious, did not squeeze him, but he made him pay his way out. It ended up with CBS having regained 100 percent of its stock and a good lode of Paramount gold along with it.

A rich man, still in his twenties, Bill Paley was riding high. He told friends that he would not become a wage slave like his beloved father. He would retire, he said, at age thirty-five. "What's the good of making money if you have no time to enjoy it?" he would ask. Paley, very much a hedonist, was full of the joy of living. Tall, graceful, handsome, in excellent health, he had the appetite of a boa constrictor. Throughout his life, he was always looking for the newest, latest "in" restaurant. Whenever he came to Paris, I had a list ready for him.

Bill, despite his youthful illusions, ended up just like Sam. He did not retire at age thirty-five. He was still sitting in his seat as chairman of the board when he was eighty-five. And even at eighty-five, he was still a restaurant buff. Whoever might wish to see Bill Paley in New York had only to go to lunch at Mortimer's, a watering hole on Madison Avenue, where writers, producers, and show business people congregate.

Paley won't last forever, of course, for he is a mortal man, however much like Superman he may appear. When he is gone, he will leave a pair of big empty shoes that no one on the scene today can fill. It is not just that Bill Paley is talented, shrewd, with good instincts and excellent taste. Others can match that. He was the right man, at the right time, in the right place, at the birth of an industry. He could grow with it, make all the rules, control it with his wealth and prestige. That, plus his native talents and qualities, is what made him one of a kind. There will never again be the same mix of talent and circumstance that makes giants.

In the first days of the new network in 1929, CBS had no reporters, only announcers doing "rip-and-read" pieces from the Associated Press (AP) ticker. That was amateurish, indicating that radio had no capacity of its own. Paley would not tolerate such an image. Whatever his company did, it had to be the best. Paley understood immediately the potential of radio. Its essence was speed. It took many hours to write, edit, print, and distribute newspapers. CBS Radio could get the news out in a split second. Paley decided to get his own news department to exploit fully radio's potential.

The early CBS, even before Paley's total ownership, had already experimented with radio news. On election night, 1928, a sportscaster named Ted Husing sat in the newsroom of the *New York World*, a microphone on his desk. As results came in on the ticker, he read them to the network and its affiliated stations. Husing told the CBS audience that Herbert Hoover had been elected, hours before the newspapers could rush out their "extras."

NBC had the jump on Paley in entertainment but Paley, always striving to be first, decided CBS could and would be first in news. He knew that David Sarnoff was not particularly interested in news. Ironically, Sarnoff was not aware of Bill Paley as a competitor. He viewed him as a valuable client: the better CBS did, the more equipment it would buy from RCA. Sarnoff loved the rivalry between NBC and CBS. The more they fought, the harder they tried to beat each other, the more orders for sophisticated communications equipment poured into the maw of giant RCA. So the door was open for Paley to build his news department. He not only valued news for itself but he sensed that people who tuned in to CBS News were likely to stay on the same dial for entertainment. Paley saw that connection long before anyone else.

Paley chose a veteran newsman to build CBS News for the network. Ed Klauber had been night city editor of *The New York Times*. For Paley that was class. The *Times* was the Cadillac of newspapers, just as Paley wanted CBS News to be the finest in radio. When the day came that some critic called us "*The New York Times* of the Air,*"* Paley's dream had come true.

Klauber was disciplined in the best *Times* tradition, which he brought into CBS. He hated tabloids and the yellow press, which proliferated in those days. He laid down basic *New York Times* standards for CBS News: accuracy, honesty, objectivity, coolness, no dramatics, no show biz of any kind. Klauber was a crusty fellow, a curmudgeon and an editor who missed nothing. Even such outstanding men as William Shirer and Ed Murrow winced under his criticism. Ed once said that Klauber was "as mean as a hungry grizzly." Both Murrow and Shirer, not yet the stars they were to become, knew they were lucky to work under so tough and professional an editor.

In the late twenties, NBC's chief newscaster was a flamboyant, globe-trotting reporter/adventurer, Floyd Gibbons. NBC had none of Klauber's rules on objectivity and coolness. Gibbons would not know what those words meant. He was a hard-drinking swashbuckler, and his broadcasts ranged from vivid to lurid. The public liked it and NBC News jolted Paley by moving ahead.

Paley had to find a rival for Gibbons without breaking Klauber's rules. He did. He found Lowell Thomas, no swashbuckler but extremely colorful, a world traveler, a marvelous anecdotalist with a rich, booming voice. Thomas was then writing travel pieces and lecturing with a slide show to illustrate the lands he had visited.

Lowell Thomas, who would become one of the most admired, best-loved broadcasters, began his first CBS News program on September 29, 1930. It was a denunciation of Europe's two bully-boy dictators, Benito Mussolini and Adolf Hitler. He warned America that these men threatened democracy and world peace. As his reports and commentaries attracted bigger audiences, Lowell Thomas continued to extol American virtues, while describing faraway exotic lands he had visited. He attracted advertisers seeking a popular sponsorship. The perfect sponsor for Lowell Thomas turned up in the person of DeWitt Wallace, founder and chief editor of one of the world's most remarkable journalistic innovations: the *Reader's Digest*. Lowell Thomas became the Voice of the *Reader's Digest* on CBS.

Thomas began to build an audience. He was an instant success, for he had the quality that would later make Walter Cronkite the beloved of the nation: he was avuncular, optimistic, and patriotic, and his voice was strong and rich as fresh-brewed Colombian coffee. Lowell Thomas was so good, so admired, that NBC called him to lure him away from CBS. NBC had the one thing Lowell wanted more than money. CBS was paying him well enough, but NBC had the highest-rated program on radio, "Amos 'n' Andy," and it offered to link Lowell Thomas in schedule to that block-buster.

I remember, as a young man of nineteen, a story in the paper reporting that the commissioner of the City Water Department was puzzled by certain times in the early evening when the water pressure fell drastically, as people, it seemed, all turned their faucets on at once. Investigation revealed that it was not faucets they were turning on. They were waiting for the first commercial break in the "Amos 'n' Andy" show to run to the bathroom and then back fast enough not to miss a second of the program. For a while it was the fad among network executives, when considering a new series, to ask: "Is it a toilet-flusher?"

Lowell Thomas succumbed to the seduction by NBC and left CBS after about six months. He made polite farewells to Bill Paley, apologizing for running out on him. Paley did not take offense. He smiled ruefully and told Thomas that CBS would get its own toilet-flusher and then maybe Lowell would come back. He did, many years later, in 1947, when CBS News had established itself as the news leader. I remember the date well, for it was the time that Ed Murrow asked me to join CBS full time as its chief Paris correspondent. Everyone was talking about the return of Lowell Thomas. (No one was the least bit aware that David Schoenbrun had joined CBS, except my mother, father, and my Uncle Joe, who said to me: "You're staying in *Paris*? When are you coming home and getting a *real* job?")

Paley and Klauber were still trying to build a news staff. It was difficult to persuade veteran newsmen to wash the ink off their fingers and practice rounded tones. Few of them could master the microphone even when they were willing to come over. But Paley persisted. In 1935, he hired a young reporter, Fred Wile, to go to London to cover a disarmament conference. Wile was inexperienced in radio and the ways of the world. He was confused and exhausted keeping up with the time difference between London and New York. If New York wanted a report on the ten o'clock news, it would require Fred to be in the London studio at 4:00 A.M. Conversely, if Fred wanted to send through a report of a major event occurring at 8:00 A.M., London time, New York would be fast asleep at 2:00 A.M. Later, we learned how to cope with this and in the process broke one of Ed Klauber's many commandments, the one that says "Thou shalt never record thy report; thou shalt always broadcast live." We did continue to broadcast live as often as possible, but there were some times and some events that had to be carried on tape.

Wile had too much to do as the only CBS newsman in London. He received permission to take on another body and hired a well-regarded journalist, Caesar Saerchinger. Caesar, who had some of the imperious manner of his illustrious namesake, promptly had cards printed identifying himself as "European Director of the Columbia Broadcasting System," a somewhat grandiose title since he had no one to direct but himself.

This did not bother the man named for an emperor. Caesar took his newly printed calling cards to the British Broadcasting Company and persuaded executives there, in the biggest broadcasting system in the world, to make their studios and facilities available to CBS News. It was a coup that gave CBS News immediate standing in elitist and standoffish London, where pushy Americans were not appreciated.

Saerchinger kept trying to catch the ears of the public and his bosses in New York. He did it when he persuaded George Bernard Shaw, the famed Irish playwright and wit, to do a "talk" for CBS. Shaw had earlier filmed a newsreel in which he strutted around, wearing a tweed Norfolk jacket and knickers, sticking out his tongue at the camera and wiggling his fingers at the tip of his nose. He matched that for CBS by saying "Hello America! How are all you dear old boobs who have been telling one another that I have gone dotty on Russia?"

Loud complaints hit CBS from politicians and the general public, chastising the network for letting a foreigner insult Americans on our airwaves. Delighted to find the nation talking about them, CBS News executives promptly invited the Reverend Edmund Walsh of Georgetown to reply to Shaw. This kept the argument humming along nicely and all America talking about what they had heard on CBS. This was not exactly a great issue, but views on the Soviet Union were the first national and world issues with which a network had dealt. CBS News, still in its infancy, was finding its voice.

Meanwhile, the money was in entertainment. Very few agencies were willing to advertise on news programs. It was a time for stars, for Kate Smith, Bing Crosby, Frank Sinatra, Russ Columbo, George Burns and Gracie Allen, Jack Benny and Mary Livingston, the "Hit Parade," the big bands, Guy Lombardo, Tommy Dorsey, Glenn Miller. In the Depression, radio was the only free entertainment, and people gathered around their Atwater Kents, tapping their feet to rippling rhythms, laughing at "Amos 'n' Andy," forgetting their troubles. Big Money was pouring into CBS and Bill Paley, not content with banking it, was looking for ways to build an even bigger network in the future.

As early as 1931, Paley began experimenting with a new medium of communication that engineers called television. That fall, CBS presented its first television program, introducing New York's mayor, Jimmy Walker, Kate Smith singing "When the Moon Comes Over the Mountain," and George Gershwin at the piano playing his own composition, "Liza." Only a few hundred sets were in public hands. The broadcast went mainly to professionals who had built receivers. It was only an experiment and was soon abandoned. But it was a brief glimpse into a future of the most powerful means of information and entertainment ever devised.

In 1936, the advent of television was advanced when RCA built a transmitter for NBC on top of the Empire State Building. Not to be outdone, Bill Paley ordered a CBS transmitter atop the Chrysler Building. NBC's tower was taller; Paley demanded that CBS's be bigger. Paley had been introduced to a young Hungarian, described to him by CBS engineers as an "eccentric genius." Paley thought that somewhat redundant. He interviewed the genius, Peter Goldmark, and was impressed by the man's visions of television, new ways of recording music, a whole exciting science-fiction world coming true that Goldmark promised. With his almost faultless instinct about people, Paley not only hired Goldmark, he raised a million-dollar fund for him to build the transmitter on the Chrysler Building as his first assignment.

Peter Goldmark never stopped sparking ideas. Some of them made CBS millions. Some of them cost CBS millions. It was Goldmark who designed the CBS color-compatible system for TV and got Paley into a one-on-one fight with David Sarnoff and the industry giant, RCA. There could only be one end to such a contest. Paley had made a mistake that cost him many millions. Then Goldmark invented the long-playing record, a great improvement over the old 78 revolutions per minute that was standard for records. Goldmark's LP records were made at 33 rpm. It permitted finer tone and more music on a record.

Sarnoff knew that Paley had beaten him with Goldmark's LP, and could take over the lucrative record market. So he had his engineers make a 45 rpm record. Not as good as Goldmark's 33, but RCA could force it upon its nationwide chain of retailers. That was illegal restraint of trade, of course, but no one seemed to mind or try to stop it. Finally, CBS and RCA agreed to exchanges of patents, standardization at 33 rpm, and a sharing of a market big enough even for the two colossi and a dozen and more medium and smaller record companies.

The contest with Sarnoff on the records had cost Paley many more millions. He would more than earn them back. Columbia Records, wholly owned by CBS, became one of the most successful and profitable in the world, up to the day in 1987 when CBS sold Columbia Records to Sony of Japan for $2 billion.

One of the results of the early contests between Paley and Sarnoff on color TV and long-playing records led to a CBS legend. A vice-president of CBS came to a board meeting and announced that their resident genius, Peter Goldmark, had come up with a new invention. Paley turned white, held up trembling hands, and pleaded: "No, no, not another Goldmark invention. I can't afford it."

CBS had already corralled for its records and programs the singing star of the era, a man with a voice as sweet as honey and as soft as velvet, a deep, melodic baritone with both a sigh and a chuckle in it, a voice that made the heart beat in rhythm. It was a voice that Bill Paley had heard aboard ship on a cruise to Europe, a disembodied voice coming out of a neighbor's cabin. When Paley met his neighbor and asked who it was that he kept playing, the man replied, "Oh, it's a new singer. His name is Bing Crosby."

Paley, never one to lose a second when it came to advancing the interests of CBS, rushed to the purser's office and sent off a telegram to New York: HIRE SINGER BING CROSBY. He then relaxed and continued on his European tour. When he returned, he asked to see the Crosby contract and wanted to know what programs were being prepared for him. Paley flushed with anger when he was told they had failed to carry out his order, on purpose.

Nervous executives hastened to tell Paley that they had been protecting him. They did not question his judgment about Crosby as a singer. They heaped praise on the man. But Crosby had a bad reputation as a heavy drinker and an unreliable performer, who often failed to show up for a recording or a nightclub spot. All their praise for Crosby's voice did not appease Paley. He let them know in words that had icicles on them that when the head of the company gave an order, it was to be followed without question. He thanked them for their concern but warned them that their principal concern must be to do what they were told to do.

CBS executives rushed to find Crosby's agent and sign him to a contract. The agent had already heard rumors of Paley's interest, and asked for the then outrageous fee of $3,000 a week. Paley argued him down but still gave Crosby the highest pay any performer was making. It was a good investment, even if the executives were proved right: Crosby did not turn up for his first show.

"The Bing Crosby Hour," once it got rolling, shot to the top of the ratings, and the advertising money soon turned Crosby's big fee into nothing more expensive than popcorn. For all his achievement in building a national network, for years Bill Paley would be proudest of his acumen in literally picking Bing Crosby's voice out of the air, in making him the premier singer of America, indeed the world. I still recall the day forty years ago when my wife and I were strolling through the Rastro—the Flea Market—of Madrid, a colorful foreign scene, when suddenly we heard that magic voice crooning "Pennies from Heaven."

News was still the stepchild of the networks, small, unsponsored, controversial. But it was making progress and gaining respectability. In March 1932, at the invitation of the new president, Franklin Delano Roosevelt, the networks came to the White House to install their gear so that the chief executive could talk to the nation. FDR suggested they put their microphones in the Diplomatic Reception Room in front of a fireplace, so that, in the president's words, "I can sit down in cozy, informal surroundings and just have a chat with my friends and neighbors, instead of a windy speech."

The CBS manager in Washington at the time was a bright, perceptive young man, Harry C. Butcher, whom I would meet years later in Algiers on General Eisenhower's staff. Harry, a public relations wizard with a sure touch, called Roosevelt's talks "a fireside chat." The name caught on and is part of the Roosevelt legend.

Thanks to Roosevelt and his intuitive understanding of the unifying power of this new medium, radio began to play an ever increasing role in national affairs in every sector. One of the most popular of programs in those early years were "Talks" programs, on which prominent scholars, scientists, explorers came to the microphone to tell about their interests and discoveries. These were considered "educational" programs.

A young man, in his twenties, was making a name for himself in these educational circles: Edward Roscoe Murrow. An impressive man, topping six feet, his hair dark over a high, wide forehead and thick black brows, he had a lean, saturnine face and a deep, resonant voice. He carried himself with grace and radiated an energy under control but ready to burst forth. He had been born in North Carolina, raised in the Northwest, where, in his youth, during college vacations, and even briefly after college, Murrow worked as a lumberjack and roved the Big Sky country. But he was no athlete, no macho man. Murrow revered education above all else.

He worked for the National Student Federation and then for Stephen Duggan's Institute of International Education. For the Institute, Murrow created a radio program called the "University of the Air." Ed Murrow debuted in broadcasting as host of the program. He brought famous world names to the microphone of his "University": The Indian poet Rabindranath Tagore, Albert Einstein, Mahatma Gandhi, and, in a direct broadcast from Berlin, an unusual event in those years, a talk by the president of Germany, General von Hindenburg.

Murrow traveled the world to arrange exchange programs for the International Institute. He would broadcast from the capitals of Europe. Inevitably, his broadcasts came to the attention of Ed Klauber, who told Bill Paley that he thought he had found just the right man to help build the CBS News Division. Paley listened to some of the recordings of the Murrow broadcasts and agreed. He told Klauber to hire that fellow Murrow. Ed's voice had reverberated over the same sensitive antennae that had helped Paley pick Crosby out of the air. In 1935, at age twenty-seven, Edward R. Murrow joined CBS News as director of talks.

When Murrow joined CBS in the mid-thirties, it was a time of rapid growth. A number of highly talented men all joined CBS News within a year or two of each other. Rarely have so many men of extraordinary ability and drive joined together in a new industry to create a remarkable institution.

Ed Klauber hired a newsman as tough and uncompromising as himself. Paul White was an editor of the wire service, United Press. True to the traditions of that service, he was dedicated to the proposition "get it first but get it right." He was a hard-news man, insisting on straight, declarative sentences and no dramatics. White had a vision of radio news penetrating into every household in America. He foresaw big radio consoles in the family living room for entertainment, and small radios in kitchens and bedrooms to carry music and brief news reports.

When the news agencies threatened to withhold their services from the networks, White asked Paley for enough money to build his own staff of reporters. He wanted CBS to be independent of any service, to develop its own resources and find its own voice. He was willing to pay United Press and Associated Press for their reports, but only to supplement CBS News's own organization.

Ed Klauber backed White all the way and got the money from Paley. They knew they were making their mark when Hollywood forbade its movie stars from appearing on radio programs. Box office was declining in cinemas, newspapers were losing circulation and advertising linage. They blamed it on the competition of radio.

The politicians in Washington also wondered with apprehension where this new, aggressive medium would lead them. CBS had startled the capital on election night, 1932, with a decision by Ed Klauber to cancel all regularly scheduled programs and give all its time to election returns. The networks had made a powerful entry into politics, although no one could imagine then that one day network television would dominate elections and become a major participant rather than just an observer. Klauber and White were instrumental in making this fateful decision.

Another man who was to become the major architect of CBS came to the network within months of Ed Murrow, in the spring of 1935. He was a well-built man, with platinum blond hair, blue eyes, a square jaw, a big brain, and limitless energy. Second only to Bill Paley himself, Frank Stanton created CBS.

Frank Stanton had majored in industrial psychology and earned his doctorate in that field. He was proud of his Ph.D. degree and would become known thereafter as Dr. Stanton. No one ever dared call him Mr., and very few would risk calling him Frank. Stanton, in the course of his doctoral studies, had devised a system to determine what he called "Radio Listening Behavior." He was convinced that people remembered what they heard better than what they read. He believed that radio was the ultimate means of entertaining, informing, and educating the American people.

He sent his study to CBS where it was read by Klauber and Paley. No theory could delight them more than Stanton's. Advertisers were also impressed. If Stanton were right, then radio was where they should put their money. But there was a problem that had to be solved first, and Klauber decided to call in Stanton to work on it. He hired him for $50 a week to do research on determining audience reactions. There were no reliable ratings services at the time, and advertisers were demanding proof of radio's listening audience. Also, CBS itself did not want to spend a lot of money developing programs without knowing whether the programs would attract listeners.

Stanton devised a system of desks with attachments like those in schoolrooms where students have a writing arm curving out of their chairs. Stanton installed lights and push buttons on the chairs. He then invited some two hundred people graded by different categories of earnings, ethnic background, and other demographic data. He asked them to listen to a projected new program. By pushing buttons, the listeners could register approval or disapproval of the program. By today's standards it was a fairly crude market test, but in the thirties it was a sensation. At the same time, others, sensing a lucrative market for their services, were devising means to determine as accurately as possible how many people in the country were listening to a given program at a specific time. It was the beginning of what has remained a highly controversial ratings system.

Stanton was a highly organized, energetic workaholic. He was the first one into the office in the morning, the last one to leave at night. He even enlisted his wife, Ruth, a gracious, intelligent lady, in his endeavors. His work at CBS left him little time for his own cultural education. He knew that dining out in New York he would be facing a number of culture "vultures," who had time to read every book, see every play and opera, be "into" everything. So Ruth Stanton would read the books for Frank and give him summaries and critical comments. She would scan the reviews of plays and concerts, attend performances, and give Frank explanations of it all.

Stanton was a quick study, and could soon hold his own in any conversation. In a very few years, Frank Stanton became president of CBS while Bill Paley moved up to become chairman of the board. Together they built the CBS network with studios and outlets from New York to Hollywood. They plunged beyond networking into a vast multibillion-dollar conglomerate of radio, television, manufacturing, records, publishing, and real estate.

During this same fecund period of Murrow, White, and Stanton, a fifty-year-old newspaper reporter who would be heard eventually in every home in America joined the network. His name was H. V. Kaltenborn. Despite the ring of the name and a continental accent, Kaltenborn was a born American, a graduate of Harvard. His distinct phraseology, his crisp, precise, somewhat Teutonic delivery, like a German officer snapping out orders, gave rise to the myth that Kaltenborn was a famed German scholar, a voice of authority on world affairs.

He could not have appeared on the scene at a more propitious moment for his qualities. War clouds were forming over Europe. Adolf Hitler was goose-stepping around Germany, while Benito Mussolini was posturing on Roman balconies. Something extraordinary and dangerous was happening in Europe, and the public turned to H. V. Kaltenborn, the authoritative "German scholar," to explain it all. He did so on the CBS network twice a week. CBS paid him a fee of $50 per broadcast.

When General Franco's colonial mercenary troops invaded Spain from North Africa and launched an attack to overthrow the Republic, Kaltenborn went to Klauber and asked to be sent to Spain to cover the war for CBS News. CBS had no foreign staff beyond Fred Wile and Caesar Saerchinger in London and Ed Murrow, who traveled around Europe setting up talks programs and negotiating contracts with the Vienna Philharmonic Orchestra and other cultural institutions. There were no network war correspondents in 1936. For once, visionary newsmen like Klauber and news director Paul White failed to see the opportunity. They turned Kaltenborn down.

Undaunted, Kaltenborn quit his twice-a-week network spots and went to Spain on his own, paying his own expenses. Hard-driving men with vision are often lucky men. Kaltenborn had a stroke of luck, but luck that he had earned by his own professional insight. He studied a map and discovered that there was a small protrusion of French territory into Spain. Spanish territory lay both east and west, but the enclave itself was French, attached to the French southern border. Kaltenborn set himself up in this French enclave.

General Franco's troops closed in on the western side of the enclave. Loyalist Republican troops moved in on the eastern side. They began lobbing artillery shells and firing bullets at each other over the French territory. Crouching inside a protective haystack, H. V. Kaltenborn set up his recording equipment and captured all sounds of the battle: bullets whistling past his haystack, shells screaming over him.

During the days of fighting, wounded soldiers, deserters, and frightened civilians sought a haven in the French enclave. H. V. Kaltenborn was there to interview them all. It was a sensational debut for war reporting and the programs seized the attention of all America. Kaltenborn, ever resourceful, persuaded a French engineer to put him through on a line to Paris and a transmitter to relay his recordings to New York. CBS promptly hired H. V. Kaltenborn—not on a fee basis, but as their first full-time staff foreign correspondent.

Kaltenborn's live battlefield report, the first of its kind, set a new standard for the reporting of breaking news as it happened. It demonstrated the enormous potential of radio as a news medium.

Everyone in CBS News was alert to the need to spring into action whenever a major news event occurred. They were ready when the story of the century broke: the affair between the King of England and an American divorcée, Wallis Simpson.

Ed Murrow went into action at once. He got Klauber and Paley to give him an open budget, no limits, to cover every detail of a story that Ed knew would mesmerize the American people: the King of England and an American commoner, in love! Romance defying all the taboos and authorities! What a story!

Murrow practically lived on the phone to Caesar Saerchinger in London, exhorting him several times a day to milk every drop out of the story. Saerchinger kept coming to the studio with a legion of Englishmen and women: barristers and King's Counsel on the law of royal wedlock; members of Parliament from every political party, left to right; churchmen, sociologists, psychologists, psychiatrists, novelists, anyone and everyone who had an opinion on whether the king could or should "marry the woman I love."

Every day was a field day. CBS had been ready and was far ahead of any other journalistic institution. Ratings for the CBS News shot up and the switchboard was delayed with callers asking questions or praising CBS for its initiative. Ad agencies frantically demanded commercial time on previously unsponsored, spurned news programs. Murrow was spending the company's money like a drunken sailor on shore leave, but the advertising money was rolling in and CBS prestige so high that Paley's chest swelled by inches.

Paley learned early on that a major newsbreak, well-handled, would bring him more kudos than the best entertainment show. He used to tell us in later years: "I dine out on CBS News." After giving Murrow his "open budget" and seeing how much it brought back, Paley never worried about the budgets of the News Division. He never insisted, as executives do today, that the news department earn money for the corporation or be severely cut if it loses. In my years with CBS, budgets were targets that we bureau chiefs were urged to meet, knowing that we did not have to do so if we had a real story to run.

The increasingly large audiences for the daily reports from London were rewarded for tuning in to CBS when Saerchinger, with the scoop of a lifetime, got through to Murrow by phone and breathlessly told him "Ed, the king has abdicated." Murrow, startled, told him that there was no sign of any such decision from any other source. "You sure you've got this right, Caesar?" he asked. "Stop wasting time," Caesar shouted. "He's quit his throne to marry the woman he loves, Wally Simpson. He told the Archbishop of Canterbury that if he was not given permission to marry Simpson, he would abdicate. The archbishop would not relent and the king has given up his crown."

Taking a deep breath, crossing his fingers, Murrow called the network, told technicians and executives he had an urgent news bulletin to put on the air. They broke into the program being aired and Murrow announced the news. It was sensational. No one else had the story.

Ed switched from his studio in New York to Saerchinger in London and Caesar confirmed his report in a direct broadcast from the House of Commons. The American people heard the news before the British prime minister could officially inform members of Parliament and the British people. CBS News was made. It instantly became number one in network ratings and would stay number one for decades. Saerchinger's coup and Kaltenborn's exploit were only the beginning of a series of incredible newsbreaks by CBS correspondents.

All credit was due Caesar Saerchinger. It was his diligent legwork and digging deeply into his sources that produced the break. But he could not have done it without the full backstopping support of Ed Murrow and the open pocketbook of Bill Paley. This would set the pattern for what would become the CBS team trademark: men in the field digging deeply into their beats, winning friendly sources who would feed them information and views, backed up by first-rate news executives in New York and full support by the highest levels of the company. That is what made CBS a winner from the start.

Everything was in place by February 1937: the basic foundation stones on which a skyscraper of a network could be built. Paley, Stanton, Klauber, White, Murrow in New York, Saerchinger and Kaltenborn in Europe. War was only two years away, a world war that would glue every ear to the radio set for every news program, a horrible convulsion of cruelty, treachery, lunacy, cowardice, and unparalleled bravery, all at the same time. No entertainment program, no soap opera, could match the drama and power of news.

It was in February 1937 that Bill Paley and Paul White, reviewing the way Murrow had so skillfully handled the management of foreign news broadcasts and talks, decided to ask Ed to go to London to become the European director of CBS News. Caesar Saerchinger, exhausted by his round-the-clock efforts, exhilarated by his tremendous success, had asked to come home where he could relax and reap the rewards of his fine work. It was a happy decision for everyone. Caesar had been splendid and earned a break. Murrow was like a caged tiger looking at a herd of antelopes, raging to get out and into the hunt.

Murrow was ready and the story was ready for him and CBS News—the incredible story of the heroic Battle of Britain. A small, dedicated band of young men of the Royal Air Force and the Royal Navy had pledged their lives to defend the British Isles from a Nazi invasion. All Europe had fallen under the Nazi tanks and Stuka dive-bombers. Hitler was massing his seemingly invincible forces for Operation Sea Lion, a massive assault on British docks and ports and cities to pave the way for a cross-Channel invasion by triumphant German soldiers.

Ed Murrow brought the American people an hour-by-hour, sometimes minute-by-minute account of the bombing of London, the fighting in the air between British Spitfires and German Messerschmitts providing a fighter escort for the Luftwaffe's heavy bombers. Murrow would stand on the roof of the broadcasting studio and record the sounds of bombs falling and exploding, describing searchlights trying to pierce the clouds, suddenly seeing a plane go down screeching in flames, not knowing for sure if it was German or British. The stakes were no less than the survival of democratic, free civilization against the dank dungeons, torture cells, and Nazi death camps. The outcome was in doubt, the suspense almost unbearable. Many a listener would begin to tremble as Murrow's voice came over the air: "This is London." His broadcasts were so thorough, so colorful, so much on top of the news, that the British people would tune in on shortwave to catch the Murrow broadcasts to America instead of listening only to their own highly competent BBC News. Murrow became the Voice of America abroad and CBS became America's ear on the world.

The German Navy shelled Britain's Channel ports, their U-boats hunted convoys bringing supplies to England, and the bombers of the Luftwaffe hit London night after night. Many Londoners spent the night sleeping in air-raid shelters. Those who went home could not be sure they would wake in the morning. Whole blocks of houses would be hit and destroyed. The pubs were filled every night, and when closing time came and the barmen sang out "Ladies and Gentlemen, time please," everyone would drink up, shake his neighbor's hand, and say "Good night and good luck. Hope to see you tomorrow." That was the origin of Murrow's signature line after the war on his evening news program: "This is Ed Murrow, good night and good luck."

The British stood alone against the full might of the German onslaught. America still clung to its illusions of neutrality and isolationism in 1940. Europe had succumbed to Hitler. Only the British, magnificently, unquestioningly, fought back, never admitting the possibility of defeat. Murrow reported their noble struggle with his powerful baritone voice that always seemed to have a throb behind it, as though he were fighting back tears. He told Americans about the British youngsters, many in their teens, who would scramble at airfields as soon as the sirens wailed the approach of Luftwaffe bombers, rush to their fragile little Spitfire airplanes, and throttle up to meet the bombers and the Messerschmitt escort fighters over London's skies.

In a few months of constant dogfights in the air, some three thousand German bombers were shot down. About seventeen hundred Spitfires fell in flames. The Germans could not take any more losses and pulled back. The Battle of Britain had been won, Hitler's invasion called off. But the killings, the burnings, the flames were not over. The Germans developed V-2 rockets and buzz bombs that came without warning. London burned but would not surrender. The struggle deeply moved the American people, but not enough for Roosevelt to persuade Congress to make war on Hitler. It took the Japanese, in an act of folly and infamy at Pearl Harbor, to bring us into the war. When that happened and Hitler committed the strategic error of attacking the Soviet Union, there was no doubt left that Germany would be defeated. But it would take years and millions of lives before the bloodletting ended.

Other networks had good men reporting out of London. So did the newspapers. But none came even close to matching Ed Murrow, the American Voice of London. Ed, himself, knew that he could not continue alone, that America would be coming into the war and that CBS News would need a full staff of foreign correspondents. As European director it was his responsibility to find those men and train them. He was as successful in that mission as he had been in his own reporting.

Murrow had met and been impressed with a professional journalist, an excellent writer and clear thinker named William Shirer. Shirer was the Berlin correspondent of the International News Service. He hoped he would soon realize his dream of becoming a staff reporter for *The New York Times,* the ultimate goal of almost all journalists.

Murrow flew to Berlin and dined with Shirer at the Adlon Hotel. He told Shirer that CBS News was the *Times* of the air, that it offered a fabulous future of high pay and prestige. He offered Shirer a starting salary of $125 a week. Murrow was not authorized by CBS to hire anyone, and certainly not for that salary. But Ed, looking ahead to full coverage of the war that was coming, knew that he had to get highly competent professionals. He never doubted that he could persuade Paul White and Ed Klauber to back his offer. He was right. They did. But they also insisted on an audition—a voice test for Shirer. That almost blew the deal. Bill's voice was high-pitched, tended to squeak or crack when excited or making an emphatic point. White was very critical of Murrow's choice.

Murrow fought hard for Shirer and won out. He told his bosses in New York: "We can't risk using men with pear-shaped tones or pretty faces who know nothing about the world or reporting. We must have highly competent professionals. I can teach a brain how to broadcast but I can't teach a pear-shaped voice how to think and write." Murrow followed his convictions thoroughly. Sometimes he was lucky enough to find competent reporters who were also handsome men with good voices. Charles Collingwood, an American Rhodes scholar at Oxford, was one of the early lucky finds. Eric Sevareid was another. Charles was a tall, graceful, elegant blond. We called him "Bonnie Prince Charlie." Eric was even taller, with thick black hair and craggy features that looked as if he had been carved out of Mount Rushmore. Eric's voice and delivery were not good. He was always nervous and gulped a lot. No matter, he was top-grade and would become one of the great stars of national radio and television.

Murrow found another Rhodes scholar, Howard K. Smith, a graduate of Tulane University, a softspoken southerner, the only American ever elected as president of the Labor Club at Oxford. Howard was an intellectual, an excellent writer, and an athlete. He broke the world record in the hurdles, although running second to Spec Towns of Georgia. For his feat, he was named to the Berlin Olympics team but refused to go. He said he would not perform before Hitler and the Nazis. He went to work in London for United Press. Ed met him and hired him for CBS. Collingwood, Sevareid, and Smith—what a trio!

CBS News was well on its way to putting together a remarkable worldwide news staff: Sevareid in Washington, Smith in London, Schoenbrun in Paris, Winston Burdett in Rome, Bill Downs and Richard C. Hottelet in Germany, Alexander Kendrick and Dan Schorr in Moscow, Bill Costello in Tokyo, George Herman and Lou Cioffi in Korea. *Variety,* the industry bible, wrote a rave review of our first year-end show and said that CBS had typecast its men: Sevareid, tall, broad-shouldered, very American in Washington; Smith, a tweedy pipe-smoking Englishman; Schoenbrun, a dapper little mustached Frenchman in Paris; Burdett, so knowledgeable about Rome and the Vatican that he was known as "Cardinal Burdett." We were all to make television history when the war ended and television came into its own.

We all met Murrow during the war, worked closely with him, and began to build reputations. The entire country waited anxiously for every newscast during the war, and we became household names. When the war ended, we were already so well known and admired for our battlefield reports that we were in place, experienced and familiar, ready to take advantage of the postwar opportunities opening up for everyone.

I had met Murrow briefly when I had worked at the Monitoring Station of CBS in the late thirties. I went on from there to the Voice of America, becoming one of its editors and broadcasters in French to occupied France. From there, I went into the army, assigned to General Eisenhower's headquarters in Algiers. It was there that I renewed my acquaintance with Murrow.

I was in the Supreme Commander's office, delivering a report to him on French-American relations at headquarters. They were terrible. De Gaulle was proud and stubborn and would refuse orders simply to prove that France was independent. In the midst of this conversation an aide stuck his head in and said: "General, your next appointment is here." I got up to leave but the general said: "No, sit a moment. It's Ed Murrow, one of America's greatest reporters. I'd like you to meet him."

Ed did not remember me. I had only delivered some monitoring copy to him years before. But he was gracious and asked me to meet him at the end of the day at the bar of the Hotel Aletti, where he was staying. He said he wanted to know more about General de Gaulle and had been told that I had close contacts with the general and the French Committee of National Liberation.

We met at six at the bar and Ed grilled me about de Gaulle. Then he regaled me with stories about Churchill. We hit it off. Ed asked me what I had done in civilian life. I told him of my few years of teaching French and Spanish in New York schools, then my articles for *PM* and my work at the Voice of America. He was clearly interested and took a few notes. Then he got up, wished me luck, and told me to keep in touch with him. I was elated. He had not made a job offer but he had clearly opened the door.

Ed filled me in on the rapid expansion of CBS News and the one hundred full- and part-time correspondents he had recruited around the world. John Daly was the correspondent in Algiers assigned to General Eisenhower's headquarters. Murrow had found Eric Sevareid working as city editor of the Paris edition of the *Herald Tribune*. Tom Grandin was the Paris correspondent, the job I dreamed of having one day. Cecil Brown, an able, aggressive reporter, was in Rome, then sent to Asia. Larry LeSueur was in Moscow. Murrow was ecstatic about the progress of CBS News and the great audiences it commanded.

Despite the successes, there were growing pains and serious problems between the reporters and news director Paul White. White was a brilliant, innovative journalist but a hard taskmaster and editor. He had an obsession about totally objective, factual reporting, and would not abide the slightest deviation from his fundamental rule: no personal opinion. Many of the reporters felt strongly about the stories they were covering and it was extremely difficult to keep any hint of opinion out of their copy. The FCC, the regulatory agency of broadcasting, permitted opinion only if clearly labeled as such; White did not permit it at all.

White clashed angrily with his Asian correspondent, Cecil Brown, a strong-minded, outspoken, and highly competent reporter. Brown, in a broadcast, had stated that support for the war effort back home was "evaporating." White called to tell him he had no right to express such an opinion and had no evidence to support it. Brown blew up, told him to go to the devil, and resigned from CBS News.

Paul White was determined that this would not happen again. He sent out a directive to all correspondents, warning them what the rule was and insisting on compliance from all. He wrote that CBS News would not allow its reporters "to tell the public what they, themselves, think and what the public should think." He told his correspondents that they "were not privileged to crusade, to harangue the people, or to attempt to sway public opinion."

His memo became known and was commented on in the press. It did much to impress the public with the seriousness and objectivity of CBS News, but was the source of constant friction with frustrated correspondents, who not only worked hard to get all the facts of their story but felt that they had earned the right to reach an opinion on them. Murrow discussed this with me and tried to describe the fine line between what he called "news analysis" and "commentary." Commentary was opinion and forbidden. You could not say that it was a good idea to create an allied coalition. That was for the public to judge based on your analysis of the pros and cons of such a coalition. We were never referred to as "commentators," only as correspondents or news analysts.

Paul White's strict rule became the CBS News standard and endured long after White had left the company. It is still, today, in theory at least, the ruling doctrine, but it is no longer applied as strictly as in the early days. Today's news director has much less power over correspondents than White and Klauber exercised in the early years. Dan Rather, Peter Jennings, and Tom Brokaw are the stars of their networks and run their news programs very much as they wish. They all do strive to meet high standards of fairness in reporting, alert to any personal prejudice or partisanship. But their opinions do break through, and bias does occur, although less often and less flagrantly than the frequent complaints from a public that itself is not committed to fairness or objectivity. We did our best during the war, as the network expanded, but it was just about impossible to be "fair" or unbiased when reporting on Hitler, the Nazis, Mussolini and his Fascists, to say nothing of Tojo and the Japanese.

When the war ended, CBS News was well established as the leader in network news. NBC and Mutual and ABC lagged far behind. CBS had gotten off to a faster start than the others. In fact, when CBS began expanding its European coverage, just before America entered the war, NBC and Mutual canceled their European reports. America had proclaimed its neutrality in the war, and the two networks, behaving as if they were under government regulation, decided that reporting from Europe would violate our neutrality. This absurd conclusion permitted CBS to forge ahead of the others. They worked hard to catch up to CBS during the war and, with excellent reporters, managed to close the gap a bit. But CBS remained the acknowledged leader for a decade. The others kept trying and finally did match CBS, and at times surpass it in the ratings, but never managed to win the prestige and renown of CBS News.

Murrow and the "Murrow boys," his devoted team, a kind of brotherhood (in fact we did all call him Brother Ed) were all ready to capitalize on their wartime success to forge further ahead in peacetime. Radio was still king of the airwaves, but we had all heard of the development of television and could sense that it would open new opportunities. We had no idea how great those opportunities would be.

3

THE BIRTH
OF TV NEWS

A year after the war ended, a young man from Alabama walked into a CBS studio on a Saturday night, sat down, looked at a camera and said, "Good evening, I'm Doug Edwards, and this is the Saturday news." TV news was born that night.

Until that Saturday in 1946, all television broadcasts had been experimental. "Douglas Edwards and the News" was the first regularly scheduled television newscast. It went on only once a week and was seen only in New York City. There was no network, no coaxial cable linking the cities of the nation coast to coast. There were only a few thousand sets in the hands of the public. But it would mushroom beyond any imaginings into a giant force that would unify the nation, break down regional differences, and provoke public debate about its influence on our society.

Edwards was almost born to be a broadcaster. Radio was his passion in his childhood, and he first went to work in a radio studio in Troy, Alabama, at the age of fifteen. At eighteen, he was a staff announcer at a station in Atlanta, Georgia. In 1938, Doug moved on and up to a major station in Detroit, WXYZ, as a newscaster. He worked with another youngster who hugged the microphone as if it were a beautiful girl—his name was Mike Wallace.

Edwards was a natural. He had a warm, melodious voice and flawless phrasing. Doug was completely at ease in front of a microphone or camera. He never flubbed, was never flustered, never missed a beat, and maintained a rhythmic delivery easy to listen to. They could hand him a script with a minute to go to air and, without having read it in advance, Edwards would sit down, face the camera, smile, and in his rich, baritone voice deliver the script without a glitch. He was and has remained for fifty years the consummate newsreader in the history of radio and television.

His reputation as a technically perfect newsreader irked him. He did not want to be just a newsreader. He wanted to be a genuine newsman, one of the correspondents overseas or in Washington who were beginning to build glamorous reputations for daring and brains. Some people, including the man who directed Doug Edwards on his evening news for many years, Don Hewitt, who became the most influential producer of CBS News, began to denigrate Edwards as a mere reader, not a legitimate journalist. It was a harsh attack on a fine man, a professional, a gentleman, who had done everything he could to get over to Europe and become a war correspondent.

Doug is a sensitive, intelligent man. He knew from the start of the war that it was essential to get to the war fronts. It was wrong for a young, healthy man to stay home and read the news while others were out in the field with the armed forces. Doug kept begging his superiors at CBS to send him over. They were reluctant to let him go. He was the most able, most professional newscaster on the staff and could pull together all the war reports into an exciting newscast.

Finally, when Doug threatened to quit if they didn't let him go, they surrendered to his demands, but only in 1944 when the war was almost over. They sent him to London under the wing of Ed Murrow. Doug would pace back and forth in the London office, begging Ed to send him to Europe to the war front. He pleaded for a chance to prove himself, to earn a reputation as a war correspondent and an intellectual.

Murrow knew that Edwards was frustrated and embarrassed by his lack of background and formal education, for he had been "a radio brat" since his early teens. He told Doug, "You know, Doug, there's nothing highly intellectual about getting shot at." Doug's mournful face prodded Murrow's conscience. He sent him to Paris to report from General Eisenhower's headquarters. The Hotel Scribe in the heart of Paris, one block down from the Opera House and the rue de la Paix, was not exactly a battle front. But it was Supreme Headquarters and that gave Doug stature and the opportunity to break away from Paris to cover a front. Edwards was delighted.

It was there that I met Doug Edwards and got the break that led to realizing my dream to be the CBS News Paris correspondent. It happened in the lobby of the Hotel Scribe one night in November 1944. French national elections for Parliament had been held that day. The reporters at Eisenhower's headquarters covered all news and not only the military fronts. So a blackboard had been set up in the lobby and the returns were being chalked up as they came in.

I saw a young man in a uniform, with a correspondent's identification disk in his lapels, standing in front of the board. His cheeks were puffed up, his lips pursed. I thought he looked like a chipmunk storing nuts in his cheeks. A deep frown creased his forehead, a look of bewilderment was on his face. I knew exactly what he was experiencing, for I had seen these signs on the faces of many of my fellow countrymen when they were confronted with the complexities and inanities of a French election.

There were some fifteen political parties listed—not two or three as back in the States. Some of the parties' titles were not to be believed. The Party of Defense of the Automobilist. The Socialist Monarchist Party, whose emblem was a flaming red fleur-de-lis. There was a complicated system of counting votes. Totals were posted for party lists but not for individuals, as in an American election. For anyone who had never experienced the special madness of a French election it must have been a nightmare. Quite obviously that was what was troubling the young correspondent.

I walked over, offered him my hand, gave him my name, and said, "I've been around here awhile and am familiar with this lunacy. If you want a quick briefing, I'll be glad to fill you in over a drink downstairs at the bar."

A big grin wiped away his frown lines. "Thanks, I'd love it. I'm Doug Edwards of CBS."

I was delighted. I didn't know Edwards or what he did for CBS and had approached him as an unknown needing help. It was wonderful to discover that he was a reporter for my dream network. I felt that luck had struck. Sometimes good deeds are not punished.

Doug was a quick study. As I briefed him on the elections, he took notes, and in a short time he had it straight. He thanked me and said that he had to go to his studio to do a broadcast for the evening news in New York. He asked me what my room number was and suggested that we have lunch the next day.

I told Doug that I was working for a small but well-regarded news service, the Overseas News Agency (ONA), and that I had met Ed Murrow many times during the war. I had landed in the invasion of southern France with two CBS correspondents, Eric Sevareid and Winston Burdett. I also told him that my wife, an artist and illustrator, was with me. She was covering headquarters for a digest magazine called *Scope*.

Doug said, "Great, I hope she'll join us at lunch." He grinned, and to show me that he knew where he was and what he was doing, he added with a smile, "*A demain*," in a debonair French manner. I replied, toasting him, and pronounced his name in the French manner, Doo-*glahs*. He toasted me back calling me Dah-*veed*. We became close friends.

My wife, Dorothy, and I became very fond of this amiable southern gentleman. Doug never complained even when he was being hurt. He never bragged even when he was the premier television anchorman in the nation.

From his first regular newscast at WXYZ, Detroit, in 1938, Doug Edwards was still anchoring radio and television newscasts fifty years later in 1988. He is a remarkable survivor in a field where wild animals prowl ready to bring down any prey. He has survived because he is good at what he does and doesn't play the political game at all. Doug just comes in, does his job, and goes home. No office politics. He was on the top rung of the ladder in the first decade of television news. In the hearts of those of us who know and admire him, he is still top-rung.

Doug came to me one day and said that the air force had offered him a place on a "junket" to Turkey and the Middle East, to do a series of reports on its bases. "I'll be away for about two weeks, maybe three. How'd you like to be the CBS man in Paris while I'm away?"

I wanted to jump up and hug him. My face lit up and I told him I would cover for him. He told me the procedures for cabling Paul White in New York and how I would receive broadcast assignments. I had accompanied him to his studio and knew what was needed. I had also been "stringing," that is broadcasting part time, for the Mutual Broadcasting System and was sure I could handle the CBS broadcasts. I was all keyed up to meet the challenge but a little frightened, for if New York did not like my newscast reports it might kill my chances to get the Paris job one day. However, it was a challenge I could not resist.

All went well. On my first broadcast Paul White himself got on the air with me and asked whether I was the same fellow who had worked in the Monitoring Station some years back. When I said I was, White seemed pleased. "Well, good. Welcome aboard." About ten days later I received a brief note from Ed Murrow in London, saying he had heard I was subbing for Doug and doing a good job. "Keep it up and be patient. I'll call you one day. Best personal regards, Ed." I treasured that note and read it several times a day.

Doug came back, excited by his trip. He was becoming a world traveler and getting good experience, just what he wanted. We went to dinner at one of our favorite restaurants on the boulevard Montparnasse. His favorite dish was pure American: a thick, rare steak topped by fried eggs and a bushel of potatoes.

The woman who owned and managed the restaurant had a son who was running a high fever. Her doctor said he needed one of the new antibiotic drugs just discovered. They could only be obtained from the Army Medical Corps and with great difficulty. I had a war buddy in the corps and got the needed drugs. Her son was cured immediately and from then on our steaks grew bigger and thicker and the eggs on top increased from two to three. In front of our plates was a butter dish with an illegal black-market slab of butter on it, covered up by a lettuce leaf, one of the silliest but most amusing subterfuges.

We wondered what an inspector would think if he entered the restaurant and saw on every table a mysterious lettuce leaf to the right of the main dish. We ate, drank, and laughed for hours. Those were the happy days of victory in war and a bright future, which we were sure belonged to us. It was a time of hope and dreams. We were tomorrow's children and tomorrow was ours.

For Doug Edwards, tomorrow came in the form of a summons from Paul White to return home and take over the anchor position on the most popular and most important daily CBS News program, the 8:00 A.M. "World News Roundup." Correspondents from different capitals would be called on each morning to report some news development in their capitals, Doug would coordinate the reports and write summary news items on events that we were not covering: an earthquake in Peru, a typhoon in the China Sea, a plane crash in a jungle. Any significant news event always had a CBS staff report.

Doug was also told that he had been chosen to work on television. He was not happy about that at all. No one wanted to hear about television. There were not enough sets, too small an audience, and, therefore, no sponsors and no money. In radio, in addition to a staff salary, a broadcaster received a fee for each appearance on a sponsored show. Doug did a two-minute insert news brief at noon on a soap opera called "Wendy Warren and the News." It was a highly rated, well-sponsored program, and Doug was making a lot of money. He did not want to be shifted over to a television program barely beyond experimental.

CBS President Frank Stanton, who believed in television's future and in Doug Edwards's capacity to succeed in TV, called him in and gave him a visionary talk about what television would rapidly become. To sweeten the pill during the early stages, Stanton told Doug he would give him a raise in his staff salary to make up for the radio fees he would lose. Doug, a good company man, was not going to reject so fair an offer from the corporation president. It was one of the wisest decisions he could have made. Doug would become the first of the "evening stars."

In those primitive days of 1946 and 1947, CBS had only one television team, a cameraman and a soundman. Their equipment was heavy and cumbersome. It took hours to develop film, cut, and edit it. Thus, there were never many film reports on the evening news program. The program depended mainly on Doug himself, reading the news in his faultless style, interviewing celebrities and political leaders who came to the studio, or fellow correspondents who were passing through New York.

It was a thrill for me when, reporting back to my agency home office in New York, I called Doug to say hello and he promptly asked me to come to the studio and be interviewed on his TV program. He said that there was great public interest in General de Gaulle and since I knew him well that would make a good interview topic. It was my good fortune that night to become one of the pioneers on this new medium, television news.

The producer and director of the Edwards show was my cousin, Henry Cassirer, who had first worked with me at the CBS Monitoring Station. Henry did a good job in minimal conditions. He had to devise props, maps, anything to visualize items that were not on film. Henry was too much the scholar, too serious to cope with the somewhat theatrical demands of television. He would leave CBS and join me again, in Paris, as chief of television for the United Nations Educational, Scientific and Cultural Organization (UNESCO) in the great days of that institution under its brilliant director-general, Julian Huxley, the famed British biologist.

I was astonished at the lack of facilities for TV. Doug's studio was a few floors above Grand Central Station. To get to it, you had to walk down steel-lined corridors under overhead iron beams. I felt like the Hunchback in the towers of Notre Dame. Doug had no lab there for developing film. That was done a few blocks away in a former German glee club and concert center called Liederkranz Hall. Technicians had to drive through traffic jams or run on foot through crowds to get film to Doug's studio. Once, in a rush, they pulled film out of the developer, still wet, and spread it out all over the floor, waiting eagerly for it to dry so that they could run out and carry it to Grand Central Station.

After appearing on the evening news, I called Ed Murrow the next day. He had told me to be patient and that I would hear from him. A year and more had gone by without a word. Doug had told me that Ed was unhappy with his current assignment and advised me not to prod him.

Bill Paley had made a serious error concerning Murrow. His vaunted instincts went awry in this case. Impressed with Murrow's success in recruiting and directing the foreign news staff, Paley got it into his head that Murrow was a natural executive. Then Paley learned that at one point in the war, Churchill had offered Murrow the top job in the world-renowned British Broadcasting Corporation (the BBC). This served to confirm Paley's own judgment. He called Murrow in London and asked him to return to New York as vice-president in charge of news.

This was a fundamental mistake. A great broadcaster with a national following should broadcast and not handle budgets and administrative duties. Paley soon discovered his error when his new vice-president canceled the richly sponsored and popular Kate Smith show one night in order to carry a news report on some issue before the United Nations. Ed was always quick to call the network and preempt time for a major news development. This was the instinct of a dedicated newsman—but not of an executive of a commercial network. It cost CBS many thousands of dollars to preempt a commercial show.

Ed himself was miserable when he was told one day that the sponsor of William Shirer's program had decided to cancel it. Shirer felt that the sponsor was a right-winger, that he did not like Shirer's outspoken commentaries. Shirer charged he was the victim of censorship. Murrow told Shirer it was not true. His ratings had been slipping, Murrow argued, and he was losing audience. Paley ordered Murrow to fire his old friend and wartime buddy. Firing Shirer was one of the hardest orders to follow, but Murrow had no choice but to do so. Trouble was brewing with another old friend, news director Paul White. White was hitting the bottle a bit too hard and committed the ultimate sin of appearing on the air several sheets to the wind. Murrow had to fire Paul White.

The final blow came when Paley agreed to let Murrow resign as VP and go back on the air where he belonged. The sponsor of the major evening news program was Campbell's Soup. The sponsor said he would be delighted to have Murrow do the show. But the newscaster was another old friend, Robert Trout, the man who, years earlier, had showed Murrow how to do a news broadcast.

Trout, who had expected his contract to be renewed, for his ratings were high, had just bought a yacht, a dream he had cherished for years. He was getting big money and could afford it. At that point they cut his legs out from under him and gave his show to Ed Murrow. Trout, enraged and feeling betrayed, left CBS and was taken on at once by NBC, for Bob Trout was one of the best of the broadcasters. He would eventually return to CBS, but the bitterness never completely disappeared.

None of these events had yet erupted when I called on Ed in New York in 1946. He was clearly not happy at being an executive but he felt he owed it to Paley to give it a try. Mindful of Edwards's warning, I said nothing to Ed about a job with CBS. He knew, however, how much it was on my mind. When I left his office and said good-bye before returning to Paris, he smiled and said, "Patience wearing thin? Not to worry, the call will come." I was elated, for, as vice-president, Murrow was the man who could give me the Paris post. I knew the man they had then, Don Pryor, was not happy and that they were not happy with him. I went back to renew my waiting and do my job so well that my dispatches would come to Ed's attention and encourage him to call me.

The ONA editors asked me to go on a reporting trip to Czechoslovakia to find out how the Czechs were doing in their dangerous effort to cooperate with the Communists, while keeping the Soviet Union, on their borders, happy, but remaining a democratic state with friendly ties to the West.

The foreign minister, Jan Masaryk, son of the Czechs' "George Washington," Tomás Masaryk, had lived in the United States, spoke fluent English, was a dedicated democrat and anti-Communist. He would have to walk a high wire without a net to keep the Russian bear off his back. He had told me one day in Paris: "I don't want to be a bridge between East and West because I've seen what horses do on a bridge." He had a marvelous sense of humor and said: "I worked for the Crane Company in Chicago. They make toilets. I feel that was good training for a foreign minister."

Except when heading into a shooting war zone, I would always invite my wife to join me on my reporting missions. She is a talented artist/illustrator and would sketch the scenes wherever we were. She is also an excellent editor and helped me with my dispatches. But I was reluctant to take her to Prague because she was some six months pregnant. It was winter, bitter cold in Czechoslovakia, with little or no heat, and rationed milk and food. Dorothy insisted, telling me, "They have babies in Prague, don't they?"

We arrived at the Hotel Washington after midnight in February 1947. It was below zero and there was no heat. The washbasin on our dresser was frozen solid. Dorothy and I put on several pairs of stockings, pants, and sweaters. We snuggled down under the wonderful Eastern European eiderdown, thick, soft, and warm.

At about seven in the morning, there came a knock on the door, someone shouting *"Telegrammski."* A yellow cable form was then slipped under the door and into the room. Dorothy nudged me and said, "Get up and get it, it could be important." I growled that I would not budge from beneath the lifesaving eiderdown just to get a cable from some pesky editor telling me what stories he wanted covered. "It can wait," I asserted.

Dorothy punched me in the ribs and said, "You're not going to let your pregnant wife get out of bed and walk across that freezing floor?"

"Certainly not," I countered. "I forbid you to get out of bed. Stay put for at least an hour."

I felt the covers torn off me and heard Dorothy's feet padding swiftly through the glacial room. She jumped back into bed and put her freezing feet on my behind. I shrieked in pain. She laughed and then tore into the cable. A moment's silence, and then I heard her shriek, "Oh, my God!" My heart almost stopped until she went on, "Hear this. 'If you would like to be CBS News Paris correspondent and are free to join us call me collect soonest. Best regards, Ed Murrow.' "

I sat up, grabbed the telegram and began rereading it. Then I jumped out of bed, pulled Dorothy out with me, and whirled her around the room in a waltz. The room was no longer freezing. The news had heated our blood. We were young and strong and now we knew that the future was ours.

I finished my Czech mission for ONA, went back to Paris, called my editors, and thanked them for the two years I had worked for them. They were nice about it. They said they understood that I could not turn down a bid from Murrow. They wished me good luck.

CBS kept me busy in Paris with two and three newscasts a day, one for the 8:00 A.M. morning news, one for Ed Murrow, and some for a variety of special programs. One of these was a breakfast show, the "Mike and Buff" show, with Mike Wallace and his then-wife Buff Cobb. There was no television reporting from Paris in 1947. We were not yet ready to hire expensive camera teams. The satellite for live broadcasts was years away from development.

Since there were only a few thousand TV sets in use in those days, with very little sponsorship money, TV news had a minimal budget in 1946 and 1947. The top-name CBS newsmen all spurned television, following the lead of Ed Murrow, who had nothing but disdain for the new medium. Ed refused to appear on TV. He said that news was essentially based on ideas and that television could not handle ideas. It needed visuals. That meant, Ed argued, that it was good only for wars and sports. "TV is action, and it is mindless," Murrow proclaimed. He obviously had no idea that he, himself, would become the nation's most successful, most admired television broadcaster. Even then, he stuck to his guns. He would not do television news. He charged that news programs were unduly influenced by pictures rather than words or ideas. Ed would only do documentaries and, reluctantly, political conventions.

The first big breakthrough in public acceptance of TV news came at a convention in the summer of 1948, a presidential election year in which, everyone knew, Tom Dewey would become the first Republican president since the triumphs of Franklin Roosevelt in the thirties and forties. No one gave the slightest chance to FDR's vice-president and successor, a small-town man of no charisma, blunt-talking Harry Truman, whom some dismissed as "that haberdasher."

Radio was still by far the major medium in 1948, but television was beginning to show the potential that Frank Stanton had seen when he talked Doug Edwards into becoming the TV standard-bearer of CBS News. Philadelphia had been chosen by the Republicans as their convention site because the new coaxial cable, linking cities to the TV images, was being laid down, snaking along the Atlantic seaboard through the heavily populated cities. It did not yet reach the Middle West or the Pacific Coast, but it would very quickly. Politicians were fast to sense it as a powerful medium. They wanted to appear on camera, striking heroic poses. Philly was the place for it.

Paul White and Bill Paley persuaded Murrow to join the convention-coverage team for both radio and television. They did not try to argue him out of his criticism of television. Instead, they appealed to his loyalty to the company, saying that he could help them launch television by lending his name and audience appeal to the coverage. Grudgingly, he agreed to do television reports during the convention.

Murrow rebelled when he discovered that to do reporting from the floor he had to have a heavy backpack strapped on him with "rabbit-ear" sound antennae sticking out over his head, in addition to a clumsy battery-operated voice transmitter. Reporters lumbering over the convention floor looked like men from Mars who could not cope with Earth's gravity. Murrow waved away technicians and growled that he would not be turned into a monster out of H. G. Wells. He did agree, as a compromise, to offer political analysis on convention events from the Doug Edwards anchor position.

Even that concession was hard for him to make. He had promised his friend Bill Paley that he would help, but he cursed as he made his way to the anchor position. Doug was located in a small, overheated cubicle. To get there, Ed had to climb a steep, twisting route to a point under the rafters of the arena, overlooking the floor far below. Murrow sweated so heavily that he looked as if he'd been walking in the rain.

Murrow was a sweater. Even in his own air-conditioned radio studio at 485 Madison Avenue, he would jiggle his legs nervously, as sweat began to break out, until it would drip, drop by drop, from his chin. It was an unbelievable sight to see this fearless man—who had been through the worst of the blitz of London, who had recorded reports from a Flying Fortress over Berlin, as the plane rocked in the shock waves of ack-ack explosions—sweat during a perfectly peaceful and comfortable broadcast.

The stars of CBS News, Robert Trout, Charles Collingwood, Ned Calmer, were all reporting on radio. At the time of that convention in 1948, there were about 500,000 TV sets in public hands. Allowing for as many as four viewers per set, that meant an audience potential of 2 million. Any newspaper would be happy to have that circulation. But radio men were used to a potential audience of 100 million and more. TV was still some years away from reaching national audiences and big advertising money. CBS executives knew the potential was there, but CBS correspondents were willing to wait until it had been achieved.

To everyone's surprise, despite the poor working conditions, CBS News was highly praised for its coverage of the convention. Even the elite *New York Times*, which looked down on both radio and television, condescended to praise the CBS efforts. It wrote of the "accuracy" of the TV reporting, the speed of its communications, the excitement of seeing as well as hearing what was happening on the floor. Politicians who had been only names and still photos had become real, live human beings. It was a new dimension.

In later years, realizing what a formidable competitor the networks were, the *Times* became somewhat less generous in its praise. It is often severely critical of TV's shortcomings, which are real enough. But in 1948, TV was still too small to threaten the power of the press or drain away a large amount of advertising money.

Frank Stanton's promises to Doug Edwards began to come true. Unflappable as always, Doug acquitted himself more than well as anchorman of the convention coverage. He was adept at getting the floor reports of the sweating Martians down below him, and skillful at interviewing the political leaders who all made their climb to his cubicle so that they seemed to be a long line of ants struggling up a mountain face. Doug was so successful that Stanton and Paley, seeing a chance to capitalize on his new fame, decided to drop his weekly Saturday-night program and have him anchor a Monday-to-Friday, five-times-a-week news show. It would run for fifteen minutes, from 7:30 to 7:45 P.M., close to prime time.

Doug balked at this at first. He was earning the then princely sum of $400 a week on his radio shows. TV could not match that, even at five nights a week. But Stanton again talked to him, told him that he was already on his way to becoming the "biggest star" of CBS News. He said, "In a year or two you'll be the most famous name in America and earn three times as much. TV will be a bonanza, the biggest money-maker in the history of communications." Meanwhile, he would double Doug's staff salary. He had made Doug an offer he couldn't refuse. Doug had no idea how fortunate he was.

Doug consolidated his good fortune by doing a good job anchoring the weeknight news. He did so well, in fact, that after two years CBS changed the title of the program from "CBS TV News" to "Douglas Edwards and the News." However, he never did fulfill Frank Stanton's prediction that he would become "our biggest star." Murrow, Collingwood, and Sevareid remained the most stellar CBS broadcasters. Doug did, however, become nationally known and admired. Most important, he was listened to. Each week a new station hooked into the coaxial cable and, by 1951, the coaxial finally reached the West, permitting Doug to begin his evening news broadcast by announcing proudly, "Good evening from coast to coast." TV had become a national power, its cable hookups spider-webbing across the nation.

Doug was King of the Airwaves at the start, but NBC came up with a rival newscaster who began to challenge Edwards. His name was John Cameron Swayze, and his program, "The Camel News Program," was sponsored by Camel cigarettes. Edwards's program was sponsored by Pall Mall cigarettes, but Paley would not permit the sponsor to impose its name on the program.

Swayze was much older than Doug and a totally different personality. He was flamboyant, wore a flower in his lapel, and seemed to me to look like a broken-down ham actor. He seemed no match for a clean-cut southern boy, but there is no accounting for the tastes of the American public. How they could simultaneously applaud an Ed Murrow, a Fulton Lewis, Jr., an Elmer Davis, and a Father Coughlin baffled me. For a time, they preferred Swayze to Edwards. Doug eventually caught up and pulled ahead again to number one, but it was a warning to CBS not to try to rest on its laurels. There were other networks working the field and they were good.

There had been different directors assigned to the Edwards program after my cousin, Henry Cassirer, went off to Paris. No fewer than three different directors took turns in the control room on alternate nights. The most effective of them was a young dynamo named Don Hewitt who would, in a long career, make television history with the "CBS Year-End Report" and "60 Minutes."

Hewitt was a fireball of energy, an electric generator of ideas, who seemed to radiate sparks as he jumped around shouting his orders to the cameraman. Sitting in his control room and watching him direct the program was a seat at the most dramatic, funniest show in town. Don would bellow, "Get Ready and ROLL." When he yelled "ROLL" it sounded like a ten-letter word. Then, "Take One! Goddamn it, ONE, hit it, HIT IT." When I watched him screaming, waving his arms, red in the face, I wondered if he would last through the fifteen-minute show. He did. He lasted almost forty years as the most successful, biggest-money-earning producer in television history.

If Doug Edwards was a natural broadcaster, then Don Hewitt

was born to be a journalist. He was, from an early age on, a "media brat." His father sold ads for the Hearst papers. Young Don's childhood idol was Hildy Johnson, the wisecracking, "scoop" reporter in the play *The Front Page*. At nineteen, Don was impatient with his college studies. He quit, threw away his books, and got a job as copyboy in the newsroom of *The New York Herald Tribune*.

Bright as a newly minted penny, Don was no deep-thinking intellectual. He was and has remained an activist, a man of action rather than ideas. If not an intellectual, he was nonetheless highly intelligent, imaginative, and innovative. He would make and break every rule and invent exciting new techniques for telecasting. What others might consider absurd was ordinary fare to Don Hewitt.

Don had noticed that Doug was having trouble reading his script and looking into the camera at the same time. Doug was adept at looking down and up and not losing his place, but Don disliked the almost constant bobbing of Doug's head. So he invented cue cards with the script written on them so that Doug could direct his eyes at camera level, keeping his head up. That did not work as well as expected, for the cue cards were placed to the right and left of the cameras so that Doug was still not looking directly into the lens and at the public. Don brooded about this until the day that a brilliant solution came to him. He shouted at Doug, "I've got it, I've got it! You'll have to learn Braille. Then you can finger your script while looking into the camera."

Doug, of course, did not learn Braille but, soon enough, an ingenious technician invented the TelePrompTer, a device that fitted just above the camera eye and moved the script on a roller, which an operator adjusted to the rhythm of Doug Edwards's delivery.

At about the time that Don Hewitt was jumping up and down over Grand Central Station, another superkinetic overachiever was moving toward CBS News. Eventually he would become even more powerful than Hewitt, although he would not last as long, for he had a tempestuous, outsize ego bound to clash with top management.

Fred Friendly would team up with Ed Murrow and become Ed's producer on Ed's entry into television. Together they would win high praise and vast audiences across the country. They would make TV history, have a profound impact on CBS News, and shake up the faithful Murrow "Brotherhood," something none of us would believe could happen.

Like Don Hewitt, Fred Friendly was a product of the sidewalks of New York, a tough, ambitious, streetwise fighter. He was born in German-Jewish Harlem on 113th Street, on the border of Italian and Irish Harlem. Just trying to go to school safely through roving street gangs was a daily adventure. I know what it was like for I was born the same year, 1915, in the same neighborhood, at 119th Street. Around the corner, on 118th Street, were two men who would become highly successful entertainers, George Jessel and Milton Berlinger, whom we know and love as "Uncle Miltie" Berle. In the fifties, Milton Berle was the biggest star on TV.

Fred Friendly's name at birth was Ferdinand Wachenheimer. When he was hired at a radio station in Providence, Rhode Island, in 1937, the station manager grimaced when he heard his name. "Don't you have a middle name?" he asked Ferdinand. "Yes," said Ferdinand, "my middle name is Friendly." "Fine," said the manager, "from now on you're Fred Friendly."

In Providence, Fred learned his craft the hard way through painstaking work for very little money. He was assigned a series of micro-mini documentaries, no one of which could exceed five minutes. The documentaries were profiles of great men and women in history. To tell their life stories in five minutes gave Fred invaluable training in tight writing, tight editing, making the most of every second of air time. For this they paid him $8 per five-minute piece.

Fred learned more than he earned and, when war broke out, he left the station in Providence and joined the army. With his radio background he was assigned to an Information and Education section in Europe. He was then transferred to Asia, as army correspondent for the China-Burma-India theater (CBI). Friendly was one of the reporters who witnessed the dawn of the atomic age when he reported the dropping of atom bombs on Hiroshima and Nagasaki.

Mustered out in 1946, Fred came home to his native New York City with great ambitions. He was part of my generation of men who had fought hard to victory, had faith in ourselves and in our country, and were ready for any challenge of the future. Fred had been thinking about radio and his postwar role all through the war. On arrival in New York he went promptly to NBC, where he had an introduction from a friend. He sketched out for the NBC news people a TV show based on a panel of famous names who would be asked to identify the source of a quotation taken from the weekly news, a sort of "Who said that?"

CBS executives caught the show, liked it, and asked Fred to come over, promising him a bigger audience and more money on CBS radio. Fred, who had soon realized that CBS was the premium network, came willingly. Not only did he bring his show with him, but he sparked ideas for other programs. Fred radiated ideas. There were no limits to his imagination and his curiosity. Friendly was an intellectual searcher with a far-ranging mind. He cared little about technique and gimmicks.

Friendly was just the right kind of man for Ed Murrow, who had criticized TV for being a mindless picture gallery. One part of Fred, his mind and his soul, yearned to be a scholar. Another part drove him to action. Fred did not have the temperament for scholarship. With his unbounded energy, he could never have passed his life in library stacks. He admired scholarship and used scholars on his programs. This again was an ideal complement to Murrow's own temperament. The two men were bound to hit it off well.

One day, Fred Friendly met a softspoken young man named "Jap" Gude. Jap was an agent, representing Ed Murrow, Elmer Davis, and Walter Cronkite, three of the all-time greats of radio and TV. Fred spoke to him with passion (he never spoke except with passion) about a wonderful book he had just read that was just screaming to be adapted for radio and TV. The book was *Only Yesterday* by Frederick Lewis Allen, one of America's top editors. It was a socio-political-cultural recounting of the period that historians called the Roaring Twenties.

Fred was convinced that he could adapt the book to sound and pictures. He pleaded with Allen to give him the rights to the book and to agree to narrate Fred's script. Allen, a print man with ink in his veins, was appalled at the idea of doing anything on radio. He agreed to sell the rights to the book but not to narrate the program.

Fred pondered on his next step. He went to Gude and told him that Ed Murrow, with his background in educational programs, his interest in history, and his great fame, was just the man to make the project a huge success. Gude agreed to talk to Ed about it. He then brought Fred to Murrow so that Fred could plead his own case. To Fred's delight, Murrow enthusiastically endorsed his idea.

Murrow had lunch the following day with the president of Columbia Records, Goddard Lieberson, a sophisticated executive. Murrow told him of the idea and asked what he thought of it. Goddard said he liked it and, moreover, that he would be willing to make a Columbia record album of it ("Hear It Now"). Then, if successful, it could go on to radio and TV. He offered Murrow $1,000 in advance to make a pilot record. Thus was born one of the most remarkable series in communications history, "Hear It Now."

Ed Murrow called on me on several occasions for contributions to the *I Can Hear It Now* album. First, he asked me to try to find a good recording of President Woodrow Wilson at the Versailles Conference after World War I. Good recordings were not easy to find in those days, but I was fortunate in discovering an excellent recording of a Wilson speech calling for self-determination for all peoples and promising a postwar world of freedom and democracy. Ed was delighted; he thanked me and sent me a generous fee.

We had less success with Ed's later request, but it turned out to be highly significant. Ed wanted a recording of General de Gaulle's famous speech of June 18, 1940, made in London after the Nazis had overrun France. De Gaulle, in a broadcast to France, said that he and other Frenchmen overseas would never stop fighting against Hitler and would one day liberate France. He called for "resistance" and said that its "flame must never be extinguished." Most importantly, there was a phrase that caught the imagination and was quoted all over the world. It was particularly admired in the United States, which is why Murrow wanted it for his album. De Gaulle had said, "France has lost a battle, not the war." However, the historic phrase had never been uttered. I was not disappointed. I was elated, having made what I knew to be a breakthrough in history, correcting a global myth.

What General de Gaulle had actually said was, "This war has not ended with the Battle of France. This war is a world war." He then went on to talk of France's allies in Britain and America, their power, their factories and tremendous resources that would eventually throw back the Nazis. But some reporter in London, sending back a summary of his speech, had written: "General de Gaulle declared today that France had lost a battle not the war." This was the reporter's paraphrase, not de Gaulle's own words.

The phrase had caught on so well that de Gaulle's propaganda people began to print placards saying FRANCE HAS LOST A BATTLE, NOT THE WAR, as if it were a quote from the general. De Gaulle would actually use the phrase himself in a later talk over Radio Luxemburg. But it was definitely not in the historic broadcast of June 18, 1940.

Murrow had told me to check it out with Friendly. Fred asked me to go and see de Gaulle and persuade him to re-create the speech including the phrase. I was about to tell Fred that there was no way that de Gaulle would consent to reenact a scene and rewrite it. He was a man with a deep love and sense of history. I said nothing, however, for I recalled that one day, years earlier when I was working for Mutual, their aggressive news director, Abe Schechter, a Friendly-type volcano, had asked me to invite de Gaulle to participate in a kiddies program for Christmas. I told Schechter it was impossible and he snapped back, "I want de Gaulle's refusal, not yours." He got it the next day.

I did have access to President de Gaulle, more than any other foreign correspondent except perhaps Cy Sulzberger of *The New York Times*. De Gaulle knew how important the *Times* was. My agency was not important but de Gaulle was loyal to men who had been his comrades-in-arms on the long fight back. I had been one of Eisenhower's liaison officers to de Gaulle's embryonic government in Algiers. I landed on the southern beaches in the first hours of the liberation campaign and fought alongside the French all the way to Vienna. This meant something to de Gaulle.

When I saw the president and explained what we needed, he looked at me through his hooded lids and shook his head. "No, that is impossible. I cannot rewrite history and I am astonished that you should ask me." I blushed, apologized, and told him that I was under instructions to do so and had warned my editors that he would refuse. I was angry with Friendly for forcing me to do a foolish thing.

Friendly was furious when I called to tell him of de Gaulle's refusal. He stormed over the phone, protesting that de Gaulle was a nit-picker, a purist, a holier-than-thou fanatic. Fred was in a tantrum. I simply hung up. It was at this point that I began to have doubts about Friendly's commitment to accuracy. I would have other occasions to confirm this. Fred and I did not get along.

One of the main reasons for conflict was his lack of respect for the correspondent. As producer, he felt he was the boss and we were his employees. He did not hesitate to interfere with the story line, to edit our work as he saw fit. Unlike Don Hewitt, who did everything to support the reporters, Fred thought we were there to support him. I recognized his imagination and creative ability, his brains and drive. I know he admired my control of my Paris reporting beat. But we were two strong-minded men with different goals, and were bound to conflict. The same would happen between Fred and Howard K. Smith.

Fred was building his own empire inside CBS News, riding as the tail to Murrow's high-flying kite. At the same time, he was challenging the power and the bonds of the Brotherhood of the Murrow boys. Murrow needed Fred, who would make Ed famous on TV. Ed refused to choose between his new and his old friends. By not choosing and not putting his hands on the reins, Murrow let us pull in different directions.

Friendly was overweening, dictatorial. He regarded the correspondents not as valued colleagues as Murrow did, but as slaves to carry out his orders, no matter how wrong-minded or unrealistic they often were. When I complained once about his tendency to twist a story to fit into the view he wanted, that it was not moral to do so, Fred paced up and down the studio floor, like an angry grizzly. I thought he might hit me and I stepped back, for he was a big heavy man. He shouted, "Don't talk to me about morals, I've got the morals of a mink." I never did understand why he thought that was a standard to proclaim with pride.

Accurate and moral, or not, Fred, in his own field, was close to being a genius. He had every quality except balance and total news integrity. The *I Can Hear It Now* album broke all records. More than 500,000 albums were sold, an astonishing, unprecedented sale of a talking, not a musical, record. They went on to make three more albums.

One day, many years later, in 1963, when I was chief correspondent in Washington, I walked into a bookstore in which records were also sold and saw an array of *I Can Hear It Now* albums. I noticed that the first one proclaimed in bold print "Edward R. Murrow—I Can Hear It Now." Then, in small print, at the bottom of the album, it said "produced by Fred W. Friendly." The second album featured

"Edward R. Murrow and Fred W. Friendly—I Can Hear It Now." The third album reversed the original order. "Fred W. Friendly presents Ed Murrow . . ." Murrow had long since left CBS. Friendly had ridden high, thanks not only to his undoubted talents, but also on Murrow's back.

A serious problem developed out of the techniques used in making the record. A bright, young sound engineer, Joe Tall, had invented an editing machine. It was a rectangular slab of what looked like heavy stone, with a narrow ditch running along its width, and a slit in the center. Joe would lay a strip of recorded tape into the ditch and feed the tape into a playback machine. This permitted him to hear what was on the tape and locate exactly where each sound emanated. He would take a razor blade, draw it through the slit and cut the tape anywhere he wanted, eliminating extraneous material that slowed up the narrative.

This made it easy to take a speech, cut out its long-winded or complex passages, and keep only the most dramatic phrases. This meant that, in unscrupulous hands, you could take the word *not* out of a sentence and turn its meaning around. No one would dare do anything so obvious, but the opportunities for distorting a statement were limitless.

There was a real concern about the integrity of the tape-editing system. I was told, for example, that on one program, a report on Eisenhower during a visit to Mexico, a producer did not like the weak applause after Eisenhower's speech. So he went to his tape files and took a recording with enthusiastic applause, substituting it for the real scene. I was never given any proof of this, so it would be unfair to mention the producer's name, but the possibilities for such tricks were evident.

I Can Hear It Now was the sound diary of an extraordinary period of history, from the entry into power in 1933 of Franklin Delano Roosevelt and Adolf Hitler, through the blitz of London, Churchill's rallying of the brave British people, Charles de Gaulle's Free French movement fighting back, up to 1945, V-E Day and the surrender of the Germans and the Japanese. It carried the recording of Roosevelt telling us that "the only thing we have to fear is fear itself," to Churchill's assertion that "If the British Empire lives a thousand years, this will be its finest hour." We could hear again Edward VIII giving up his throne to marry "the woman I love," all the glorious, poignant, tragic moments of that unforgettable era. It was superbly done, and overnight Fred Friendly, deservedly, became one of the most respected producers of radio—gearing up for even greater fame and power in television.

Charles Dickens had introduced his *Tale of Two Cities* by noting that "It was the best of times and the worst of times." The same may be said of the era in which television came into its own, the 1950s. It is to those times that we now turn.

4

TV COMES OF AGE

Victory over the Japanese ended World War II but it did not bring the peace for which a war-weary world had hoped. The shooting war was soon followed by the Cold War, a split in the ranks of the victorious allies, with Russia and the United States standing eyeball to eyeball, snarling at each other. Stalin, challenged by America, tightened the already cruel repression of the Russian people. America, fearful of Russia, turned upon itself, looking for Communists and saboteurs inside the Republic. We had nightmares about the "Red Peril" of Russia and the "Yellow Peril" of China, and turned viciously on anyone who dared dissent from official policy in such dangerous times.

Inevitably, this anti-Communist hysteria, far in excess of any hard evidence of a genuine internal threat, turned against the most powerful means of public communication, the networks. A book called *Red Channels*, published by a rightist organization called Counterattack, accused almost two hundred men and women of transmitting "pro-Sovietism" over the air. Counterattack charged that the Communist aim was to conquer the world by the use of fifth columns, saboteurs, and mercenaries. This charge was "confirmed" for them when North Korea, a Soviet ally, invaded South Korea.

The nation was convinced that the Soviets really aimed at world conquest and might even achieve it. Absurd as that thought was, it has remained, even today, almost axiomatic for millions of Americans. American conservatives turned upon their own president, Ronald Reagan, when he negotiated a historic treaty of nuclear arms reduction in December 1987. Fear and hatred of Russia has dominated the American political scene for the past forty years and more. It became a major crisis for the networks in the fifties.

Some of the most talented men and women in radio, television, the press, books, and the performing arts were listed in *Red Channels:* Leonard Bernstein, Howard K. Smith, Alexander Kendrick, Orson Welles, Irwin Shaw, Dashiell Hammett and Lillian Hellman, Garson Kanin, Edward G. Robinson, and stripteaser Gypsy Rose Lee who, apparently, kept taking off her clothes and baring her breasts to subvert America. No absurdity was too gross, too ridiculous for the maddened witch-hunters of the day.

CBS was dubbed the "Red Network" by Counterattack. Because of this, and heavy sponsorship pressure, the most liberal but objective of the networks joined the slavering witch-hunters. All the networks bowed down to the anti-Communist terrorists of the right. CBS hired former FBI agents to investigate staff employees. CBS producers used the *Red Channels* list of "subversives" to blacklist actors, writers, and all performers. Ed Sullivan, who emceed the most popular entertainment show on television, would not book an act for his program before checking with *Red Channels* to see if the performers were on their "Red list."

The worst moment came in December 1950, when CBS executives sent a questionnaire to all employees, asking them whether they had at any time or were now engaged in any Communist activities. We were asked to swear, under oath, that we never were and were not now members of the Communist Party.

This "loyalty oath" was an offense to all American citizens, a grave violation of our civil and constitutional rights and our protection against having to testify against ourselves. That there were undoubtedly, in any huge organization, some Communists, could be assumed. But no other network asked their staff to sign a loyalty oath. The Communist Party existed legally in the United States. A pillar of American jurisprudence and philosophy held that we enjoyed freedom of speech and of assembly. Thomas Jefferson had proclaimed that democracy would flourish in a free marketplace of ideas, convinced as he was that democracy was the best of ideas and would conquer all others. In the 1950s, there were few Americans willing to uphold those principles or share Jefferson's faith. We lived in a paroxysm of fear, a paranoia of suspicion and hatred.

The correspondents were furious and said they would not stoop to sign such a humiliating loyalty oath. We were astonished and bewildered when we heard that our idol, Ed Murrow, had signed it and called on all of us to follow his lead. I was angry, disappointed in Ed's action, but agreed to follow him and sign, for I had no right to be more Catholic than the Pope. Ed had made it clear that the continued existence of the CBS network was at stake. Sponsors were threatening to cancel all advertising. CBS was in mortal peril. That is why Ed surrendered to the anti-Communist hysteria.

The loyalty oath and staff investigations, carried out with loud baying of the hounds, turned up just one CBS staffer who confessed that in his youth he had been a member of the Communist Party and had sent reports to the Soviets on the morale of the people in Finland during the Russo-Finnish War. He admitted to youthful "idealism," anger at the suffering during the Depression, and that he foolishly believed the rhetoric of Communism. When he matured, he realized that Soviet deeds did not carry out the promises of Communist slogans. He had broken with the Party as soon as his eyes were opened. That was the one "witch" found by the witch-hunters.

Ed Murrow stood staunchly behind all the newsmen accused, without evidence, in *Red Channels*. He also supported the one man who admitted he had been a Communist. "Everyone is permitted a youthful indiscretion," Ed argued. "The man is one of our best correspondents and his work reveals no sympathy for Communism or the Soviet Union." Senator Dodd, head of the committee investigating subversion, publicly applauded the frank confession and the full cooperation of the man in question. I do not give his name now. Many will remember it. After thirty years, I do not think it right to dredge up an old scandal to embarrass a man and his family who suffered terribly during the event.

The witch-hunting would increase in fervor when it was discovered that Klaus Fuchs, a scientist who had helped build the British and French atomic arsenal, had, at the same time he was helping us, passed on secret nuclear data to the Soviets. This confirmed all the accusations about the "enemy within." When Senator Joseph McCarthy arose to pick up the anti-Communist banner, the hysteria swept across the nation. Reputations were ruined by smears without any proof. Don Hollenbeck, one of CBS's most respected newscasters, under constant pressure that amounted to persecution, put his head in the oven and turned on the gas. His was not the only suicide in the nation.

It was then that there occurred an event that would be one of three or four major developments that would provide a big breakthrough for TV, which came of age in the 1950s. The event was the introduction on the network of a new weekly series, a TV adaptation of the very successful "Hear It Now," to be called "See It Now."

The "See It Now" series first aired in the fall of 1951. It was an instant success. Producer Fred Friendly used the medium perfectly, opening the show with a scene that no other medium could duplicate. He had Murrow sitting in a TV control room, surrounded by TV monitors. Ed pointed to one of the sets and said, "You are now looking at the Atlantic Ocean." Then he turned to another set and said, "That is the Pacific Ocean." At that point, the pictures were brought up together on a split-screen, the Atlantic on the right, the Pacific on the left. It was the first time in history that people could see the two oceans simultaneously. It might not change the fate of nations or the lives of people, but it was an extraordinary breakthrough, pointing up the still unknown and untested potential of this phenomenal new medium. Friendly, who had not worked much in television, seemed to have a perfect sense of the medium— natural, instinctive, realistic.

From the waters of the oceans, the cameras panned over to pictures of the Brooklyn Bridge in New York and the Golden Gate Bridge in San Francisco, strengthening the point already made about television's ability to span the continent and unify the nation. The oceans and bridges were only symbols of a far more significant truth projected that day: that television would in fact span the nation and unify the country profoundly, in its politics and culture, and not always with the best results. At its best, which the Murrow-

Friendly team would attain, television fulfilled its promise of informing and educating the nation. At its worst, it became intrusive in the political process and mindless in its so-called entertainment programs. If the fifties were the best and worst of times, TV became the best and worst of the media.

"See It Now," an immediate hit, would last on the air for seven years, highlight years of the big breakthrough period of the fifties. For all of Friendly's undoubted technical skills and understanding of the medium, the show was, however, made by the personality and powerful presence of Murrow. Murrow literally broke through the tube and entered the living rooms of America as someone of enormous prestige who was personally visiting every American family.

Fred Friendly, no modest man, admitted that he was not the man who really made "See It Now" the phenomenon it was. Murrow was that man. "There is a magic about Murrow," Fred said. "When he spoke in his deep and vibrant voice, listeners knew that he believed every word he spoke and was certain it was so important that you had better listen carefully." Murrow convinced us all that he was making us personal witnesses to history and that, if we understood, along with him, what had happened and was happening, somehow we would find a way to control our own destinies. It was an illusion, but such a powerful one that it seemed real, compelling.

The program was only thirty minutes long and at least five of those minutes were allocated to commercial messages. In that limited space of time, Murrow would present from three to four reports each week or, on rare occasions of overwhelming importance—as in the case of Senator McCarthy, his most famous "See It Now"—the entire half-hour would be given to one subject.

The "See It Now" on Joe McCarthy shocked the television audience and the nation, and caused bitter splits among friends and family. No one who was not alive in those days can understand what had happened to America and to the democratic process. One man, totally irresponsible, making sweeping charges without a shred of evidence, terrorized the media, Congress, even the White House.

When Senator McCarthy called a news conference and waved a paper in the air, shouting "I have here the names of seventy-nine Communists in the State Department," not one newsman, not one member of Congress demanded that he show the paper and reveal the names. In fact, McCarthy did not have a single name on his list. He did not uproot any dangerous spies and saboteurs of the Republic, but he did smear, calumniate, and destroy the careers of hundreds, while striking fear into the hearts of millions.

Ed Murrow had long resented the networks' subservience to government. Licensed by the FCC, unlike newspapers which were not regulated by government, the networks felt vulnerable and insecure, always fearful that a station license might be revoked or a major advertiser offended or angered. That is why Paley laid such emphasis upon factual reporting and a total interdiction of personal opinion or editorializing.

As a member of the board of directors of CBS, Murrow had obligations to the network that clashed with his own ethics and morals. It pained him every time he was obliged to write to J. Edgar Hoover, head of the FBI, to advise him of the substance and themes of new CBS programs, inviting Hoover to express his views on the programs. The "Murrow boys" knew nothing of his correspondence with Hoover. It would have shocked and saddened us to see Ed bow to the worst kind of censorship, to what seemed like the beginning of an American police state.

Murrow, telling us about it much later, explained that his real error was accepting Bill Paley's proposal that he become a vice-president and join the board of directors. "That made me an executive of the company and not a reporter or editor. I had an obligation to Paley and CBS, which had given me my career. I had to do what they thought was needed to protect them. Once I resigned to go back on the air, that rather shameful period came to an end."

Murrow admitted that he felt nauseous when he discovered that President Frank Stanton had also sent a message to Hoover informing him of a new program, "See It Now," and invited Hoover to listen to it and tell CBS what he thought of it. That CBS would ask the director of the FBI to judge a Murrow program sounds incredible, aberrational, but it was true, a low point in the history of CBS. Writer Richard Rovere commented, "In 1953, the very thought of Joe McCarthy could shiver the White House timbers and send panic through the whole executive branch."

It certainly sent panic through the ranks of network officials. Knowing that neither the White House nor the Congress was ready to challenge the monster from Wisconsin, the networks were afraid to report at all on McCarthy. It was a no-win situation. If they praised McCarthy or treated him favorably, they would alienate millions who feared and hated him. They would not soon forgive the networks. But if they criticized McCarthy, he and his rabid cohorts in Counterattack and various un-American activities groups, in and out of Congress, could destroy the networks.

Murrow brooded about this. He burned to tell the truth about McCarthy, to find ways of exposing his distortions, lies, smears, without expressing editorial opinions. Murrow was determined to find a way. He was convinced that nothing less than the fate of American democracy was at stake.

Murrow dipped his feet in the icy waters with a first attempt to cope with the witch-hunters. He reported the case of Milo Radulovich, a young lieutenant in the air force, who had been denounced as a security risk because his father and his sister were allegedly involved with Communist organizations. It was a clear case of guilt by association, and unproved associations to make it worse. Joe McCarthy was not involved, it was the air force itself that had brought the charges. For Murrow it was a clear example of the infectious disease of McCarthyism. The Radulovich affair would be a test case for Murrow and Friendly.

One of the brightest, most talented reporter-producers of CBS, Joe Wershba, was assigned by Murrow to research the case. Wershba was thorough and his findings convinced Murrow that a grave injustice and travesty of democracy had occurred. Radulovich had been accused but never granted a hearing. For Murrow this was a star-chamber proceeding, typical of dictatorships. Instead of fighting Communism, the McCarthyites were turning Americans and our institutions into secondhand imitations of the totalitarian states.

On October 20, 1953, Murrow devoted the entire half-hour of "See It Now" to the Radulovich affair. Murrow gave the facts first, then he stated that CBS was unable to determine whether or not the father and sister were involved in Communist activities. No evidence had been presented to back up those charges. And, even if true, the activities of a father and sister could not be visited upon the son and brother, who was totally innocent and who had not been charged with any activities unbecoming an officer. "How," Murrow asked, "can an American officer be punished for something that someone else did, no matter who that someone else was?"

The program, in the climate of the day, was an act of courage by Murrow and by Paley. Their judgment was confirmed by a wave of laudatory reactions. Jack Gould, the critic of *The New York Times*, wrote that "a major network, CBS, and one of the country's most important industrial sponsors, the Aluminum Corporation of America, ALCOA, consented to a program taking a vigorous editorial stand in a matter of national importance and controversy." The air force, surprised and disconcerted by the public support for Radulovich, hastily called for a review of the case and withdrew all charges against the lieutenant. It was a triumph for Murrow, Paley, and, above all, for ALCOA. It was the first sponsor willing to advertise its products on a highly controversial program. Without such support, CBS might not have dared give Murrow a green light.

Bill Paley told several of us, years later, that he had been terribly ashamed of the way CBS stroked J. Edgar Hoover and made its staff sign loyalty oaths. "This was perhaps my biggest mistake," Paley confessed. Because he was so torn by guilt feelings, he saw Murrow almost daily. He listened but did not advise. He let Murrow know that Murrow could function as a kind of autonomous entity inside the network. Network rules would not be rigidly applied to "See It Now." Paley knew that Murrow was a responsible man and would do nothing that was really off-base. He gave Murrow a free rein.

After the air force's mistreatment of Radulovich, Ed Murrow became enraged when Joe McCarthy viciously attacked Brigadier-General Ralph Zwicker, a war hero, again with no evidence of any kind. Murrow became convinced that no one was safe from the inquisitor from Wisconsin. He was right. McCarthy would go on to attack our most illustrious soldier, five-star General George C. Marshall, the overall commander of American forces in World War II, the superior officer of Eisenhower, the man who chose Eisenhower and jumped him over dozens of senior men to be Allied Commander in Chief in Europe. If McCarthy could attack General Marshall and denounce the entire army hierarchy of being soft on Communism, then whom would he hit next, the President of the United States? Democracy itself? He had to be stopped. The question was, How?

Murrow told producer Fred Friendly to start building up a file of newsreels and TV clips of McCarthy in action. The only way to beat him, Murrow guessed, was to let him disgrace himself with his outrageous behavior and unsubstantiated accusations. It was a shrewd guess. Murrow knew that he could not make a direct attack, that would violate all fairness and editorial dicta. By letting the camera expose McCarthy, Murrow could then, in few words, string up the noose for the madman.

All through February 1954, Murrow and Friendly viewed hundreds of feet of McCarthy film, winnowing out the inconsequential, selecting those scenes that showed McCarthy at his most vicious and his phoniest, including one memorable scene when the camera, close up, caught McCarthy wiping away a crocodile tear in a dry eye.

As they worked away planning the program, Ed consulted almost daily with Bill Paley. The twentieth floor was vibrating with fear—not Paley himself, who stood firmly behind Ed, but all other executives.

When the program was finally edited and ready to air, Murrow asked Paley if he wanted to see it first. Paley asked Murrow if he was absolutely sure of his facts. Murrow confirmed that he was. "Okay," said Paley, "then go ahead. I'll see it on the air like everyone else." Paley stood solidly behind Murrow and made only one stipulation. He insisted that CBS offer McCarthy free time to reply. Paley knew McCarthy would demand such time, so he thought it better that Murrow offer it before it was demanded of him. Murrow agreed at once. The historic program, one of Murrow's and television's greatest accomplishments, went on the air Tuesday night, March 9, 1954.

Murrow and Friendly knew that they were in fact all alone on this program. Despite Paley's statements of support, they suspected that he had not accepted an advance view of the program in order to be able to disassociate himself from it if it went badly. This may have been an unfair suspicion but it seemed to be confirmed when news director Sig Mickelson also refused an advance viewing, as did the sponsor, ALCOA. Murrow and Friendly were walking on the ledge of a skyscraper in high wind with no safety net under them. If the public reacted badly, if McCarthy went into one of his rages, their careers could come to a crashing end.

Fred Friendly was so nervous that his hand was shaking and he missed the button on his stopwatch when he signaled Murrow to start the show. Ed pulled no punches; he had decided to go for broke. There would be no traditional "balancing" the program. Ed had said, in advance, that asking him to be fair and balanced about "Jumping Joe" would be the equivalent of asking him to be fair and balanced in a report on Goebbels, Hitler's wartime minister of propaganda.

Ed would cue up a clip of McCarthy making some wild and uncorroborated accusation, and then he would give the true "facts," rebutting McCarthy point by point. At the end, Murrow threw aside the fundamental CBS rule against editorializing. Murrow believed that McCarthy was a threat to destroy the Republic and no journalistic rule was going to gag Ed or prevent him from stating his case. He did so, putting his final words slowly, solemnly, with all the force of his being behind them.

"We will not walk in fear, one of another. We will not be driven by fear into an age of unreason, if we dig deep in our own history and our doctrine and remember that we are not descended from fearful men. Not from men who feared to write, to speak, to associate, and to defend causes that were, for the moment, unpopular. . . . There is no way for a citizen of the Republic to abdicate his responsibility."

As I watched and listened, I saw Ed as a true descendant of Thomas Jefferson, of Tom Paine, of Benjamin Franklin. I asked Friendly for a kinescope of the program, which I then showed to the top journalists and officials of Paris who had so often looked down on us for failing to stand up to the witch-hunting demagogue. I was proud to be a member of the Murrow team.

As the show ended and the picture faded away to black, Murrow was totally depressed, in the grip of what he called his "black Murrow" mood. Producer Joe Wershba was one of the first to rush over in the studio to congratulate Murrow, who was still sitting, brooding and sweating on the set. Joe's wife, Shirley, a news editor, was there too, heavy with child. She rushed to embrace Ed and tell him, "Ed, if it's a boy, I'll name him for you." Grim-faced, unsmiling, Murrow replied, "Do you really think that this was all worth it?" At the most glorious, bravest moment of achievement and triumph, he always felt that he had failed to live up to his goal.

He need not have worried for a moment. Within seconds, the CBS switchboard lit up as thousands of calls flooded in. With rare exceptions, they were all congratulatory, some almost embarrassingly worshipful. Murrow could never take praise gracefully.

He was essentially a shy man, a pessimist, and, despite his fame, a modest man. When his radio newswriter, Jesse Zousmer, a cynic, was annoyed at all the adulation of Murrow, he started a Murrow Ain't God Club. Several newsmen wrote in to join. But the club disbanded abruptly when Jesse received a letter from Murrow, asking to be a member.

One thousand phone calls were logged in in the first hour, two thousand in the next. The switchboard broke down. Western Union messengers were run bow-legged carrying huge bundles of telegrams in the days when telegrams were still delivered. The calls and telegrams ran ten to one in Murrow's favor. A full day after the program the CBS switchboard still could not handle the torrent of calls. The hate-mongers, the McCarthyites, screamed in rage, but their screams were drowned out by the cheers of the public.

Within a week, the Gallup Poll showed a big drop in McCarthy's approval rating. At a dinner in Washington, Murrow's wartime comrade, President Eisenhower, came over to his table. The president rubbed his hand up and down Ed's back, as everyone watched. Then he said loudly, "Just wanted to see if there were any knives sticking in there." Everyone laughed and applauded. The day had been won in that ostentatious act of presidential approval.

Murrow, never one to take a step back once he had plunged forward, got up, shook hands with the president, and said strongly enough for the others to hear, "From here on in, it's up to you Mr. President." It sounded to some like a direct challenge to Eisenhower to climb down off the fence and come out against McCarthy. Murrow told me that this was not his intention at all and that the president, who knew him well, understood that Ed was only saying that television alone could not end the threat to democracy. McCarthy had to be destroyed by his peers in the Congress and the White House.

Murrow's early depression lifted as more and more congratulations poured in. He was amused by all the CBS executives who had never said one word to him, who had, in a sense, walked across the street when they saw him coming, suddenly appearing to offer him a drink and handshake. Ed particularly appreciated one honest executive who said to him, "Great show, Ed. Sorry you did it."

The "See It Now" show did not immediately floor the senator, but it certainly greased the skids for McCarthy, who lost his ability to terrorize the public. McCarthy denounced Murrow wildly in his reply on his CBS show. Murrow, accepting all-out war, hit McCarthy even more fiercely on his radio evening news show. All rules against editorializing or personal opinions disappeared. Murrow and McCarthy were engaged in a bitter personal feud, and Murrow was winning every round of the fight.

Much later, at a dinner in our apartment in Paris, my wife, Dorothy, asked Ed for his final thoughts on the McCarthy broadcast. Ed looked sad as he answered, "I know it had to be done, and it was done well. But I am troubled and have real reservations about it. Did I use and abuse the power of TV? Did I act responsibly with total integrity? I'm truly not certain." Then he threw back his head, the cloud lifted off his face as he laughed and said, "You know and I know that I'm the guy in the white hat. But what could a guy in a black hat do if he had the power of this medium in his hand as I did?" His comment rang true. It testified to his diamond-hard integrity, despite his self-doubts. Those self-doubts by this superlative man were perhaps his most redeeming feature; they earned our love as well as our admiration.

After Senator McCarthy's scorching attack on Murrow in his CBS reply, reporters came to Murrow's office and asked him for a comment. He said it would be his last word on the subject. This is what he said: "When the record is finally written, as it will be one day, it will answer the question 'Who had helped the Communist cause and who has served his country better, Senator McCarthy or I?' I would like to be remembered by the answer to that question."

More than thirty years have gone by since Ed asked for that ultimate verdict of history. There is no doubt about the verdict. McCarthy is remembered with revulsion and shame. Edward R. Murrow is revered.

Despite the great success of "See It Now," tensions had built up between Murrow and his oldest friend and backer, Bill Paley. As CBS had grown into a multibillion-dollar industry, with many interests beyond broadcasting and news, Paley had become increasingly irritated by what he felt were personal crusades by Murrow. What really bothered him, beyond the controversial nature of some programs, were the constant complaints from big-money advertisers and affiliated stations. When Murrow did one of his greatest reports, an exposé of the cruel, inhuman treatment of migrant farm workers in the South, "Harvest of Shame," southern affiliates "blacked out" the program, that is, refused to carry it.

Conflicts of this kind caused Paley to tell Murrow one day "Every time you come up with another of your controversies, I get a pain in my gut." Murrow could have turned that back on Paley, saying, "I remember the day when your guts were stronger." But, as Murrow told me later, "There was no point in ending an old friendship with insults and bitterness. I knew then that my time at CBS had run out."

Despite the nationwide applause for his TV work, Murrow still hated it. He disliked the pancake makeup on his dark beard. It only made him sweat more. He hated the glaring lights and the glitz of TV. All during his TV successes, he clung desperately to his real love, his evening radio news program, where he and he alone was in control. On radio he didn't have "a dozen yapping hounds snapping at my ankles and barking at me. On radio, between me and the American people, there was only one engineer, who flipped a switch and pointed a finger to let me know I was on the air. On TV, there were a dozen people blocking the public away from me."

Ed was wrong, for he really did break through all the obstacles and screens of TV, but he hated every minute of it. Despite his feelings, he was a natural television performer. As CBS foreign correspondent Alexander Kendrick wrote in *Prime Time*, his biography of Murrow: "His eyes, deep-set and grave, his mouth and chin, clean-cut, purposeful, a baritone timbre of voice and straightforward address, serious content, heightened by an occasional Mephistophelian smile."

On the opening program of "See It Now," Murrow had said: "Good evening. This is an old team trying to learn a new trade." Those were modest words for what, in fact, was the beginning of a new journalistic dimension. The joining together in one picture of the two oceans was not just a technical gimmick. It held out the promise of more electronic miracles that would bring the world into the American home. It was one of the first steps toward making the world a global village.

In those days CBS did not even give Murrow a budget to live within; he had no budget at all. Friendly, as producer, could spend whatever it took to put the show on the air. Murrow's okay was all he needed. He did not report to any CBS executive, a procedure that today would be unthinkable. In those days, it didn't matter. CBS was proud of Murrow. He brought tremendous prestige to the network, and that prestige created a CBS aura that was a powerful magnet for all talent, producers, and advertisers. Paley figured that Murrow was more than worth anything that his programs might cost. Eventually, the "See It Now" programs would cost about $100,000 each. Today it would be three or four times that much.

In the extraordinary decade of the fifties, we were all trailblazers, exploring uncharted territory, expanding the horizons of a miraculous new land of sight and sound around the world. Because the company was smaller, devoted only to broadcasting, news was bigger, more important. Paley did not care how much money news spent, for it was a relatively small sum for the giant returns it brought. The network was a gold mine, a license for making money, and Paley felt that news was the license fee he had to pay for that privilege.

We excelled, not because we were all more talented than today's competent men and women, but because we were a privileged few, allowed to explore our potential without strong supervision or restrictions. Paley would tell us, on our visits to New York, that he "dined out on the News Division." Wherever he went, to the most glamorous cocktail and dinner parties, people would talk to him about CBS news programs. He walked tall among the mighty and the powerful who ruled our society. We gave him the prestige that money alone could not buy. He held the reins lightly and gave us our head.

Christmas 1952 was a landmark date for "See It Now" and TV news. Murrow and a technical crew had gone to Korea. It would be the first war that would be seen as well as heard in American living rooms. "See It Now" was expanded to a full hour for the war report. Murrow covered the story as he had covered the London blitz; there was no glossing over the harshness of combat in Korea. You could almost feel the cold, see the frozen ground, the towering mountains, the tight, drawn faces of frightened soldiers, the blood and guts of war. Until "See It Now" went to Korea, the war had been reported mainly by reports from Washington on how the fighting was going, illustrated by Army Signal Corps film, carefully vetted to show the best of our military efforts. Murrow and his teams got down into the freezing mud, the foxholes, and showed us the terrible trials of our fighting men. Murrow revealed the misery, the hopelessness of the Korean War, which had become a deadly no-win stalemate, a tragic war, with no glory, no nobility, no end in sight.

With Ed in Korea were four toughened World War II veteran reporters: Bill Downs, husky, big-bellied but muscular, with a voice that could carry over bursting shells; a buddy of Murrow's from the days of the London blitz, Larry LeSueur, a cool, down-playing wit; Bob Pierpoint, the youngest of them, a competent journeyman reporter, never dramatic but always precise and accurate; Lou Cioffi, a tough, streetwise New York Italian, sardonic, wisecracking, recklessly brave. Lou, who would become my colleague in the Paris bureau, was wounded in Korea and sent back for a quieter spell in the New York newsroom.

Each reporter had been assigned a camera team on the Korean front. For the first time, pictures and sounds were recorded together and the war, in all its horrors, was brought home to the American people. It was a forerunner of network coverage on an even greater scale in a later Asian horror, the war in Vietnam. The CBS teams, in the bitter cold of winter, would lug their heavy equipment, which had not yet been miniaturized as it is today, up and down mountains. They hauled and pulled their cameras and sound machines to the top of Pork Chop Hill to interview a young soldier from Nebraska trying to dig a foxhole out of the frozen ground. Today, this would be routine. Then it was a revelation. Murrow's "See It Now" team set the standards.

The "See It Now" Korean report aired on December 28, 1952. Jack Gould, the acerbic TV columnist of *The New York Times*, the most authoritative critic of television, whose word could make or break a program, wrote that "See It Now" in Korea was "one of the finest programs ever seen on TV." *Variety*, the bible of the industry, hailed it as "The New Journalism." In fact it was simply the best journalism of old journalists.

There had been conflict over Korean War coverage even before the "See It Now" report of 1952. Back in the summer of 1950 there had been a serious quarrel between Murrow and Bill Paley. Paley, always insisting on his "no-opinion" rule, had warned Ed before he flew to Korea to stay within the bounds of the guidelines for war coverage laid down by the Pentagon. Murrow had told him he would do his best but that the Pentagon guidelines were designed to shield the military from any criticism and that CBS would not want to be a party to any cover-up. Paley agreed but warned him again to avoid personal opinion and editorializing.

Inevitably, the clash would come. You could not be an honest, probing reporter and live within the restrictions that Paley and the military sought to impose. Murrow would not tolerate anything but the most truthful, realistic reporting, no flag-waving, no covering up mistakes. There was no scarcity of mistakes by the High Command in Korea. Murrow did a taped report from the frontlines in 1950 in which he asserted that the American High Command had wasted men and material in a useless offensive action because, in the words of one officer, who was in a position to know, "we decided that we needed a victory."

Murrow raised questions that others did not dare touch. He told of our soldiers "moving up through dead valleys, through villages to which we have put the torch by retreating. What then of the people who live there? They have lived on the knife-edge of despair and disaster for centuries. Their pitiful possessions have been consumed in the flames of war. Will our reoccupation of that flea-bitten land lessen or increase the attraction of Communism?"

There was little doubt that Murrow had broken military guidelines and had flouted Paley's dictum against editorial opinion. Even Ed's friends and admirers in CBS News felt he had gone too far. There was no doubt whatsoever about Bill Paley's reaction. He was furious and he gave the order to "kill" the Murrow tape from Korea. The entire news operation went into shock. No one had ever dared censor Ed Murrow. Now there would be a clash between the chairman and his greatest broadcaster. It looked like bad days in the News Division.

Paley and Murrow did have an angry quarrel. But both men were devoted to each other and to the progress of CBS. They put the quarrel behind them and got on with developing CBS.

In those early days of the 1950s, the network was alive with new ideas, new men, and new procedures. It was growing at a fantastic speed. Radio was still the major medium but TV was catching up and would soon surpass it.

During this period, CBS News had a personality split between the demands of radio and television. Stanton decided to give each medium its own news director, to have radio and TV function as distinct entities under the overall jurisdiction of CBS top management. The radio director was a crusty but lovable veteran newsman, T. Wells ("Ted") Church. Ted was a political conservative or, as he liked to claim, "Jeffersonian Republican." He was devoted to his men and, conservative that he was, would defend newsmen against the detestable attacks of right-wingers. When one agent of Counterattack complained to Ted that one of his reporters was "un-American," Ted growled at him and said, "So are you! In fact, I am the only real American around here. I'm a Mohawk Indian." Ted's family background was part-Indian.

The television news director was an amiable and devoted fan of CBS newsmen. Sig Mickelson had been news chief of CBS station WCCO. He was highly competent and would move up to become vice-president of CBS News until, as happens to almost everyone, he was fired after a bad season and a convention in which NBC had beaten out CBS for first place in the ratings.

One of the men that Sig developed, which should have earned him considerable gratitude from management, was a young reporter who had been a top war correspondent. His name was Walter Cronkite. Cronkite had been born in St. Joseph, Missouri, then moved to Kansas City, and finally to Houston, Texas. Texas, Kansas, and Missouri would all claim him as their native son. If you listened carefully to his accent, you would know he was basically from Kansas. He had that Plains twang and the inability to pronounce "ing." Walter always said "go-een" for "going."

Cronkite attended some classes at the University of Texas but was not an enthusiastic student. He quit school and was hired by the *Houston Press*. He went on from there to a reporting job with United Press in their Kansas City bureau. He was working round the clock for what he later called "coffee and doughnuts." U.P. was not the most generous of employers. But Cronkite, barely out of his teens, loved every minute of it—it sure beat hitting the books at school.

When war broke out, Cronkite was sent overseas to cover the battles. He took to war correspondence like a pig to truffles. He loved the excitement, the danger. He would fly in bombers, slog along with the "dogfaces." He was among the first to hit the beaches at Normandy, and was right up there with General Patton's men in the Battle of the Bulge. Walter would crawl down in the mud with the GIs, talk to them when the shooting had died down, doing his "Ernie Pyle" bit of hometown interviews. He snaked over to one young soldier in a foxhole and asked his name and his hometown. The soldier looked at him in surprise and said, "I thought you knew that, Mr. Cronkite, I'm your driver."

Walter had met Ed Murrow in London before the invasion of Europe. Ed had liked him and had heard good things about his accuracy, honesty, and speed of reporting, the essential characteristics of the best wire-service men. Ed offered him a job with CBS at $125 a week, more than double his U.P. salary. When Walter told his bureau chief, he offered him an immediate raise to stay with the service. The raise did not match Murrow's offer but Cronkite accepted it. He knew exactly how to function for the service but knew little or nothing about radio reporting. He thanked Murrow and explained why he would stay with U.P. Murrow understood and wished him good luck and continued success.

When the war ended, Cronkite tried to get a job with a big-city paper, but no one would take him on. He went back to Kansas, went around to see a number of papers in the Midwest that were not by themselves able to afford a full-time Washington correspondent, and suggested to each that he be taken on and work for them all in a kind of small, personal syndicate. They agreed, and off to Washington he went.

In 1950, when the Korean War broke out and Murrow was preparing to fly there, he met Cronkite in Washington and, knowing of his excellent war record in Europe, again offered him a job with CBS, as a war correspondent in Korea. This time Cronkite jumped at it. He had listened to radio and felt he could easily learn the needed techniques. Besides, he was an expert war correspondent and knew he could do the job.

His wife, Betsy, was pregnant and Walter asked Ed if he could delay his flight to Korea until the baby was born and his family was safe. Murrow agreed immediately, and Walter was assigned to the CBS station in Washington, WTOP, until he was ready to go to Korea. At WTOP he had general assignments at first, until Sig

Mickelson, the TV news director, came to see him one day with an idea.

Sig was frustrated because Ted Church, the radio director, jealously guarded his precious "stars," Collingwood, Sevareid, Calmer, Smith. They all had well-paid radio programs and were still hesitant about the new medium, television. So Mickelson had no big names to put on his television programs. He had met Cronkite when Murrow hired him and was impressed with his professionalism and, above all, by his rich, warm, baritone voice, his optimism, his supreme confidence without arrogance or vanity, his no-nonsense attitude. Walter had never made any bones about his lack of formal education. "I am not an intellectual, not a deep-thinker," Walter told Mickelson, "but I damn well know a news story when I see one and I'm a good reporter."

Sig thought he would give Cronkite a tryout on the local 11:00 P.M. news. Cronkite was an immediate hit. He read his script with an easy, relaxed manner, yet managed to get a punch into his delivery. When a fast-breaking story came up in the middle of the newscast, he would glance at the slip of paper handed to him by a floor manager and read the news "bulletin" with ease. His eye-mouth-brain coordination was just what was needed in an anchor-man of a news show. In fact, he was so good that Sig canceled his assignment to Korea and kept him at WTOP, planning to use him on the network. Walter was furious. He felt that he had been "sold down the river to a lousy local TV station and I was ready to quit, on the spot."

In that same period, 1950, the distant future of CBS was coming into bud, although neither he nor anyone else could know that. Cronkite's eventual successor, Dan Rather, had just been hired for his first job in radio, on KSAM, Huntsville, Texas. Dan, a twenty-year-old Texan, a graduate of Sam Houston State University, had majored in journalism. KSAM paid him forty cents an hour to do everything from broadcasting sports to sweeping the newsroom floor.

By then all the building blocks that would bring CBS News to its heights of prestige and profit were in place. There were Murrow and Friendly with "See It Now," then "CBS Reports," then Murrow's unexpected spinoff from a "See It Now" episode, called "Person to

Person," the least prestigious but biggest money-earner of Murrow's career; Doug Edwards, the evening anchorman, and his dynamic producer-director, Don Hewitt, who would become the most successful producer of this first television century; Walter Cronkite, preparing his own extraordinary future by trying out in different programs—"The Man of the Week," "You Are There," "The Twentieth Century," the latter produced by two of the brightest men in television, Burton ("Bud") Benjamin and Ike Kleinerman. And a long list of lower-level editors, cameramen, sound men, cutters, assignment-desk men, the mechanics who kept the great machine rolling and ready for the biggest breaking stories, so many of which were ahead.

ABC lagged far behind, but NBC was working hard to close the gap with CBS, the leader. Edwards fought neck to neck in the ratings race with John Cameron Swayze and finally pulled a length ahead by 1953. But NBC came up with a winner that would overtake CBS News and win first place: the team of Chet Huntley and David Brinkley. They achieved fame in the 1956 conventions and took over the evening news, with Brinkley anchoring his section in Washington, and Chet in New York. Their closing lines, "Good night, David," "Good night, Chet," became a national catchphrase used by comedians and politicians as if it were the very soul of wit.

Television was ready for a big jump forward in the first year of the decade. In 1950, there were 40 million to 50 million radio sets in American homes. TV was behind but moving up fast, with a more than respectable 10 million sets in use. TV had become the younger, not the poorer, brother of the networks. One year later there were 40 million TV sets in use and weekly sales were surging to reach a peak of 5 million a year in the mid-fifties.

Our inaugural year-end show in 1950, called the "Mid-Century Report," became an annual classic, an eagerly awaited and applauded feature. The senior correspondents would fly in from around the world and sit at a round table, with Ed Murrow as the moderator posing questions about our beats and the events of the year. There were some amusing highlights in every show, for the discussion was freewheeling, unrehearsed, and the participants were men of wit and perception.

One amusing moment occurred in an exchange between Winston Burdett, our Rome and Middle East correspondent, and me, in from Paris. When Winston was talking of the misery of homeless Palestinians, I asked him why some super-rich Arabs, like King Ibn Saud, didn't spend some of their oil billions to help their so-called brothers, the way the Israelis, without oil or resources, did everything they could to help Jewish refugees.

Winston started to say, "Well, Ibn Saud isn't all that rich . . ." He saw a storm cloud coming up over my face and hastily added, "Just a minute, David, just a minute! I want you to know that I don't agree with what I just said."

The most hilarious, if somewhat ribald, moment occurred off the air, not on the show. Bill Downs had gone to the men's room just before airtime. A page ran in and shouted, "Mr. Downs, sir, one minute to air." Bill, a big powerful man, hastily yanked his zipper and pulled it right out of his fly. He ran to the round table and carefully crossed his legs and wrapped his jacket around his front. In the course of the spirited discussion, he forgot what had happened and spread his legs wide. At the show's end, Don Hewitt, in the control room, called out, "A fine show, gentlemen, and you, Bill Downs, really put on a spectacular show. Just look down at your crotch." Bill looked down at a gaping space. He looked around the table and in his big, gruff voice said, "Well, for the first time in the history of television, the public can legitimately ask, 'Who was that prick?' "

Television received its first major test as a medium with equal rights of access to all news events, against the powerful opposition of the traditional, established press, suspicious of, even disdainful of the new medium. It came in the presidential election campaign of 1952, and I found myself, on my first assignment in the United States, right in the middle of a tempest. It was not of my seeking or my making. It was thrust upon me. It almost broke me and ended my career, but, at the critical moment, I came out of it with renewed prestige. It was a close call for a day or two.

It began with a series of conferences at CBS News headquarters in New York. Top management, while insisting on total objectivity in covering the election, nonetheless had its own favorites. Paley and Stanton were, after all, citizens, as well as executives. They split on whom they favored for the presidency. Paley, who had been a wartime colonel, had worked with and come to admire General

Eisenhower and was an enthusiastic Eisenhower supporter. Frank Stanton was just as committed to Adlai Stevenson. There were a lot of cynical comments about how clever top management was. CBS could not lose the elections, no matter who won.

There would certainly be no favoritism on the air, but we all knew that top brass was more than interested in how we would cover the candidates. Sig Mickelson talked to Paley about the right man to be assigned to General Eisenhower. Sig gave him a list of possible candidates. Paley said, "You're the news chief, who is your choice?" Paley was not going to commit himself. Sig did not hesitate. "I'm planning to call Schoenbrun back from Paris and put him on the Eisenhower campaign."

Paley made no comment; he just asked questions. "Why David? He's a foreign correspondent, a specialist on French affairs, he's never covered politics in America." Paley told me later that he was delighted at Sig's choice but would not reveal it. "I could not interfere with the head of News. If I had named you, it would have put an unfair burden on you to have been selected by the chairman, and made things awkward between you and Sig." In those days Paley was truly a sensitive and understanding executive.

Both Sig and Ted Church, the radio director, told Paley that I had a long history of working with General Eisenhower in Algiers and again after the war at SHAPE (Supreme Headquarters, Allied Powers Europe) just outside Paris. I had even briefly been a TV coach for Eisenhower, who hated the medium and was awful on it, his bald head gleaming while his rambling sentences did not parse and never seemed to end. We had a good relationship, which would be important to CBS, giving me ready access to the candidate. "Besides," said Sig, and it was the clincher, "for anyone who manages to understand French politics, American politics should be a breeze."

I got the assignment in a phone call from Ted Church instructing me to wrap up current assignments in Paris, bone up on American political procedures, and accompany Ike back home whenever the general decided to launch his presidential bid. It was the biggest challenge in my life since the glorious moment I had received Ed Murrow's telegram asking me to take over the Paris bureau of CBS News.

General Eisenhower decided to open his campaign in his

hometown, Abilene, Kansas. Bill Paley had asked Sig Mickelson about the problems involved in televising Ike's first campaign speech nationally. Sig checked it out and reported back that AT&T could lay down cables and telephone connections, but that it would cost $5,000. Paley sensed that it could be a giant step forward for television. He approved the cost. He was also an admirer of Eisenhower and felt a special tie to his wartime chief.

When I arrived in Abilene, Ed Murrow was already there, but he had refused to participate in television coverage. He was there to do his regular evening radio news show. He grinned at me and said, "It's all yours, buster, you're the man on the spot." Neither of us knew how right he was.

Technicians had laid their cables in a barnlike structure just off the local ballpark. A rostrum had been set up for Eisenhower at one end of the grounds. People were already pouring into the field to see and hear Ike, their "Man from Abilene." Some fifteen to twenty thousand men and women had come in from farms all around Abilene. Fresh from Paris, I was astonished at the expanse of the wheat fields stretching to the horizon. I thought to myself that in all my travels I had never seen so far and yet so little as the great plains of the Middle West. As an easterner I had always resented the phrase "the heartland of America," for the Midwest. I thought of it as the belly of America. But I was impressed with the awesome scope of our farm output. We could not only feed ourselves but produce enough for the whole world as well.

Overhead the sky was ominous, leaden, with black thunderheads rolling down upon us. I feared a sudden downpour that would ruin the inaugural speech of the campaign. I checked our microphones on the rostrum and walked over to my camera team. They were ready for action.

I stood in front of the camera, nervously checking the sky, and did a brief introduction to the speech, setting the scene. When I saw the general approaching the rostrum, I turned my head and said, "Here now is General Eisenhower." The quick, clever cameraman had panned over as I turned, and then he zoomed in on Eisenhower. I stepped away and the camera moved in on the general, who had mounted the rostrum.

Booming cannons began exploding. The sky lit up with flashes. It looked like a fierce battle was being fought. A sudden storm had broken over us. Rain poured down, soaking the crowd and the general. Ike's sparse hair was plastered over his bald dome, while water flooded his spectacles and ran down his nose. It was a disaster.

I rushed over to the rostrum and signaled to Eisenhower to follow me to the barn, where we were keeping our cameras dry and where he could find shelter from the storm. He stomped inside, swearing. Like de Gaulle, Eisenhower would on occasion revert to the barracks language of his soldiering days. He was in a temper and he blew up when I said that we had just enough light in the barn to televise his speech. He bellowed at me, "Damnation, I'm not going to hide away here while twenty thousand people get soaked waiting to see me."

I had forgotten how much he hated and mistrusted radio and television. He was bad at both, but worse at television. He would always keep his head down, presenting his bald dome to the camera. I had tried to coach him back in Paris, but it always ended with his shouting at me and throwing me out of his office. I had tired of reminding him of Roosevelt's highly effective fireside chats on radio, and of de Gaulle's extraordinary success in making himself a hero of France, although most Frenchmen and women had never seen him, by the force of his oratory in broadcasts from London to France. De Gaulle had created himself uniquely on radio waves.

I had chosen a bad example. Eisenhower disliked de Gaulle's pomposity, his ego, his manipulation of the masses by his oratory. "Don't you see how frightening this is?" Eisenhower had asked me. "A clever demagogue, a Huey Long, a Hitler, could use radio for evil ends."

"But, General," I protested, "you know CBS. You are a good friend of Bill Paley and Ed Murrow. You know they are men of the highest integrity and commitment to public service without prejudice."

"Well, I don't like or trust radio or TV. I don't like the idea of something where you have to depend on the integrity of the men who run it and not the basic integrity of the institution itself. It can fall out of good hands and into evil hands. I don't like it."

Those words, spoken months before, were running through my head as I watched him stride purposefully back to the rostrum in the rain. It did not presage well for my assignment as the radio-

TV reporter on the Eisenhower campaign. Eisenhower may have had some friendly feelings about me personally but not about what I was doing. I knew I would have to walk a careful line in dealing with him.

We hastened to lug our heavy equipment out of the barn and back onto the field. Ike was getting ready to speak and, quite evidently, didn't give a damn whether our cameras were in position to carry his speech beyond the fifteen to twenty thousand people in the ballpark to the many millions waiting to hear and see him across the nation.

The storm mercifully abated and only a misty spittle of drizzle was falling on the general. The wind whipped the pages of his speech and occasional thunderclaps would muffle his voice. He fought on doggedly, asserting that this election was about liberty versus socialism, an assertion that astonished me. I had never once heard him say anything like that back at his military headquarters outside Paris. Eisenhower called for cuts in government spending and elimination of proliferating federal agencies. He wanted to end government controls over business and to turn civil rights responsibilities over to the state.

It was a rockbound, hidebound, old-line, right-wing Republican litany. Eisenhower sounded like his adversary for the nomination, Senator Robert Taft, leader of the conservative wing of the party. This was not the Eisenhower sought after by the more liberal eastern establishment, the Henry Cabot Lodges, the Rockefellers. Perhaps being in the Middle West, a conservative heartland, had influenced the general. Perhaps his contest with Taft made him reach for the Taft supporters. But I suspected that I was hearing the true Eisenhower, the man from Abilene, the military conservative, who had for so long rigorously excluded politics from his duties that we had not known what he really thought. It was a revelation that disturbed me, although I still had great admiration and trust in him as an honest man and a man of peace. I felt relieved when he called for an armistice in Korea and pledged that, if elected, he would fly to Korea to seek peace.

I returned to my miserable, coffinlike "sleeperette" in a train parked on a siding outside town. The hotels of Abilene, about two or three of them, did not have enough rooms for the hundreds of reporters who had come to cover the event. As I climbed onto the train, Ed Murrow was there signaling me to join him in the lounge car. I moved quickly to get out of my sodden clothes and joined him at his table, where he was drinking bourbon and branch water. He offered me a glass but I refused. I could never stomach whiskey, hated its taste and bite. After so many years in Paris, my tipple was wine. They had none in Abilene so I settled for a sour-tasting beer.

Murrow, his head down, looked up at me from under his black brows, his face somber. He said, "David, there's a small problem about tomorrow's news conference in the Abilene theater. And, it's on your shoulders."

Murrow went on to explain that Jim Hagerty, Eisenhower's press chief, a veteran *New York Times* reporter, had told Murrow that TV would be barred from the general's news conference. "Your lights and cameras would turn the event into a kind of circus," Hagerty had said, adding that Reston of the *Times* and other top Washington journalists had demanded that TV be kept out.

Murrow, who had no use for TV himself, nevertheless was outraged at the discrimination by the written press against TV, and shocked that a candidate for the presidency would dare black out an important American medium of communications with the people. He told Hagerty, "Wherever a pencil goes, so will go our microphones and cameras. Radio and TV will not be gagged and blacked out."

Murrow then set up a conference call with the three chief executives of the networks, Bill Paley of CBS, David Sarnoff of NBC, and Leonard Goldenson of ABC. Paley said, "We want a live camera broadcasting to a joint network pool, all three networks transmitting the pictures and sounds across the nation. We want those cameras focusing directly on Schoenbrun when he walks into the theater and challenges the security guards.

"Schoenbrun has been named all-networks pool correspondent. Backing him up will be Frank Bourgholzer of NBC. David is to march right in, forcing his way through any barrier, with the camera on him. If the guards stop him and order him out, he is to defy the order. I don't want to see Schoenbrun walk out of that theater. If they won't let him in, he must force them to carry him out, while our cameras show the entire nation that the American people are being prevented from watching the Eisenhower news conference. The voters will know whom to blame and it won't be Reston of the *Times* or anyone else but Eisenhower himself."

Paley may have been an Eisenhower advocate but he was, above anything else, the chief of a network that was being challenged in its very right to exist as an equal medium. Goldenson and Sarnoff completely concurred with Paley's decision. They had put me in the toughest spot I had ever been in.

I felt like a subaltern leading the Charge of the Light Brigade as I slowly walked into the theater, Frank Bourgholzer some steps behind me, the cameraman on my heels. Up ahead, at the entrance into the theater, I saw some security men huddled in conference with one of Hagerty's assistant press representatives. I kept walking right up to the guards. They stepped back but then fell in step with me, one on each side, another leading the way. As our strange procession entered the theater, I could see a few hundred reporters already seated in the orchestra. To my left was the balcony. The guards closed in on either side of me and steered me toward the steps leading up to the balcony. "You can sit here," they muttered.

I thought to myself, "Well, the back of the bus for TV, but at least I'm in. I followed Paley's instructions and they did not dare keep me out." I looked around and realized that the balcony seats were a much better vantage point for TV than the orchestra. The orchestra curved downward and was crowded. The balcony was empty except for our team and it was elevated, so that our camera would get a good sweeping view of the orchestra and the stage where Eisenhower would speak. I began to relax. "I've done it," I thought, mistakenly.

Our technicians had installed mikes for me and for Bourgholzer. Then I froze as Jim Hagerty walked on the stage. Not because of anything that Hagerty was doing, but because I suddenly saw that the technicians had not installed a television monitor or a return-cue line from New York. I therefore had no way of knowing whether a TV picture was being transmitted or whether the sound from the stage was being carried to a network line. I was sitting in limbo, blind and deaf on the biggest story of my life. My heart and my stomach crowded one another trying to jump out my throat. My "backup," Bourgholzer, a kindly man, looked at me with a sad smile. He shrugged his shoulders and looked to heaven imploringly.

Hagerty began to talk. Not knowing whether the national audience was hearing him, I began to tell them what he was saying, apologizing for talking over Hagerty. I did not know it then but Murrow would tell me later that all the top brass of the network, Paley, Stanton, Church, Mickelson and a gaggle of lesser executives were gathered in the office of Hubbell Robinson, vice-president in charge of programming, one of the key men of CBS. They were watching a TV set. Ted Church, my immediate boss and friend, was groaning. He stood up and shouted, "David, shut up, for the love of God, shut up." My voice was muffling Hagerty's and his voice was coming in strong, so it was hard to hear me. All across Manhattan, the giants of TV, Paley, Sarnoff, Goldenson, were cursing me. Thank my stars that I did not know that until later.

Then General Eisenhower came out of the wings walking toward center stage and a standing mike. I said, "I still don't know whether you will hear the general." I paused, while back in New York the groaning and imprecations doubled. "But," I continued, "I don't dare talk over the general. I'll keep silent and when he has finished I'll summarize his remarks for you." Cheers broke out in Hubbell Robinson's office. My career had been saved, but only barely.

Somehow I got through that ghastly scene. I staggered onto the train and collapsed. About an hour later, Murrow came to see me. "It was touch and go, David. At the beginning, they could have murdered you. But you showed good judgment when Ike began speaking. And none of this was your fault. The technicians fouled up and the top brass in New York now knows that. No one is angry with you. It's going to be a long campaign and you'll get plenty of chances to make your mark, while this will soon be forgotten. What is important is that we have won a great victory today. You brought us in and no one will ever try to bar TV again."

How wrong he was. TV would still have a crucial fight ahead at the convention in Chicago, and once again I would be in the middle of it, but this time without a disastrous foul-up.

If I had almost lost my job, Eisenhower had almost lost the election by the bad judgment of his aides in Abilene. Eisenhower, in his mistrust of television, had not realized that television was his main hope of winning the nomination that Senator Taft and the party regulars had all but tied down before the convention even began. For them, Eisenhower was not a party stalwart, but an outsider without ties or debts to those who ran the party. He owed no one anything and they had no leverage on him for appointments and patronage. If he could beat Taft, he would be the master of the party without ever having been a party man. He could turn the party upside down, clean out a lot of dinosaurs, bring in his own men, a terrifying thought to those who had been running it.

The regulars knew that they had a better chance to beat the Democrats with Eisenhower as their standard-bearer. But Eisenhower was an invention of the eastern big-city sophisticates, tainted with liberalism, and many of the party Old Guard would rather lose with Taft than win with Ike.

The only way that Eisenhower could break the grip of the good old boys would be to force open the doors of the smoke-filled room where a few leaders picked the candidate of their choice. The way to do that was through television cameras that would bring the American people into the convention hall. The people across the nation cared little about party lines or controls. They revered Eisenhower as their conquering hero, Democrats as well as Republicans. Only television could bring all the people into the hall. With a ground-swell of voter pressure, Eisenhower could wrest control from the Taft Old Guard, and only television could generate such a ground-swell.

The Old Guard knew this and feared TV. As the Eisenhower train made its way from headquarters in Denver to Chicago, I called CBS News, New York, at every whistle-stop. At one stop, my editors informed me that the Taft people had decided to bar television from the proceedings, particularly from the key meetings of the credentials committee. This committee was stacked with Old Guard Taft supporters. Its vote was crucial to the nomination. They would validate every Taft delegate and challenge the credentials of the Eisenhower delegates. In Texas and most of the southern states, the Republican Party barely existed. A few machine men could hand-pick the delegates without primaries or any expression of the public choice. They could pack the convention with Taft delegates, freezing out Ike on the first ballot.

I raced out of the whistle-stop station and just managed to jump aboard the train as it was getting up steam to roll on. Breathless, excited, caught up by the drama of the moment, without any thought of the ethics of my action, I made my way through the cars toward Eisenhower's private car. Passing through the cafeteria car, I saw Hagerty having a cup of coffee. I sat down and told him what Taft's people were planning and explained how the barring of television could end all hope of the nomination for his candidate.

Hagerty understood at once. He jumped up, thanked me hastily, and said he would tell Ike. I asked him to wait a moment, for I had an idea. It would do no good to talk to Ike without a plan to offset the Taft faction. I suggested that Ike could address a small crowd of Americans at the next whistle-stop, and tell them that he had been in Europe and seen the death of freedom in the East as an Iron Curtain descended from the Baltic to the Mediterranean, right through the heart of Europe. Then, he could say, "Now I've come home to see an Iron Curtain clanging down in our own heartland, in Chicago, at the Republican Convention. They want to ban television there. You, the American people, are being blacked out. They don't want you to see them picking their own candidate by party rule, instead of the will of the people."

Hagerty gave me a bear hug and rushed off to tell Ike. I sat there smugly proud, not thinking at all about what I had done. Instead of being an objective, strictly neutral reporter, I had entered the political fray in support of one candidate against another. If I had stopped to think about it, I doubt that I would have done what I did, although I could argue that I was fighting for television more than for Ike. I had been caught up in the sweep of events. And, as a citizen, I far preferred Ike to the reactionary Old Guard of the GOP. That was no excuse at all, I know. A reporter acts like a reporter, according to the rules of our game. I had no right to invoke my citizenly interests, to breach the rules of objectivity and fairness. Days later I realized what I had done and had serious misgivings about it, but the deed was done and could not be undone. I realized that day just how powerful television, young as it was, had already become and wondered just how far we would go to influence the political process of the nation. Today we know its awesome dominance of politics.

After two false starts, in which Eisenhower's rhetoric got so tangled that no one knew what he meant, he finally got off a brief, coherent statement about an Iron Curtain in Chicago blacking out the American people. It made headlines in every paper in the country, highlights on every radio and television news program. Telegrams, phone calls, and letters flooded the Chicago stockyards and Republican headquarters, demanding an "open convention."

The Old Guard surrendered and we marched in with our TV cameras prying and probing into every corner. The old smoke-filled room, the old bosses were finished. Politics would never be the same again. From smoke-filled rooms, we would go to proliferating primaries—the whole process controlled and magnified by television. It began at that landmark convention of 1952. No one would ever again try to ban television.

In that big breakthrough, another national phenomenon emerged, one that would win the American people for the next quarter of a century. A new star was born at the convention, the young man from Kansas whom Sig Mickelson had hired when he was unable to get any of the radio stars to work for him on TV. Sig chose Walter Cronkite to be the anchorman of the convention. In 1948 it had been Doug Edwards who had done so well that he was made anchor of the prime-time evening news. By 1952, Doug was so enshrined in that stellar role, so occupied with it, that he would have no time for a convention role. That opened the door for Cronkite, who wasted no time stepping through it and making the most of his opportunity.

Walter was magnificent in his new role. He called the story, play by play, straight, clear, factually, just the way Paley wanted it. He had no visible ideology, no personal opinion. After twenty-five years on the air most people did not know whether he was a Republican or a Democrat. Cronkite was strictly nonpartisan. As a U.P. reporter he had learned early to be first, fastest, and accurate. No punditing, no larger meaning of it all. As he had told Sig years before, "I am no intellectual. I'm a damned good reporter." He was.

Cronkite, unlike the more sophisticated Charles Collingwood, Eric Sevareid, and Howard Smith, worldly intellectuals all, was pure, unadulterated Middle America. He was fascinated by what was taking place on the convention floor and managed to project that fascination to his audience. He was so excited by what he was doing that he came close to becoming a sort of "Gee Whiz" kid. This naïveté was charming, and appreciated by millions of Americans. Walter didn't talk down to them from lofty heights. He talked to the people in their own Middle American accents and mispronunciations. He was one of them. He made listeners feel that they could do what he was doing. Paradoxically, that lifted him in their eyes, where they sometimes resented a Murrow or a Sevareid.

Walter became a family friend, the "most trusted man in America." They trusted him because he told the news straight, without any partisanship or prejudice for or against anyone. This corresponded exactly to the thinking of millions of Americans. Sig Mickelson knew that he had backed a winner when the radio stars who had snubbed TV and Cronkite for a year and more began coming around to his broadcasting booth above the convention floor to suggest, too casually, that perhaps they could be of some small help in the coverage.

Eisenhower had little trouble sweeping the convention. He won 590 votes to Taft's 500 on the first ballot. It was all over. Before a second ballot could be called, delegates were jumping up changing their first ballot vote. Taft's floor manager surrendered and moved to make the Eisenhower nomination unanimous. The military hero had won. Television had done much to help him win. Walter Cronkite had chronicled the story and jumped to national fame. And, in that historic breakthrough of 1952, another name that would make American history emerged. Republican advisers had chosen a running mate for Eisenhower, a freshman senator from California named Richard Nixon.

I had made a difficult but successful debut in national political reporting, but I was anxious to get back to my beat in Paris where I knew the ropes better than in Washington, and where I lived a life of glamour spiced occasionally by hardship and terror.

5

THE DARK SIDE OF GLAMOUR

In ancient times all roads led to Rome. In the 1940s and 1950s, all roads led to Paris. Paris had become the world's international capital. It was the site of the United Nations Educational, Scientific and Cultural Organization (UNESCO), with delegates and staffers from every corner of the world. The director-general, Julian Huxley, noted biologist, brother of the famed author, Aldous Huxley, attracted scientists and writers, poets and musicians, the leading world figures of education, science, and culture. Hemingway once wrote that Paris was a "moveable feast." It was that and more. It was a carnival, a never-ending spectacle of lights, color, beauty, wit, of rose petals in champagne, a strange mix of idealism and cynicism. It was exhilarating, irritating at times, and never dull.

In addition to UNESCO, other institutions established in the late forties and fifties would draw the world to Paris. The North Atlantic Treaty Organization (NATO) pulled together the Western democracies and brought us General Eisenhower, who, at the height of the Cold War, returned to Europe to rebuild an allied army in the face of the threat from Russia. The powerful Red Army, never demobilized at war's end, needed "only shoe leather to march to the Channel," according to an expression of the day. The democracies had eagerly and thoughtlessly dismantled their own military forces after Hitler and the Japanese were defeated.

NATO and UNESCO together could have provided a correspondent all the stories needed for a full day's file. But they were not lone institutions. There were many more: the Organization for Economic Cooperation and Development (OECD), where the heads of the big central banks of the world would come to confer. It had a brilliant staff of economists, trade and labor experts, specialists of every kind, each with a story to tell. Then came one of the historic changes in European politics, the creation of the European Economic Community, better known as the Common Market. It was the brainchild of a Frenchman, Jean Monnet, a man I came to revere as the most commonsensical, compassionate, peace-loving leader in the world. He never commanded a single soldier, but he changed the history of Europe more than Napoleon, Hitler, and Stalin. He persuaded the Germans and the French to integrate their heavy industries and their economies in the Coal and Steel Community and the Economic Community of Europe.

After having fought three wars in some seventy years, the French and Germans abandoned their fratricidal aggression and moved to swap minerals for coke, instead of making them booty in a war of conquest. The Rhine River, swollen with the blood of Frenchmen and Germans, became at last what nature had intended, a source of power, generating electricity for industry, and a water highway for moving goods and products between the countries.

I was close to Monnet, saw him regularly, listened to him explain his ideas for the new Europe. It was an ideal running story, dramatic, optimistic. I plunged into the stream of those events, immersing myself thoroughly in the exciting, hopeful developments of the postwar world, a world, we thought, of peace and prosperity for all. In the aftermath of victory in Europe and Japan, we really believed that. Being a foreign correspondent in Paris was having a privileged reserved seat, front row, at the greatest show on earth.

Not only did we have our choice of stories, we could pick and choose among the celebrities of the world. They all came to Paris, from Broadway, Hollywood, Harvard, Cal Tech, Washington, the movie stars, singers, violinists, opera stars, generals, scholars, senators, prime ministers, kings and queens, diplomats from every country in the world. Almost daily the phone would ring in my Paris office at 33 Champs-Elysées and it would be someone famous calling to say hello and asking when I would be free for a drink or a meal. That was the great advantage of being a newscaster. They heard me daily on radio, saw me two or three times weekly on television. I was like an old friend to many who had never met me in person. It has never ceased to astonish me to note the magnetism and unifying quality of broadcasting.

I hope I will not be accused of vulgar name-dropping if I mention just a few of the remarkable men and women who called me in Paris. Some became friends for years. The list is very long and the following is only a sampling of the legions of accomplished people who came to Paris in the 1940s and 1950s to join the talented group of Americans reporting from Paris:

Lauren Bacall and Humphrey Bogart; John Foster Dulles and General Eisenhower; Lawrence Tibbett of the Met; Princess Grace and Prince Rainier; Harold Macmillan, Prime Minister of England; Winston Churchill; Lily Pons and André Kostelanetz; Ernest Hemingway; John O'Hara; John Steinbeck; Irwin Shaw; T. S. Eliot; James Thurber; e. e. cummings; Elizabeth Taylor; John Huston; Grace Moore; Fredric March; J. Robert Oppenheimer; and Ho Chi Minh. It was a galaxy of suns, the international stars rivaled in brilliance by the talented and beautiful Parisians: Picasso, Georges Braque, Brigitte Bardot, Jean Cocteau, André Malraux, Jean-Paul Sartre and Simone de Beauvoir, Albert Camus, and, towering over everyone, the giant figure of Charles de Gaulle.

Paris was eternal springtime, handsome men courting beautiful women in flowered dresses at a round-the-clock garden party. Time stood still. We were all forever young, would never age, would drink champagne and dance in the streets always, for there were no tomorrows, only the glorious todays. Ah, but it was good to be alive in Paris in a springtime with no end.

It did end, of course. Nothing so wonderful could last for very long. But it did last for more years than I had the right to expect. There was a coterie of highly talented, witty men and women, the finest corps of journalists ever gathered together in one capital.

They were young and not yet well known, but many of them would make their marks and become legends in our cultural history, in writing, photography, dancing, movies, ballet. Gene Kelly lived around the corner from me on the Quai d'Orsay, near the Pont de l'Alma. He would invite us to his house to meet Serge Lifar and Jean-Louis Barrault. Robert Capa, the man who invented himself, was one of many famous photographers. We would all dine together several times a week, Capa, Chim (David Seymour), Henri Cartier-Bresson, men who would capture the world in photos.

More than forty years have passed but I still recall vividly some of their pictures. They were not only photojournalists, they were essayists and artists. Dr. Huxley asked Chim to do a special study of the children of Europe who had lived through the war. He did a photo album that was shown at exhibits around the world, winning critical acclaim everywhere. There were two particularly meaningful portraits. One was a shell-shocked little girl of about ten, who had lived through savage bombings. She was asked to do a drawing of the war. Chim's picture showed her staring wildly at the camera, her hair tousled, while behind her on the blackboard was her "drawing," a tangled, mad scrawl of squiggles and clashing lines going in every direction with no form or shape. It was a powerful portrait of a deeply disturbed mind.

In another mood was his picture of a Greek boy, his head shaven to rid him of lice, his feet bare and his clothes ragged. But a smile wider than his face and his shining eyes showed us a very happy boy. Dangling on his chest was a pair of new shoes, the laces tied behind his neck so he could wear the shoes as a necklace. It was obvious, as he stepped barefoot through the dust, that the new shoes were far too precious to be worn. No description of the scene could equal Chim's picture.

Henri Cartier-Bresson had sketched so many scenes around the world that it is difficult to signal any one as exceptional. What remains in my mind is a scene he shot in Shanghai during a panic. Hundreds of Chinese men and women had rushed to the Shanghai Bank to withdraw their savings. They were pushed into a line by the police and the line writhed in a serpentlike manner as they pushed and shoved. The panicked line looked like a giant centipede with one body and thousands of feet. No description of the Shanghai panic could have matched Cartier's photo.

Robert Capa had landed at Normandy in the first assault wave. He jumped off the landing craft before anyone else and dashed up the beach *ahead* of the troops, then whirled around to take head-on pictures of the assault force breaching the German lines, while machine-gun bullets whistled and hissed all around him. Back in New York, some clumsy fool fogged his film in the lab and few of the prints could be saved. But Capa's bravery made him an overnight hero, and *Life* would publish thousands of his films in the years ahead, making him the premier photojournalist of our times.

There was a man of exceptional and unique talent in Paris, neither a journalist nor broadcaster. His name was Art Buchwald, and he became one of the greatest humorists or satirists of America. Janet Flanner was a veteran from the heady days of Paris in the twenties, an intimate of Gertrude Stein, Hemingway, Cocteau and the literati of Paris. Janet was the author of the magnificent "Letter from Paris" published regularly in *The New Yorker* under her pseudonym Genêt. All of the men and women working in Paris in the forties and fifties were destined to set new standards of excellence for journalism.

A young Harvard graduate, a classmate of John F. Kennedy, a man of breeding and class, was briefly press attaché at the American embassy. Ben Bradlee had no desire for a diplomatic career. As soon as he could, he got the job of Paris correspondent for *Newsweek*. His office was near mine in the Herald Tribune building on the rue de Barri. We became good friends.

Ben came to me one day and said he needed to earn some extra dollars, asking whether I would use him as a "stringer" for CBS when I, or one of my staff, was not available. I agreed and shortly thereafter I called him to do some broadcasts. He said he would need a radio alias to avoid conflict with his byline in *Newsweek*. I dubbed him Ben Lenox, in memory of Lenox Avenue in Harlem, where I had been born. Ben did well until one day his phone rang and he heard the voice of his boss in New York, *Newsweek* editor Malcolm Muir. Muir told Bradlee to tell "your good friend" Ben Lenox that he ought to stop broadcasting since he sounds so much like Bradlee himself. Ben, who could not disguise his distinctive, slightly gravelly voice, assured Muir he would pass the message on to Ben Lenox. Bradlee would go on to become the premier journalist of America, as chief editor of *The Washington Post* during the hard-hitting exposés of Watergate by his staff reporters Woodward and Bernstein.

Another young reporter in Paris in those days who would make journalistic history was Theodore H. White. "Teddy" White had been the senior correspondent in China for Time-Life. He had a falling out with Henry Luce and left that organization. His monument to his years in China was a magnificent book, *Thunder Out of China*, a Book-of-the-Month Club best-seller, which earned not only high sales but critical acclaim. Teddy found a new job as an editor of the then liberal magazine *The New Republic*. He called me and gave me assignments to cover Paris events for the magazine. Then, when I left my agency, ONA, to go to CBS, Teddy replaced me as the ONA Paris correspondent. He was my best friend in Paris.

Teddy left Paris in the mid-fifties after his book on Europe, *Fire in the Ashes*, became another best-seller. He had captured the story of China and of Europe. It was now his decision to tackle the immensely more difficult challenge of America. Once again he succeeded brilliantly by doing what everyone said was impossible. Despite the intensive coverage of the Kennedy-Nixon election contest, Teddy set out to write a book re-creating the election from beginning to end, telling us what really did happen.

The book, *The Making of the President, 1960*, became a national sensation, instituting a new kind of journalism and launching a title that would be imitated a hundred times and more. There was a flood of "makings," of "sellings," of "greenings" of America. In fact, the title was not original with Teddy White. He took it from a book written in Paris in the twenties by Gertrude Stein, *The Making of an American*. But it was White, not Stein, who made the term a byword.

A few weeks after coming to Paris to take over the ONA bureau, Teddy White called to invite me over for a drink and a talk. He told me that he had been looking over the Paris beat to acclimatize himself and to find just who were the well-informed reporters with whom he would want to associate. He grinned and said, "You passed the test with high marks, so I'll start with you. Will you join me in selecting a group of men who, while working alone and competing, are willing to join forces to achieve what we cannot do alone?"

I asked him to tell me exactly what he had in mind. "Paris," said White, "is the Mecca of the world and the most famous and powerful people come here. You have little chance to get an exclusive interview with Churchill. I can't easily get to Adenauer or De Gasperi. But if you and I and several other top bureau chiefs jointly invite one of these 'sacred cows' into our pasture there's a good chance the cow will come."

I understood at once that he was right. "Shall we draw up a list of the men we want to join us, and work out ground rules for our meetings?"

Teddy was ready—he had drawn up a list in advance, expecting my agreement. I went over his list, objected to some names, added others, until finally we had hammered out an agreed-upon list. We would keep our group small, limiting it to six. Each man had to represent an important institution. Each must be alone in his category—that is, if we chose a weekly news-magazine reporter, no other weekly news magazine would be represented. There was one daily newspaperman, one news weekly magazine, one political agency, one wire service, one radio-television network, one non-American who had clout in his own country.

We ended up with the following list: Teddy White, ONA, a special agency; David Schoenbrun, CBS network; Harold Callender, *The New York Times*; Robert Kleiman, *U.S. News and World Report*; Preston Grover, AP; and Thomas Cadett, of the BBC, former chief of British Intelligence for France in the war.

The ground rules were agreed to by all: We would assure all guests, virtually under oath, that the meeting would be for background only, with no attribution to the guest. We would not write about anything discussed at the meeting for at least twenty-four hours. We would not only respect the confidentiality of the meeting by never revealing the source, we all swore never to admit that the meeting had ever taken place. Such solemn vows were necessary to win the confidence of world leaders.

Inevitably, the existence and modus operandi of our confidential group became known—not through us, for we kept our vows. The aides of the world leaders whom we had invited could not help but gossip about it or boast of the select group of powerful journalists who had invited their boss. Someone dubbed us "The Secret Six" and the name stuck. We were not always the same six, for Tom

Cadett went back to London, Harold Callender fell ill. Pres Grover, Bob Kleiman, Teddy, and I were permanent members of the brotherhood, until Teddy left Paris for Washington, Pres Grover retired, and I was sent off on so many missions to North Africa and Asia that I could no longer consistently work with The Secret Six.

One year I had been elected president of the Anglo-American Press Association and I felt uncomfortable representing the entire press while working inside my own secret cabal to beat out all the others. The Secret Six faded away, never to be resurrected by succeeding generations of reporters. It had been the right thing at the right time with the right men. It is hard to duplicate those special circumstances, just as the job of foreign correspondent in the forties and fifties was totally different from foreign correspondent in the seventies and eighties.

Thirty, forty years ago, the capitals of Europe and Asia were sites of major news stories. In Paris we would follow the fortunes of Jean Monnet trying to unite Europe, of General Eisenhower training a new integrated allied army to stand up to the Soviet challenge, of Charles de Gaulle proclaiming the greatness of France and opposing any allied integration. France, he would thunder, is an independent nation and takes orders from no one. France is a great power, he would orate, all the more determinedly, as it became increasingly evident that France was not a great power. De Gaulle seemed to believe he could make it great by intoning its greatness.

There was no lack of political, economic, diplomatic stories on my Paris beat—to say nothing of Sartre and existentialism, Picasso and two-headed chickens, Christian Dior, Balenciaga, and Balmain's collection of "Jolie Madame" dresses. One of the first TV documentaries I did was "The Birth of an Easter Hat," which followed Pierre Balmain's original sketch to the final product perched saucily on the pretty head of a stunning mannequin. The producer of the documentary, his first assignment, was Av Westin.

Today, most stories from abroad are disaster stories, natural or manmade: floods, earthquakes, forest fires, abductions, assassinations, riots, and counterdemonstrations. Today's foreign correspondents are firemen and ambulance chasers, lacking a sense of the broad and deep sweep of our times that was inevitable in Europe from the forties through the sixties.

In early days, Howard K. Smith, in London, told Americans how the British were trying to build a new socialist future by caring for their citizens "from the cradle to the grave." He discussed the cost of such a program, its impact on production and productivity, and the effectiveness of National Health services, which was one of the most controversial subjects, hotly debated back home in the States. Howard had his share of newsmakers to report on: Churchill, Anthony Eden, Aneurin Bevan, the tempestuous labor leader and radical of the Left, and the stories of the royal family. Britain, like America, would get hysterical about Communists and spies, particularly after it was discovered that Klaus Fuchs had passed all nuclear secrets to the Russians. This was followed by the scandal of Guy Burgess and Donald Maclean, highest ranking diplomats, who knew all allied secrets. Thanks to their treason, so did the Kremlin. Britain was even more isolationist than de Gaulle. They wanted no part of Monnet's United Europe. They would eventually be forced to join in self-defense, but they kept Howard Smith busy reporting British opposition to Europe for years.

Dick Hottelet in Bonn and Berlin had a giant figure to offer to Americans: "Der Alte," the Old Man, Konrad Adenauer, who was building a democratic Germany and working toward a virtual integration of the German and French economies, so that the two enemies might never again make war upon each other but instead learn to live together as neighbors and tradesmen. With Churchill in London, de Gaulle and Monnet in Paris, Paul-Henri Spaak in Brussels, Adenauer in Bonn, De Gasperi in Rome, Stalin in Moscow, we were reporting on a world of giants.

There are exciting personalities today, too, of course, Margaret Thatcher in London, Gorbachev in Moscow. But Mitterrand is no de Gaulle or Monnet. Charismatic leaders of the forties and fifties gave us terrific stories to report and helped us all become successful. It is not that correspondents of today are less competent than those of yesterday. Some of them are outstanding, as good as the best, Pierre Salinger and Richard Threlkeld of ABC News, Tom Fenton of CBS, and many more. But if they are as good as any of us were, the stories they cover are not as varied and important. And today's correspondents do not stay long enough in each capital to become fully expert. They chase around after violent events. I was in Paris twenty years, Smith almost as long in London, Burdett longer in Rome. This gave us authority.

In addition to the outstanding men and women already noted, there were many other reporters with a high level of competence in Paris in those days. William Attwood of the *Paris Herald* and *Look* would go on to become an American ambassador, and then publisher of the Long Island daily, *Newsday*. Ed Korri, the U.P. bureau chief, also went on from journalism to be named ambassador by the president. A young Belgian whom I recommended for a job with *Newsweek*, Arnaud de Borchgrave, would become chief foreign correspondent for *The Weekly*, and is today editor-in-chief of the conservative daily, *The Washington Times*. It is a remarkable coincidence that the two men who worked as *Newsweek* correspondents in Paris, Ben Bradlee and Arnaud de Borchgrave, should end up as editors of rival daily papers in Washington.

The strong foreign press corps was equalled in drive and ability by an outstanding group of world-class French journalists. Jean-Jacques Servan Schreiber, his sister Brigitte, today a senator of France, and Françoise Giroud founded *Express* and built it up to a mass-circulation weekly news magazine, similar to *Time*, with national influence and prestige. André Fontaine, foreign editor and then editor of *Le Monde*, the most intellectual and "authoritative" of the daily papers, was frequently quoted in the world's press, while the world's ambassadors consulted him regularly. Among the best of the French journalists was the specialist on the Soviet Union who wrote for France's biggest circulation daily, *France Soir.* Michel Gordey, like André Fontaine, was admired and consulted by the journalists and diplomats in Paris. Among his other "accomplishments," Michel was the son-in-law of Marc Chagall. When Chagall's daughter divorced him, Chagall kept referring to Michel as "my son," and was furious with his own daughter for failing to save the marriage.

We were all friendly, went out to dinner together or invited friends to our homes. One night, my wife and I went to dine with the Gordeys. Michel had remarried a most attractive and bright young woman named Beverly, who became the Paris representative of the American publisher Doubleday. On arriving at their apartment for dinner, we were delighted to find that, as a special treat for us, Michel had invited Marc Chagall and his wife. My wife, a painter, loved Chagall's works and was thrilled by his presence. He was at ease, informal, and most pleasant.

After dinner, Dorothy walked to the living room to examine a large Chagall oil of a Russian village with people flying over the rooftops, a typical Chagall scene. Dorothy was studying the colors and brushstrokes with rapt attention when suddenly she heard a voice with a strong Russian accent, Chagall's, whisper in her ear, "Do you like Chagall?"

Dorothy turned and smiled warmly at the master, saying "Oh, yes, I like Chagall, very much."

The old man then said, "And do you understand Chagall?"

Dorothy said she did, whereupon he said, "I love Chagall, but I do not understand him." He then laughed uproariously and one could sense that this was a favorite joke of his.

I had walked with Michel over to his desk above which there was a kind of bulletin board with papers or memos pinned to it. When I looked closer, I saw the papers were, in fact, a series of greeting cards, for Christmas, New Year's, birthdays, anniversaries, each one handmade and painted by Chagall, who had sent them to his favorite son-in-law. It is one of the most remarkable, unique collections of a world master, and I'm sure a museum would give a lot to get Michel Gordey's collection.

Night after night in Paris we were privileged to drink or dine with people of extraordinary ability and wit. No theater, no concert, no spectacle could equal dining out in Paris. James Thurber came to dine at our apartment one night. Dorothy told him she had just read a French translation of one of his short stories, in *Elle* magazine. She said, "Jamesy, your story was wonderful in French." Thurber replied, "Doesn't surprise me a bit, many of my things lose something in the original."

Each of these men and women in Paris was a delight, each had a story or a quip of quick wit. I once dared asked Hemingway how one becomes a great writer. First he glared at me, then he growled and said, "Read great writers." Hemingway was a complex man. He had great charm with his friends, but could be caustic and cruel with those he did not like. He was annoyed with one of the nicest, brightest of the journalists, Toni Howard of *Newsweek*. He didn't like her flamboyant getup. Toni had raven hair, wore fireman-red coats, and, at night as well as in the day, wore black sunglasses. This irritated "Papa" Hemingway, and when Toni swept passed us in the Scribe bar, Papa commented, "There goes the girl whose hair is prematurely black."

Even Communists, not known for their wit or humor, were wits in Paris. The number-two man of the party, Jacques Duclos, deputy to the chief, Maurice Thorez, was short, five feet by five feet, roly-poly, a former pastry chef who had risen through the ranks to become the Communist Party's chief of delegation in the National Assembly. Duclos wielded considerable power and influence. At one point, he was truly feared and not just by neurotics, but by reasonable people who truly thought the Communists would take over France. They had become the biggest party in the country with 20 percent total of all the votes, at their peak. They have fallen since to a small 10 percent. But they were at their strongest when Duclos was reigning over their parliamentary delegation, terrorizing the other groups.

I sat in the correspondent's gallery overlooking the floor of the assembly one day, covering the debate over France joining America and its allies in the North Atlantic Treaty Organization. The speaker at the rostrum was France's slim, trim, elegant foreign minister, Georges Bidault, a former history teacher at the famed lycée, Louis le Grand.

Bidault was talking about the Soviet threat and the need to meet it, as the Communist benches hissed and booed. When Bidault paused a moment to sip some water, the strong voice of Duclos, with his almost comic deep-south accent, could be clearly heard in the silence, asking "Would the Honorable Foreign Minister not prefer to drink a Coca-Cola?" The laughter that broke out ridiculed Bidault and made him look like the American lackey the Communists always accused him of being. This, of course, is exactly what Duclos had intended with his sally. Duclos was also the man who invented the politically devastating phrase, the "Coca-colonization of France."

I was astonished one day to open my mail and see an invitation from Jacques Duclos to come to church and witness the baptism of his grandchild. Ever since the Soviet revolution, the Church had looked upon Communism as the Great Satan, a hatred equaled in fury by Communist detestation of the Church. Even before Communism, the Church and the Left in France had been at daggers with each other. Fortunately, cold-steel daggers are no longer used, but the verbal attacks and street clashes were almost as deadly between the Red and the Black. I wondered what in the world Jacques Duclos was doing in church baptizing his grandchild.

There was a huge crowd of well-wishers in the church. The French are both passionate and unforgiving in their ideological battles, yet, at the same time, able to cohabit with their enemies. It was normal in Paris to go to an elegant dinner party and find among the guests a bishop and a Communist leader, chatting amiably and sipping champagne together in a most civilized manner.

When the ceremony ended and Duclos stood on the church steps accepting the congratulations of friends, I walked over to him, shook hands, and asked, "Jacques, I've been trying to puzzle out this affair. You are an atheist are you not? You don't believe in what you call this ecclesiastical mumbo-jumbo?"

He gave me a sunny, Mediterranean smile, flashing a gold tooth, and said, "Yes, of course, this Catholic mysticism is mumbo-jumbo. As Marx has taught us, religion is the opium of the people. Can any reasonable man really believe that the sprinkling of water on a baby's forehead could guarantee paradise, or failure to do so, condemn the infant to hell?"

"But, Jacques, if this is your belief, why are you baptizing the infant in church?"

His smile got broader and sunnier, and in the rolling consonants and drawn-out vowels of the Midi, he said, while laughing, "But just suppose I am wrong? Why should this sweet child suffer hell because of me?"

His reply was typical of French cynicism and sophistication. It has been said many times that Frenchmen wear their hearts on the Left and their wallets on the Right. Many devout Catholic workers carry Communist Party cards in their pockets. Many Communists wear crucifixes under their shirts. It is difficult for most Americans to understand the mentality and self-defense reflexes of a people who have suffered centuries of invasions, revolutions, assassinations, and changing regimes with a record of a half-dozen different lines of royalty, an undigested revolution, and, by the fifties, the Fifth Republic of a series so shifting that, quite clearly, the Republic was not firmly rooted in French life.

Every Frenchman supports two or more political parties. As far back as Julius Caesar, it had been observed that "All Gaul is divided into three parts." The French count on these divisions, on something akin to anarchy, as their best defense against dictatorship. Like Americans, they constantly rail against their political representatives and then vote the same men and women back into office. Consistency is not their greatest quality, nor is the logic of which they boast. France is not, as it proclaims, the country of René Descartes, the philosopher of reason, the man who devised the formula "I think, therefore I am." It is, rather, the country of the Christian philosopher of faith, Blaise Pascal, who wrote, "The heart has reasons that reason does not know."

I had one experience in Paris that gave me what I felt was the ultimate insight into the French mentality. I first wrote about it more than thirty years ago in a book about France, as part of a chapter titled "Manners, Morals and Mores of the French." The book was successful, on the best-seller lists in both New York and Paris and published in a number of countries. But the one chapter turned out to be a phenomenon. It has been reprinted every year for three decades. I received a royalty check on it a year ago. It was included in several anthologies, including Boston University's best essays in English. It was translated into almost every written language on earth, in Chinese, Sanskrit, and Swahili. I made more money on that chapter than on the entire book. It appeared in *Harper's*, in *Life*, and in the *Reader's Digest*. It was totally unexpected and seemed to hit a nerve in different peoples everywhere. Its highlight was the story that follows.

It was midnight in Paris and I was in a cab taking me home from the CBS studio near the Opéra. There was no traffic and we were speeding along the Quai d'Orsay, that broad avenue that parallels the Seine, on the Left Bank. As we approached a crossing, the traffic light turned red. My driver slowed down, inched toward the corner and then sped through the red light. He repeated the same unnerving maneuver some four blocks further on.

On arriving safely, my limbs unbroken, I protested to the driver that it was dangerous as well as illegal to run through a red light. He looked at me almost sadly, as though regretting that I was not very bright, but what can one expect from an American.

"Monsieur," he said, snapping out his words in the clipped, rapid Parisian of Menilmontant, "do you know what a red light is?"

Surprised by the question, I replied, "Yes, of course. It is a warning sign for you to stop and permit cross traffic to proceed. It is meant to spare you the disaster of a collision at the crossing."

"No, not at all," said the driver, with the assurance of a teacher talking to a backward student. "A red light is only an automatic signal in a mechanical, preset traffic system. It is green for so many minutes and red for so many. It cannot warn me of a collision because it has no eyes and is mindless. It is simply a machine.

"But, I, sir, am not a machine. I have eyes and a brain. You noticed, did you not, that I slowed down as I approached the corner? I looked to my left. No cars. I looked to my right. No cars. What would you have me do then? Sit there while a dumb machine told me to wait? No, sir, I knew there was no cross traffic and consequently no danger. As for the law, it is just as blind as the traffic light. I, sir, am not a machine. I am a man and I use my brain, following common sense and not the automatic switchings of a blind traffic light."

I think of that cab driver often when I am driving. I slow down at all crossings. I look right and left. And, if the way is clear, I go through a red light, for I, too, am a man and not a machine. It is a most satisfying humane philosophy, but it also explains why French governments rise and fall like lunar tides and why France never realizes its full potential, but, somehow, in adversity, remains smugly happy.

By now, the reader must think that foreign correspondents do little work. We dine with bishops and Communists, movie stars and Nobel Prize authors. We pub-crawl from one bistro to the other, lunching at the Tour d'Argent, dining at Maxim's, spending the day at Georges Braque's studio, watching the master paint, dining with Chagall, lunching at Vallauris with Picasso and buying one of his new baked-clay dishes with brightly colored designs signed with his illustrious name.

Paley and Stanton and commercial-time sales directors would send me sponsors of our programs and ask me to demonstrate how advantageous it was to be associated with CBS. I would take them on the rounds of the famous restaurants, night clubs, and historic sites, from Maxim's to the historic sewers of Paris. I would wine them, dine them, entertain them, and they would go home and tell my bosses that I was a most friendly playboy who lived it up and did not work.

Paley and others, who heard my newscasts, knew that I was working around the clock, covering my beat by day, ten to twelve hours, seven days a week, then entertaining my guests, sometimes until dawn. I was young, strong, grabbing at life with both hands in a wondrous, if sometimes fearsome, world.

The day began at early breakfast at home, with a careful reading of the fifteen morning papers of Paris, looking for news stories or thinkpieces that I might follow up for CBS. After ten, in the office, I would work the telephone, which was often maddening, for French phones did not work well and often provided wrong numbers. I would check my most important news sources, talking to the spokesmen at the Foreign Office, at the Ministry of Finance, at the Atomic Energy Commission (AEC), at NATO, OECD, and all the other international agencies.

It was impossible to park in Paris, particularly near government buildings, so I had an office driver who would take me on my rounds, and drive constantly around the block until I emerged from the office I was visiting. I had a source book with more than a thousand names in every field of human endeavor, from nuclear weapons to Paris fashions, with official phone numbers, unofficial private lines, and, most difficult but important, home phones for important officials. I never knew at what hour of the night something important would break. I could not go to the theater or any public spectacle without leaving my seat number with my studio engineer, along with the phone number of the manager's office.

Correspondents today do not cover a beat as thoroughly as we did in the first few decades after the war. There is no longer the same demand for stories from Paris or elsewhere in Europe as there was yesterday. Paris is no longer the capital of the world. It is no longer the capital of art. The École de Paris has been replaced by the School of New York. The flow of stories and interests has changed.

In those days, without satellite communications, only the man on the spot could interview the prime minister. Today, Dan Rather or Peter Jennings picks up a phone, cuts into the Telstar in the sky, and calls the prime minister directly. The correspondent is more a leg-man, not the responsible chief correspondent he once was.

I am often asked by students how to become a foreign corre-spondent. I advise them all not even to think of it. If they want to become famous reporters and newscasters the place to be now is Washington, D.C.

Up until the late 1960s, all of our television reports were done with a camera-sound team, on film. We would have to write up a "dope sheet" that gave every detail of what we had filmed, plus background data on the story. We would then send the package to New York, hoping our film would not be scratched or fogged in development, hoping, too, that some editor would not cut it up so that we would no longer recognize what it was that we had reported. It was hard, frustrating work.

Our radio circuits, not yet on underwater cable, were on short waves and subject to clacking, buzzing static. Comedian Robert Klein once did a bit on the Johnny Carson show, about listening to Schoenbrun in Paris at eight in the morning before going off to teach English in high school. Klein said he would hear something like this: "A grave crisis has erupted in France today over crackle, buzz, whistle, and hiss." Klein said he would go off to school and worry all day about what the grave crisis was, and rush home early to find out what had happened.

Access to sources and communications were the lifelines of the foreign correspondent. I would spend weeks cultivating a minor official in the hope that one day he would give me a news item of importance. I took pains to ask the names of the long-distance and overseas operators and supervisors. I made sure they received fla-cons of perfume for Christmas. I would drop by the PTT building from time to time and leave behind boxes of chocolates. It paid off one day in a big news scoop on an uprising in Algiers.

There had been rumblings of dissidence among the French colonial settlers and the paratroopers in Algeria. They were fearful of Paris surrendering to Algerian guerrilla forces demanding inde-pendence and were determined to keep Algeria French, despite the "appeasers" in Paris. We all knew that trouble might soon erupt.

I would call news sources in Algiers daily, just to get the feel of the climate there. One day, the long-distance operator told me that the circuits were out, that she could not put me through. Immediately suspicious, I called a good source, Jacques Duhamel, principal aide to Finance Minister Edgar Faure. I was told he was not there. I called a top source at the Foreign Office. Not there. I called Chief of Staff, General Ely. Not there. Everyone of importance was out of his office. One secretary told me, "He is at the Elysées Palace at an emergency meeting."

My ears grew longer than Peter Rabbit's. I called the supervisor for the Algerian phone circuit on whom I had lavished perfume and chocolates. She told me, "I cannot put you through." I pressed and asked, "Are the circuits down, or is there some other reason that you cannot put me through?" She replied, "Listen very carefully to what I am saying, monsieur. I CANNOT PUT ANYONE THROUGH TO ALGIERS."

I thanked her, took a deep breath, crossed my fingers, and called my editor Bob Skedgell, in New York. I told him to patch my call into a recorder, for I had a major newsbreak for him. Then I announced a revolutionary coup in Algiers by colonialists breaking away from the French government. Skedgell came on and said nervously, "Are you sure of this, David? There is no hint of it anywhere on any wire." I said, "Yes, I'm sure, I'll stake my job on it." He dryly replied, "Yes, you might well say that. Okay, we'll go with it, but it's your neck, not mine." I sweated it out all night until the coup was officially confirmed.

Covering that Paris beat, in the chill of the Cold War, of espionage, shootings and abductions, of riots and coups was the dark side of the glamour of being a foreign correspondent. I was on duty, or available, twenty-four hours a day, seven days a week. I could go nowhere without calling the cable company and telling them where I was. There was no real relaxation. At the most glittering dinner parties, at a ball in Versailles Palace, there was always the nervous tension. Whenever a phone rang anywhere, my ears would prick up and I would wonder if it were for me. I was pulled out of my seat at the Theatre Edouard Sept one night, in the middle of an exciting second act, and led by an usher to the manager's office. It was CBS, New York, informing me that the King of England had died and they would need a reaction story in an hour.

One night, I was hosting a party of six at the Lido nightclub. It was well after midnight and I began to relax, sure there would be no call that night. Just as the thought flitted through my mind, the impresario of the club, Pierre-Louis Guerin, came up to the table and signaled me to follow him to his office. It was CBS, an excited, happy editor on the phone, shouting "It's over! It's over. The Korean War has ended in an armistice! Get your butt down to the studio and tell us what NATO thinks, what de Gaulle thinks, what General Norstad thinks. Just tell us what everyone thinks. Good luck." He hung up leaving me gaping at the phone.

How in the world was I going to get a reaction from General de Gaulle at one in the morning? Or the prime minister? Or any official? I had their home phone numbers and the end of war could be an excuse to wake them up, everyone except de Gaulle. No aide would dare wake him up, short of a Russian invasion. What to do? Then the last words of the editor echoed in my ears, "Tell us what everyone thinks." I had an inspiration. I turned to Pierre-Louis and asked, "Do you have a recording machine here?"

"Of course," he replied, "we use it for all rehearsals. Why do you want it?

I explained that the war in Korea had ended, a joyous moment, peace in the world. Wouldn't his guests be delighted if he would give me a drumroll while I would announce the great news from center stage?

Guerin, one of the great showmen of Europe, lit up and clapped his hands. "Capital! Capital! Let's do it." Within minutes I was on the stage, microphone in hand, a sound man recording. The drumroll erupted like thunder and all the people in the nightclub put down their drinks, stopped talking, and looked to the stage, wondering what was up.

I made my announcement and an uproar of cheer exploded. Champagne corks popped, strangers kissed, the Lido went wild. It was Carnival in Rio, and I was recording the whole scene while doing a running commentary.

I ran out of the Lido, clutching the tape, and drove at top speed down the Champs-Elysées, across the place de la Concorde, en route to my broadcast studio near the Opéra. I was exhilarated, but by the time I got home at almost three o'clock, I was trembling with fatigue and tension. The thrill of the story had fallen flat, something like the "little death" after coitus. Glamorous? Yes, of course. But a drain on the nervous system, the dark side of glamour.

The tensions of covering a competitive, fast-moving news beat, nerve-tingling as they were, did not match the darkest side of our lives, the dangers, even terrors of covering wars and revolutions.

I will never forget the day in Oran, Algeria, when my cameraman, Georges Markman, and I were chased into an alley by a murderous mob of rioting Arabs. As I huddled in a doorway, I saw Georges, with incredible bravery, stand up in the alley and film the thugs who were pelting us with stones. I shouted at him to come back and seek shelter, when bullets began smacking on the doorway just behind me. I don't know how we escaped that day, but I'll never forget the terror of the uprisings in Algeria. Markman and I made some twenty trips to war-torn Algeria, each of them fraught with peril.

My editors were merciless. They called me in Algiers and told me that my broadcast describing a French patrol capturing a few guerrillas in a counterterrorist operation was sensational. Now, they said, get back down there and film a combat patrol for TV.

We did. I sat in a jeep with a French lieutenant, while Markman was lashed tightly on the front fender, holding his camera out like a gun aiming at our quarry, three *fellahs*, Arab revolutionaries, running in front of our jeep and heading for a clump of trees. We caught them before they could reach the trees. Georges filmed the capture and the beatings that followed. I jumped out of the jeep and retched, while the rebels screamed in agony.

Being a correspondent was by no means all champagne and rose petals. We would gasp for breath in the furnace of the Sahara Desert, and, the next day, shiver in the cold of an Atlas Mountain top. We sat at a café in Constantine, when a cab whirled by and a terrorist threw a bomb at our tables. The bomb landed at the restaurant entrance and blew us out of our seats. Fifteen torn and bleeding bodies were twisted in the rictus of death all around us. Not glamorous at all.

There was no glamour in the Congo, where savage, maddened blacks killed nuns and children, while equally fierce Belgian mercenaries mowed down black villages with machine guns. Vietnam was a hell of sweltering heat, constant bombings by our own American planes, "friendly fire" that would hit us instead of the enemy, correspondents captured by the black-pajamaed Viet Cong and never heard of again. There was no glamour in Jerusalem when a bomb went off in a garbage can in a crowded marketplace, killing and wounding, tearing the flesh of some fifty and more shoppers, mainly women and children. All that was the dark side of glamour, the price we paid for the dinners at Maxim's, the elegant parties, the high life among the beautiful people in the dazzling City of Light.

My heart goes out to the new generation of correspondents today who have to work in areas as terrifying as anything we had to face. I am chilled when I hear about reporters in Lebanon, who risk abduction, being held as hostages, or death every time they walk out of their hotels. They labor under severe conditions of censorship in Russia, China, South Africa, and Central America. They live with violence in El Salvador, Nicaragua, the Mideast, and Afghanistan. Then they are often accused of causing the violence they are covering. Many correspondents and diplomats have become the prey of terrorists around the world, and there is little glamour or glitz in their work.

AN ERA ENDS,
ANOTHER BURSTS
FORTH

The fifties were years during which the reporters, the independent newscasters of the Murrow era, rose to power and fame, and then, like a Fourth of July fireworks spectacular, ended in puffs of smoke and faded away, leaving only the memory of their brilliance. Out of the ashes of the past, television news would rise like a phoenix, born again, but not the same. It would never again reach the heights, the crusading morality, the dedication to democracy and the quest for the truth that Murrow achieved in the "See It Now" reports on Lieutenant Radulovich and Joe McCarthy. Never again would we foreign correspondents be allowed to freewheel, control our beats, cover them as we saw fit, making the decisions on news.

By the sixties, the day of the famous correspondents had ended. Before it died, it lived gloriously and set records that can never be matched, not because today's correspondents are not as talented or dedicated, but because power has shifted from correspondents and broadcasters to editors, producers, cost accountants, lawyers, and, above all, management. Management prospered and was proud of the prestige of their newsmen, but executives always feared us, worried we would go too far, become too controversial, anger the powers that be, frighten off sponsors. They were shaken by the uproar over "The Selling of the Pentagon" and General Westmoreland's libel suit. Whatever prestige we brought to the networks was judged not sufficient to balance the headaches we caused.

After Murrow's triumph with his "See It Now" on Joe McCarthy, the comment made by a cynical executive—"Great show. Sorry you did it."—proved to be the death knell of the program. It continued for a while, becoming even more controversial, if that were possible. Murrow, who had defended Radulovich from baseless charges, decided to mount his white horse and ride off to defend another man whom he admired and who had been pilloried, the scientist J. Robert Oppenheimer, chief of the top-secret wartime Manhattan Project, "father" or, rather, chief architect of the first atom bomb.

Oppenheimer, who had suffered deep guilt about having opened the nuclear Pandora's box, opposed any further development of nuclear power, particularly the plan to make a hydrogen fusion bomb, a hundred times more powerful, more destructive than the original fission bombs that had been dropped on Hiroshima and Nagasaki. Oppenheimer was horrified by what he felt was the impending suicide of the human race in a mushroom nuclear Armageddon.

The Right shouted insults at Oppenheimer. He was accused of refusing to defend his country, of cowardice, even of treason for trying to stop the ultimate weapon that would guarantee our dominance in the world. When Murrow devoted an entire program to an interview with Oppenheimer, giving him the opportunity to state his views, insults, threats, and cancellations overwhelmed frightened executives.

"See It Now" was an expensive program in those days, $100,000 an episode; it would be at least four times as much today. So long as a sponsor was willing to pay, so long as the critics and the public lauded the program, Paley was willing to foot the bill. But when an organized Right began systematic attacks on CBS and when the sponsor, ALCOA, began complaining about bad publicity, "See It Now" was doomed. ALCOA, accused of being a trust, had sponsored the program to whitewash itself in Murrow's reflected glory.

"See It Now" was a moral shield for a giant corporation under attack. When ALCOA felt secure again, it hastened to rid itself of a shield that had become a sword at its throat, as they saw it.

Bill Paley called in Murrow to give him some "good news." He said that "See It Now" would be expanded from thirty minutes to an hour. Then Paley dropped the other shoe. "Of course, we have to make up that program time, so instead of a weekly it will become a monthly, or something like that." Ed knew at once that it was the beginning of the end of the program. It is a management trick to "promote" a program out of existence. I would discover that myself when they played the same stunt on me some ten years later.

The worst clash between the two old friends, Murrow and Paley, occurred when Murrow, asked to address the National Radio and TV News Directors at their Chicago convention in 1958, let off a blast against the TV networks. He denounced television as a hopeless mix of show business, advertising, and news. He charged that TV programs were guilty of "decadence, escapism, and insulation from the realities of the world in which we live." Murrow argued that TV should "teach, illuminate, yes, and even inspire." He challenged the networks and the sponsors to turn over at least two of their regularly sponsored programs "not to sell cigarettes or automobiles, but rather the importance of ideas."

Bill Paley blew up. It was one thing to suffer Murrow's controversial programs, but this time Paley felt, not without reason, that Murrow had stabbed him in the back, had shown no loyalty to the network that had made him rich and famous. Paley was furious when he learned that Murrow had sent advance copies of his speech to the news directors but not to his own bosses, Paley and Stanton; that was adding insult to injury. Murrow, Paley decided, would have to go.

Paley called Murrow in and was shocked to see how tired and ill his old friend was. His anger began to subside as he asked Ed with genuine concern how he was. Murrow replied, "Not great." Paley went on to discuss in calm terms where they stood. He told Murrow that it might be a good idea to take a year off to rest, read, travel without deadlines or cameras. Murrow, sensing that this was the first step out of CBS, not caring much, bone-tired, agreed at once.

Murrow took his year and came back, but he did not look rested or happy. In his absence CBS asked his producer, Fred

Friendly, to take over a new documentary series to be called "CBS Reports," without Murrow. Murrow would do a few on his return, but the name of the programs was the corporate logo, CBS, not the name of a newsman. This was symbolic of the evolving shift of power away from the newsmen to management, from issues to entertainment and big commercials.

Television had established itself as the greatest instrument for launching and selling products on a national scale. No other medium could equal it. But TV news and documentary programs that were controversial were by no means the best way to sell beer and autos. What the executives and the ad agencies wanted were programs that attracted a large audience and that simply entertained, rather than provoked or stimulated the intelligence of the people. Soap operas were popular with housewives in daytime, but something more was needed for evening prime time. A genius of show business found the key that would mesmerize Americans: greed. Everyone wants money. The thing to do was give away huge sums every week in TV contests. Money was the greatest magnet of the public.

There were a number of successful game shows—"Name That Tune," "What's My Line?"—but the blockbuster program that drew the nation to CBS was the brainchild of a man named Lou Cowan. He had first broken into the networks with a radio show called "The $64 Question." Contestants were asked questions on a sliding scale that gave them eight, then sixteen, then thirty-two dollars, up to a triumphant sixty-four dollars if they answered all questions successfully. One day Lou decided that it would make a good TV vehicle. TV did not deal in such paltry sums as sixty-four dollars. Lou decided, with top CBS approval, to call his show "The $64,000 Question."

It was an instant hit, a national sensation. A contestant would be enclosed in a glass booth where he could hear only the question and nothing else. As he pondered the answer, chewing his lips in painful thought, an unseen orchestra would play dramatic music, which came to be called greed music. Then the correct answer would come and the program moderator would shout "Right, for so many thousand dollars! Do you want to keep it or do you want to risk going ahead for more? All or nothing." The contestant would moan and groan in an agony of indecision and frustrating greed.

Then the drama would build, as the contestant answered each question correctly until the final question was posed: "Now for the Sixty-Four-Thousand-Dollar Question. Will you go? Are you ready?" The audience, transfixed, were afraid to breathe, even at home, as though somehow they might upset the contestant. When a contestant went all the way and won the $64,000, the studio audience would go wild, cheering, whistling. Even in home living rooms people would applaud.

"The $64,000 Question" broke all records until a scandal broke its back and wrecked Lou Cowan. A disgruntled participant revealed to a reporter that the show was rigged. Questions and answers had been secretly given in advance to some of the contestants. The show's drama and credibility were destroyed. It went off the air and Cowan went out of CBS.

The idea, however, was as valid as ever, and game shows that give away fortunes are among the most popular shows of today. Two of them, owned and produced by Merv Griffin Enterprises, are top-rated in the nation: "Wheel of Fortune" and "Jeopardy." They are so popular that when affiliates run either one against the network news, they beat the news shows by a big margin.

On a trip to New York I was asked to dinner by Murrow, and he suggested that, before eating, we have a drink and watch a new television show, "The $64,000 Question." I sat there amazed by the spectacle. When it ended, Ed turned to me, lifted his glass, and said in his most dour voice of doom: "Well, David, you have just seen the future, and it is not ours."

He was right about his own future. It was shortly after that evening that Paley called him in to tell him the "good news" about the "expansion" of "See It Now." But Murrow was not yet personally finished. His best work as a crusading reporter was over, but for the first time in his life he was making a lot of money and becoming even more famous and admired on a new program that was pure entertainment. It was, in fact, a TV version of keyhole voyeurism.

The new program, "Person to Person," was an offshoot of a segment that had appeared on "See It Now." Ed's writers and researchers, Jesse Zousmer and John Aaron, bright and able men, one day set up an interview by Ed of Senator Taft. Ed and the senator could not clear a date on which they could meet. So Jesse proposed that he tape the senator at home, while Murrow, back in the studio in New York, would interview over cable and telephone lines. It would be a smooth-running dialogue between the two men, even though they were thousands of miles apart, like a two-way telephone call but on camera. It ran for only about five minutes, but it was commented on as an original, exciting device.

Jesse and Johnny decided that it could be done on a grand scale in a half-hour or full-hour show, with Murrow "dropping in" and visiting famous celebrities in their homes, via TV circuits, rather than in person.

Bill Paley loved the idea, saw instantly that it would be a huge success. Murrow recoiled as though attacked by a snake. His first reaction was to feel that it reeked of gimmickry, of trivia, of gossip-mongering and Peeping Tomism. Jesse and Johnny and, above all, Paley, worked on Ed to give it a try, to make at least a pilot show. Ed, still reluctant, agreed. Paley promised him that a success in prime-time entertainment would bring him at least some keeping money.

Murrow cared little about money for himself. But he knew that he was in constant danger, both physical and political, as he flew around the world and assailed the Establishment, and he was concerned about his wife, Janet, and his son, Casey. He was earning thousands a week but paying out about 80 percent or more in taxes, while living up to his own star status. He was literally broke and needed his big weekly checks to keep up with his expenses. He got it with "Person to Person."

Murrow's guest list on "Person to Person," almost one hundred in the first year, was a Who's Who in the world. The Duke and Duchess of Windsor, Leopold Stokowski, Billy Graham, Liberace, Marilyn Monroe, Sir Thomas Beecham, John F. Kennedy and Jackie, "Betty" Bacall and Bogey, Ella Fitzgerald, Fred Astaire, Henry Wallace, Orson Welles, to name only a few. No interview program before or since could command the famed celebrities that Murrow's "Person to Person" did.

It was an instant hit, and Ed was earning $7,000 a week. Taxes in the pre-Reagan days reached almost extortionate levels at the top of the income scale. There was only one way to earn and keep money, that was to own and sell a property for millions and pay only a smaller capital gains tax. The show was owned by three men: Murrow, with 40 percent, and Jesse Zousmer and John Aaron, with 30 percent each.

Ed came to them one day and offered to buy them out. They were low-level income earners and were glad to get some keeping money of their own. They did not know that Paley had talked to Murrow about selling the show to CBS. After they sold out to Murrow, his agent, Jap Gude, then negotiated a million-dollar deal with Paley. Jesse and Johnny, faithful employees of Murrow, part of the Brotherhood, were enraged. They felt Murrow had played a dirty trick on them. He could have sold to CBS without buying them out first. Their share would have been much greater than what Murrow had paid them.

I do not know the truth of this argument. I knew and liked Jesse and John, had worked closely with them, could understand their feeling of betrayal, although I could not judge the facts of the case. It was a sad day when Jesse and John, in anger, resigned from CBS. I never dared ask Murrow about it for it was too personal, too sensitive an issue.

Murrow, who thought that by now he knew his public, was totally surprised by what happened on "Person to Person." He told me one day, "Never be predictable. Once they're sure of what you'll do, don't do it." He applied this psychology to "Person to Person." He felt he had been doing too many celebrities and switched to give his public some ordinary Americans: a mailman, a barber, a farm worker, an auto mechanic. After two weeks of presenting ordinary Americans to ordinary Americans, Murrow was flooded with letters and telegrams of protest from his audience. They told him they did not want him to interview ordinary people. If they wanted to see ordinary people, they could invite all their relatives and friends over to dinner. They wanted glamour and glitter to light up their own dull, gray lives. They wanted to see how the rich, the mighty, and the beautiful lived. They did not want to see themselves.

Murrow came to Paris in 1957 to cover the NATO summit meeting of all the chief executives of the Allied Powers. I did the news reporting, the blow-by-blow on the conference, while Ed did his analysis pieces for his evening show. The day the meeting ended, Ed came to the studio to do his wrap-up piece and final conclusions.

I sat next to him, when suddenly I saw him double over, his body racked by a hacking cough that rattled his bones. He gasped for breath. Frightened, I offered him a glass of water. He gulped it down, nodded his thanks. He looked old, tired, ill. I was thoroughly alarmed. He pulled himself together, stifled the cough, grinned weakly at me, and then went on to do his piece with a strong steady voice. Once the broadcast ended, another spasm doubled him up. He was smoking four packs of Camels a day, flying around the world, working without rest or proper diet, drinking too much whiskey. It was then that I knew he would not be with us much longer.

The coming end of the Murrow era was not by any means the end of expansion and power for television news. Murrow could not be replaced, but able men were on their way up and new techniques and technology were emerging to make television news the dominant force in national politics.

A new reporting technique had been devised at the Republican convention of 1952. Floor men, with backpacks and transmitters, could talk directly to Cronkite in the anchor booth. When a young freshman senator, Richard Nixon, was surprisingly chosen as Eisenhower's running mate, a CBS reporter started to interview him on the floor. Don Hewitt, directing the program in the booth above, cut in and told the reporter to take off his headset and mike and ask Nixon to put it on. In that way, Walter Cronkite could directly interview Nixon himself. It was one of many clever innovations by Don Hewitt, which led an admiring fellow producer, Av Westin, to say, "Don Hewitt is the man who invented the wheel."

The first shadow of significant future influences fell over the CBS studios on election night 1952. The Remington Rand Corporation had proposed a new experiment to CBS. Their engineers had built a computer that they dubbed UNIVAC. They believed that if sufficient data on previous elections were fed into the computer, precinct by precinct, plus up-to-date data on current polls and trends, the computer might be able fairly early in the evening to predict the winner, long before the polls closed or the ballots could be counted. I wonder if these technicians had any idea of the consequences of their design.

CBS researchers compiled data of voting trends of the past. These were fed into UNIVAC along with current data. CBS went on the air with its election coverage at 6:00 P.M., New York time, still 3:00 P.M. in the West, where millions had not yet voted. Within three hours, with polls still open in more than half the country, UNIVAC predicted a sweeping Eisenhower victory over Adlai Stevenson. It did this with only 10 percent of the votes counted.

Remington engineers did not believe their own creation's foresight. They tinkered with their computer, changed the data, and told Walter Cronkite that UNIVAC was predicting a close race. As more returns poured in, UNIVAC belched angrily and spewed out renewed predictions of an Eisenhower sweep, rejecting the doctored data its mistrustful masters had forced down its throat. It had been right in the first place and was right again; it was an Eisenhower triumph. UNIVAC had enabled CBS, despite one early glitch, to beat the other networks to the final election results. Remington executives apologized for their lack of faith in their own new monster. CBS was ecstatic. Serious analysts of elections were deeply troubled.

Any thoughtful observer of the election process had reason to be troubled. There was something sinister in the thought that a computer could announce the winner while half the country had not yet voted. To what extent did the announcement affect the results? This is an issue still being hotly debated today.

Since that first attempt in 1952, the process of calling results early has been considerably refined and speeded up. All the networks now have detailed voting records of just about every precinct in the nation. Reporters question voters as they leave the polls. These "exit" opinions are also fed into the computers. Instead of taking three hours, the most modern computer can predict the results in minutes. An election campaign that lasted two years and more—all the efforts, money, drama, and suspense—comes to a swift, electronic climax two minutes after the first results come in. There are some who gloomily predict that one day we will not have an election at all. They'll just feed data into a supercomputer and it will choose the president for us.

Political scientists are properly worried. Politicians are talking about a new system in which all the polls across the nation, in all the time zones, would close at the same moment, whatever their local times were, and that television would be barred from making any predictions about the winners until midnight or later. I doubt that it will ever come to anything so rigid, but unquestionably some steps must be taken to bring this runaway electronic fortune-telling from making an anticlimax of the electoral process.

It is not only computers that have an undue influence, one of the most controversial of the political tools is the public-opinion poll. No one really knows, and few agree upon, the influence of polls on the electoral process. If the polls show a man far ahead and the weather is bad on voting day, will his voters stay home, confident in victory, so that he ends up losing or having his margin severely reduced? Will a close poll spur all sides to greater efforts? Will those behind find their supporters losing faith and abandoning them? Americans like winners, and winning has a bandwagon effect. These questions remain without definitive answers today, while the debate goes raging on after more than thirty years.

The next major evolution in television news came in the presidential election year 1956. Walter Cronkite had emerged in 1952 as an overnight sensation. Doug Edwards, anchoring the evening news, was running well ahead of John Cameron Swayze of NBC. CBS was on a roll. NBC, unwilling to risk its established stars against the formidable Cronkite, virtually conceded the ratings race by choosing two unknown reporters to anchor their convention coverage.

One was, in fact, well-known and highly rated on a local Los Angeles news program, but not known nationally. He was a tall, handsome westerner, an intellectual with a voice that sounded very much like Murrow's. In fact, some critics at first called him "the poor man's Murrow." They would change their minds quickly when Chet Huntley emerged as an outstanding newscaster at that convention. He was good on his own, but he reached even greater heights as he played off against a young North Carolinian named David Brinkley. Brinkley, wry, sardonic, staccato, irreverent, was a sharp contrast to solemn, serious Huntley. The chemistry worked perfectly and to the astonishment of everyone, including the NBC executives who had decided to go with them, the Huntley-Brinkley duo won top honors, outrating Cronkite. CBS came in a weak second in the coverage. Americans, always ready to cheer new champions, sang the praises of Huntley-Brinkley.

Bill Paley was distressed. He had been first for a long time and he did not tolerate coming in second. The immediate victim of his anger was the innocent news director, Sig Mickelson, an able man, but a loser at the convention. He was summarily fired by Paley, without even a farewell meeting or any good wishes; Paley had none for him. Paley could be brutal when things went wrong.

Strangely, Cronkite was not blamed at all. Paley felt he had done his usual good job but the chemistry in the CBS coverage was not good, and that must be the fault of the news director. Mickelson was replaced by one of the corporation counsels of CBS, Richard Salant. Salant was a protégé of Frank Stanton. Paley did not think highly of him but had no rival candidate to offer, so he deferred to his right-hand man, Stanton. Salant would have a checkered career at CBS. No one lives very long in top executive jobs at the networks. Salant did last longer than usual, but he was up and down, in and out twice.

Salant, in his first two years, would make major changes in the CBS star system. He had to prepare for 1960 to meet the challenge of Huntley-Brinkley. Before that, he ran into another challenge from the new twin-suns of television. Because of their success at the convention, and because John Cameron Swayze was running behind Doug Edwards, NBC fired Swayze and tried a new, daring experiment. They put Huntley and Brinkley in as dual anchors of the evening news—Huntley in New York, handling major world and national news, and Brinkley in Washington, covering the capital's politics and the Eisenhower administration. This bifurcated anchor worked extremely well, again to everyone's surprise. An anchorman had, heretofore, always been the stellar performer of the network. No one had ever tried a split-anchor position.

It took almost two years, but Huntley-Brinkley finally outrated Doug Edwards by a clear margin. It was really a tribute to Doug that it took them two years to do it. Doug had been the CBS anchor for almost fourteen years. Americans can be fickle and unfaithful to their favorites. Huntley-Brinkley were new stars. Doug was a valued old friend but they had grown used to him. The NBC duo were the new hot rods of television.

Richard Salant took good note of what was happening. He knew Paley would not again tolerate being second to NBC. He knew, too, that he would be blamed if he took no steps to meet the challenge. He did the only thing to do, and everyone at CBS agreed.

He removed Doug Edwards as anchorman* and replaced him with Walter Cronkite in April 1962. Cronkite was the best CBS had. Salant had to go with him and hope he would win out. Salant breathed easier when the chairman, Bill Paley, endorsed Cronkite as his own choice. If Cronkite did not win, Salant would not go down with him.

Cronkite did not win right away. In the first year, Huntley-Brinkley ran ahead of him in the ratings, but not by much. Paley, watching carefully, thought that Walter was doing a good job and beginning to build audience. He particularly liked his factual style, his lack of intellectual pretension, his expertise at straight, hard-news reporting, just what Paley wanted.

Paley had had more than enough of Murrow's championing of controversial causes. Murrow had done a magnificent documentary, "Harvest of Shame," showing the wretched living conditions and ruthless exploitation of migrant farm workers by huge agricultural conglomerates. Critics raved about it, social science professors acclaimed Murrow, but southern affiliates refused to carry the program and sponsors canceled commercials. Paley told friends, "CBS is not the Ministry of Justice, not an avenging angel. We are a big business and we are being hurt."

Despite the best efforts of Cronkite, Huntley-Brinkley remained in the lead. There is an axiom in television, which probably applies to every human endeavor: The more successful you are the more successful you become, until, of course, the inevitable day that strikes everyone at the top, a downfall. Huntley-Brinkley would remain ahead of Cronkite, from 1962 through most of 1963, a long time for CBS to run second. Paley for once was patient; he had faith in Cronkite. He also knew that the more exposure a man is given, the better are chances that he will eventually win the biggest audience. As so often was the case, the chairman's judgment was correct.

Cronkite was still a few years away from hitting his peak. While he was struggling, two new luminaries began to appear in the CBS

---

* Doug Edwards continued to broadcast on CBS News radio and on TV news briefs for many years. He finally retired at the end of March 1988, after forty-six years with CBS News and a total of a half-century on the air, a worthy candidate for broadcasting's Hall of Fame.

firmament. One was still a small, twinkling star, without much light or power. It would increase in intensity and become one of the suns in the TV galaxy. The other luminary came shooting in like a comet, with the light of a supernova.

The tiny, twinkling star was Mike Wallace, the same Mike Wallace who many years before had worked with Doug Edwards in the newsroom of a Detroit radio station. His career had gone nowhere while Doug was going to the top. But Mike was enthusiastic and sure of the future, for he had, at last, been hired by CBS, not in an important post, but he was on the air for the network.

He introduced himself to me by telephone from New York to Paris. He told me that he and his wife, Buff Cobb, a young actress, were doing a morning breakfast show, a popular formula for radio. Like the established "Tex and Jinx Show," his program also used the first names of husband and wife, the "Mike and Buff Show." I listened to him with little interest, for it did not sound either important or relevant to my own job as Paris correspondent. Then, Mike came to the point. He wanted to set up a link from their studio to mine, so that Buff and he could interview me. It was at the height of the Paris fashion shows, and Buff wanted to know all about the hemlines, the colors, the new mood of fashion. Mike was eager to question me about General de Gaulle.

Mike told me that he had cleared his request with the editors in New York, who had given him approval. I said it was okay with me, and we set up a time and did the program. I am surprised that I still remember it, for it was not memorable.

I lost track of Mike until, one night in 1956, on a trip to New York, I flipped the dials of my hotel TV set and there he was. I had never seen him and was curious to know what he was doing. He was not on CBS, but on a local station, channel 5. His program was called "Nightbeat." I was impressed with his drive and gall as I watched and listened to him acting like a tough district attorney, interrogating guests whom he seemed to treat as malefactors under indictment. It was outrageous, but it drew a big audience, ratings were high, and everyone in New York knew who Mike Wallace was. Soon everyone in the country would know.

Some two years later I was back home to promote my book *As France Goes*. Frank Stanton liked the book, bought two hundred copies, and had me autograph them for friends, sponsors, and politicians. Paley and Stanton in those days were still proud of the News Division and were delighted that a correspondent had written a book that received critical acclaim. Stanton authorized me to take a few weeks from my beat to go on a publicity tour, pushing the book on radio and TV talk shows.

One of the first men I called in New York was Mike Wallace. I had heard how large his audience was. Mike was pleased to hear from me, he thanked me again for the show from Paris and promptly invited me to be interviewed on "Nightbeat." I knew that "Nightbeat" took an adversarial position against every interviewee. It was its trademark. People tuned in to see Mike Wallace beat up on a guest, the way they would tune in to William Buckley's "Firing Line," or, much later, to Mike Wallace again, on "60 Minutes," when he would cross swords with the Shah of Iran and other world personalities. He was always the tough district attorney cross-examining a victim in the witness box of his studio.

I was not concerned. I could not imagine what Mike would find to use as a sword or club against me and was willing to take my chances. The thrust came right at the outset of the interview. Mike is a killer who always goes straight for the jugular; it is what made him famous. There is nothing wrong in this. It was up to his guests, who knew what the program was like, to protect themselves.

Mike picked up my book and waved it front of the camera, as if it were criminal evidence against me. "Now, David, this book runs to more than five hundred pages. It purports to tell us *all* about France. Yet . . ."—he paused for dramatic effect, then pointed the book accusingly at me—"yet, there is not one word in all five hundred pages about sex in France." He raised his eyebrows, frowned, and then shouted at me, "Why?"

I burst out laughing, along with the studio audience who were loving it. My laughter disconcerted Mike. Most of his victims cringe or shout back. His eyes told me that he sensed I was somehow going to strike back. When I stopped laughing, I said, "Well, Mike, my book is supposed to explain all things French that Americans do not know or understand. I saw no reason to write about French sexual habits because Americans do exactly the same thing as the French. The only difference is that the French thoroughly enjoy it, while Americans feel guilty."

The audience roared, titillated. Mike, to give him credit, knew that he had been had, but he graciously laughed and, for the rest of the interview, asked me serious and intelligent questions about France. Mike puts on a fierce act but he is much kinder and more intelligent than he allows himself to be on camera.

A last anecdote about Mike Wallace. When I came to Saigon during the Vietnam War, Mike was there and we had a drink on the hotel terrace. My wife, Dorothy, joined us later. Mike's eyes widened and his expressive eyebrows rose when he saw Dorothy approach.

"My goodness, did you bring your wife along?" he asked, more an accusation than a question.

"No, he didn't *bring* me along," Dorothy snapped at Mike. "I came with him."

Mike protested that he meant nothing, he was just surprised. It was, indeed, rare to find a reporter accompanied by his wife in a war zone. But Dorothy has gone everywhere with me. She has a keen editorial mind and is a talented artist. She sketches scenes wherever we are, and her watercolors or ink sketches are as important to my work as my own diary and notes. I could see that Mike did not quite understand or approve of what we were explaining.

Many years later, we read Mike Wallace's autobiography in which he spoke, with sadness, of his divorce from a woman he had loved very much. He admitted in the book that the marriage had gone bad because he was always away on assignment.

Mike Wallace would become one of the most successful newscasters at CBS. He may have lacked the class and stature of a Murrow, a Smith, a Sevareid, but then he never pretended to be a deep thinker. He was and is a tough, hard-hitting interrogator and a professional reporter.

The other luminary who appeared in the same period, the mid-fifties, was not a newsman. In fact, he detested news and, if he could have done so, would happily have eliminated the entire News Division. He expressed open contempt of news. We looked upon him with scorn and revulsion. His name was James T. Aubrey, Jr. We called him "Jungle Jim." Others dubbed him the "Smiling Cobra." He did not last long, but, in his brief tenure, Aubrey made more money for CBS and did more damage to its reputation and its morale than anyone before or since. He was hyperactive, superkinetic, supremely confident, and utterly ruthless. Even his severest critics, however, conceded that he was brilliant, a phenomenon. He was handsome, strong, lithe, intelligent, with cobalt blue eyes and limitless energy.

Jim Aubrey was educated in the best Ivy League schools, Phillips Exeter Academy and Princeton. He won his varsity letter as an agile receiver on a winning football team and was accepted into the ultra-elite Tiger Inn. Aubrey enlisted when war broke out and became a major in the air force. While on duty in California he met and married an attractive actress. After the war, Aubrey worked for a Los Angeles station and rapidly rose to become its general manager. He was a young man in a hurry. In a world of ambitious young men in Hollywood, Aubrey pulsated with overdrive.

He came to the attention of CBS executives on the West Coast and was taken on by the network as a young executive in programming in 1955. He had an early success with a program called "Have Gun, Will Travel." ABC, hungry for new talent, jealous of Paley's ability to recruit the best, called in young Aubrey and offered him a bigger job with more opportunities than he had at CBS. He became vice-president in charge of programming at ABC in 1957. He saw it as a chance to show what he could do. He had no doubts that he was a superb showman and only needed the chance to prove it.

Prove it, he did. Although ABC could not begin to compete with CBS for the quality and quantity of its executives, producers, and performers, Aubrey went to work as though ABC were the top network. He gushed with ideas like a fountain of champagne. In a short time, he produced, to critical acclaim and big earnings, "The Rifleman," "Maverick," "The Donna Reed Show," and "77 Sunset Strip." Aubrey was on his way.

His agent, knowing that Aubrey would not realize his full potential unless he could rejoin CBS and work with its more creative and richer management, called Frank Stanton, president of CBS, Inc., and let him know that Jim Aubrey would like to return to "the best network." Stanton was not particularly taken in by flattery. He already knew that CBS was the best, but he also knew what Aubrey had done at ABC, with fewer tools. He met Ted Ashley, the agent, and offered to take Aubrey back in a key job, vice-president in charge of creative services. That position was a stepping-stone to the presidency of the CBS television network.

Aubrey jumped at the offer. He knew that CBS was in trouble after the scandal of the quiz show, "The $64,000 Question." New programs were needed quickly. Aubrey had no doubts at all about what kind of programs. Although he was well educated, had a major in English literature, and was a voracious reader, Aubrey was convinced that the public did not want highbrow programs. Nor did they want drama or tragedy. Daily life was desperate enough without watching misery and agony at night. What the country needed, Aubrey proclaimed, was comedy, a belly laugh, pure entertainment. When one associate proposed doing a TV version of Tennessee Williams's *Glass Menagerie,* whose heroine was crippled, Aubrey snorted in disgust, "Are you nuts? Who wants to watch a girl with a limp and serious emotional problems? Most of our viewers are wallowing in problems. They don't need us to give them more."

Aubrey gave Americans the kind of comedy he thought they wanted and his judgment proved correct. Ratings soared and millions poured into the CBS coffers, as Aubrey conceived such "masterpieces" as "Mr. Ed," the talking horse, "The Beverly Hillbillies," and "Petticoat Junction." It was the worst mental junk food ever presented on television. In his first big season, Aubrey's shows gave CBS the top-ten daytime shows and seven of the top-ten evening prime-time hits. Paley was delighted. He doted on Aubrey like a proud father. Aubrey, at forty the youngest network president, could have been his son.

New York sophisticates, thinking to curry favor with Paley, would sympathize with him at dinner parties about the small-town vulgarities that Aubrey was turning out. Paley would disconcert and embarrass them by saying that he did not consider the shows small-town or vulgar, but that, in fact, he liked them very much. "They're funny. They make me laugh and feel good. What's wrong with that?" asked the chairman.

Aubrey was riding high. Word spread that he had been anointed as the eventual successor to Frank Stanton as president of CBS, Inc. Stanton did not like Aubrey as Paley did. He thought him unreliable and wondered when he would go too far. Probably he didn't like to hear about someone being his successor. It was clear to us that if Aubrey made a slip, Stanton would swiftly oust him.

We all were rooting for Jungle Jim to fall on his face. Aubrey let everyone know that, in his view, the News Division was a loser and a drag on the network. Our programs cost too much for what they earned, and we brought no new audience to the network or sales of commercials. He was wrong on the record. The news programs did bring CBS not only national acclaim and prestige but also attracted many listeners who watched our news programs and then stayed on to watch the prime-time shows. People don't like to look up schedules and change dials. It's much easier to sit back in an armchair and stay with one network for the evening.

When Aubrey was calling the shots for the TV network, in 1962, I was in Washington, as chief correspondent and bureau chief, a sea change in my life that I will report on later. I was shocked to be told that Aubrey had ordered news to stop preempting entertainment shows, even for the most important newsbreakers, even a threat of war or the thrilling conquest of space. His talking horse, Mr. Ed, and "Gomer Pyle" were more important to Aubrey than the Cuban missile crisis, when the world teetered on the brink of nuclear war. We thought Aubrey was a cold-blooded, money-mad Mr. Bottom Line, who would turn down a station break on the return to Earth of Jesus unless, of course, it could be heavily sponsored.

Fred Friendly had become president of CBS News in the sixties under the reign of Aubrey. Aubrey told him one day, "They say to me, 'Take your soiled little hands, get the ratings, and make the most money you can.' Then, they say to you, 'Take your lily-white hands, do your best, go to the high road, and bring us prestige.' Balls to that!"

Aubrey's scornful version of top management's two-pronged game was not inaccurate. That is exactly what Paley and Stanton were doing. They gleefully toted up the hundreds of millions Aubrey was earning, ignoring complaints from the intelligentsia, then using Friendly and the News Division as a fig leaf to cover the shame of the Entertainment Division. They wanted it both ways.

It was perfectly true that the news operation was costly and was a money-loser. Paley had always allowed News to run virtually without a budget. In his most responsible early days, before he became chairman of a conglomerate, Paley believed that his privilege of owning a network, using the public airwaves, required him to pay a kind of license fee for making money on the air. The fee was the cost of the news and public-affairs programs.

Aubrey thought this policy was nonsense and he never stopped bringing up the subject at board meetings. As president of the television network, he was responsible for its earnings reports and for its bottom-line profits. The News Division cut into his earnings and he resented it. If Paley and Stanton wanted prestige, then let them set up News as a separate corporation and get it out of the television network's open national figures. They did, in fact, do that, setting up CBS News, Inc., with its own president.

Aubrey, who had enchanted Paley with his undeniable charm and his Midas touch in programming, began to irritate the chairman of the board. Paley did not like being lectured to by a forty-year-old executive with little experience, no matter how talented or successful. He became even more disillusioned about the "wunderkind" of TV, when Aubrey, throwing his weight around, fired two of the biggest stars of television, both finds and friends of Paley: Jack Benny and Arthur Godfrey. Firing these men, beloved by the public, was almost blasphemy. It infuriated Paley, who took it as a personal blow. It is true they had dropped in the ratings but one does not ruthlessly, summarily cancel American folk heroes.

Aubrey's "magic touch" began to escape him. He produced a series of shows that were not only vulgar and anti-intellectual but, far worse, were failures, losing ratings and sponsors. At the same time, Jungle Jim became the favorite subject of gossip-mongering columnists, hinting weekly at some "scandalous" behavior by Aubrey. As an eligible bachelor, he was characterized as a womanizer; worse, he was accused of making deals for personal gain. This was enough for Paley. He told Stanton to fire Aubrey. His era, not the finest hour of CBS, had happily lasted only about a half-dozen years.

TV had grown so quickly, had prospered and become so influential that sets were being sold at the rate of millions a year. Everyone was surprised when polls showed that the majority of Americans got their news not from newspapers or magazines but from network radio and television. TV had more than come of age. It was like a child, not yet completely mature or educated, that had suddenly shot up to six feet six, weighing 250 pounds, a powerful man with a child's mind and lack of experience. It would have to mature rapidly. It did, in a terrible decade of national tragedy.

CBS studio broadcast. *Courtesy CBS Photo Archives.*

Paris kiosk featuring Schoenbrun article on Kennedy after the assassination. 1963. *Private collection.*

David Schoenbrun reporting from Paris in the 1950s. *Private collection.*

Conversation with President Charles de Gaulle, garden of the Elysée Palace. July 14, 1959.

ABOVE: As CBS chief Washington correspondent, one of a number of conversations with President Kennedy, Oval Office, White House. 1962–1963. *Private collection.*

BELOW: Interview with President Eisenhower, Gettysburg, Pennsylvania. 1962. *Private collection.*

ABOVE: Schoenbrun on CBS Paris terrace on the Champs-Elysées. 1952.

BELOW: CBS-TV interview with Ingrid Bergman. Paris 1960.

ABOVE: The campaign meeting at the United Hebrew Schools. Southfield, Michigan. 1973. *Courtesy Benyas-Kaufman Photographers Inc.*

LEFT: CBS cameraman Georges Markman getting light reading for television commentary. Paris 1960. *Private collection.*

ABOVE: CBS Television exclusive at NATO. *Private collection.*

BELOW: CBS News reporter David Schoenbrun at an Algerian refugee camp in Tunisia; he proved, contrary to French claims, that the people were genuine Algerian refugees. March 1958.

ABOVE: David Schoenbrun with Charles Boyer, at the Lido, Paris, celebrating the end of the Korean War.

BELOW: CBS year-end panel. At table immediately in front of Schoenbrun, who is speaking, from left to right: Ernest Leiser, Alex Kendrick, Peter Kalischer, Schoenbrun standing, Edward R. Murrow, Dan Schorr, and Winston Burdette.

7

TV'S SEISMIC
SIXTIES

Upheavals high on the Richter scale shook television and the nation in the terrible ten years, 1960 to 1969. Except for the bloody, fratricidal Civil War of the 1860s, this was the most tragic testing time for America. In those ten years, while a handsome, young president proclaimed that the torch had been passed to a new generation, and that man would fly to the moon, tragedy would rack the nation.

The young prince of Camelot would be assassinated in Dallas, his brother would be shot down in Los Angeles, and the inspiring black leader of civil rights would be killed on a balcony in Memphis. A heavy-handed Texan would plunge us into the paddies and jungles of an Asian nation few Americans had ever heard of. Millions of Vietnamese and Americans would be sacrificed, the nation bled and nearly became bankrupt while inflation wiped out savings. The American people would then elect a president and a vice-president, both of whom broke the law and were forced out of office.

The true symbol of the sixties in television was the Smiling Cobra. James Aubrey had been appointed president of the CBS television network in December 1959 and began functioning in the new year, 1960. The chairman of the Federal Communications Commission, the body that regulated radio and television, Newton Minow, let off a blast against television in 1961, one year into Aubrey's reign. Minow addressed the National Association of Broadcasters and upbraided them, denouncing their output as a "vast wasteland." His attack was warranted, although his metaphor was invalid. TV was not a wasteland, it was a jungle overrun with weeds, inhabited by deadly dwarfs.

Minow warned broadcasters to police themselves or others would police them. He spoke with the powerful authority of the man who could refuse to renew the licenses to broadcast of those who dished out trivia and spurned any kind of educational or public service. Murrow had called on the news directors of the nation to realize the potential of television to educate, inform, and even inspire. Minow all but ordered them to do so under pain of punishment.

The networks responded like Pavlov's dogs. They all but salivated to do something worthwhile. All three networks agreed to combine their resources and do a special program on Telstar, a technological breakthrough. Telstar was launched by rocket into orbit. It permitted transmission of television signals from earth to the skies and back, spanning the globe. The three networks named Fred Friendly as producer of the program. At first, Telstar was "visible," could be contacted, for only a quarter of an hour, but techniques evolved so that by 1965 we had a new twenty-four-hour-a-day synchronous satellite called Early Bird.

The new globe-girdling orbital signals changed the nature of foreign correspondence. Before the satellite, which permitted direct broadcasts from foreign capitals to New York, correspondents had to work with camera teams, never knowing what was on the film, for it was never developed in our own capitals. The film would be sent to New York, delivered into the hands of lab technicians, editors, and producers, who had little knowledge of the story they were cutting up. It was television's frustration similar to the weekly newsmagazines, like *Time*, in which a foreign correspondent reading his story in the magazine would barely recognize anything he had written.

This global instant communications system was designed just

in time for the Vietnam War, which became the first war of the television era to bring its battles directly into living rooms. Since the programs before and after the news shows presented Mafia and other gangland killings or Wild West six-shooters blazing away, the Vietnam War did not seem real, but rather just another violent episode in the TV jungle.

The Early Bird did, however, have a jarring impact on the nation's press. By direct broadcasts, TV could beat the newspapers on every major news development. It took hours to write, edit, print, and distribute newspapers. It took seconds for a reporter in Paris, Moscow, or Saigon to tell the public what was happening in the world's capitals. Newspapers could not compete. They still can't. In the 1980s, David Brinkley, on his Sunday morning show, would rub it in by beginning his broadcast with the words "Now, some of the news since the Sunday papers."

With new technology, there came a changing of the guard at CBS and, at last, serious competition from NBC. CBS was losing some of the men who had made it great, while NBC, and much later ABC, were developing new men or taking on the men that CBS had lost.

Murrow was the first of the Old Guard to leave CBS. President Kennedy appointed Murrow head of the United States Information Service and its worldwide network, the Voice of America. In one sense, it was appropriate for Ed Murrow to be the Voice of America. He had been our nation's most powerful and responsible voice for so many years. It was, in another sense, totally inappropriate. Murrow was a reporter always in quest of the truth and also the White Knight of victims of persecution. As the Voice of America, he had to be the spokesman for a government whose aim was not to inform and tell the truth, but to put the best face possible on everything the American government did. It was a propaganda job, not reportorial or objectively analytic.

The next member of the Old Guard to fall from grace in the early sixties, a fall that would turn my own life upside down, was one of the most learned, able newsmen of our times, Howard K. Smith. Howard had, in the forties, replaced Ed Murrow in London as chief foreign correspondent when Ed went back to New York. Howard was almost typecast to be in London. Although a southerner, from Louisiana, he wore tweeds and smoked a pipe and looked very English. He had been a Rhodes scholar at Oxford, the only American elected president of the Labor Club, a post more important than Harvard's Hasty Pudding, more important even than being editor of the *Harvard Crimson*.

After more than a decade in London, Howard exchanged jobs with another CBS great, Eric Sevareid, distinguished chief correspondent in Washington. Eric came to London while Howard went to Washington. This was a break with CBS tradition, which was based on letting a correspondent stay practically forever in a capital so that he could develop such knowledge and so many sources that he would excel over all competitors. I was certain that we were all set for life.

I began to get nervous when Howard and Eric changed capitals and Charles Collingwood came to lunch with me in Paris and asked whether I intended to spend my life in the French capital. I sensed that Charles, one of the best of the CBS men, who had been drifting around without a special niche in New York, might be planning to return to Paris where he had been correspondent for the first year after the liberation.

The departure of Murrow had been expected. We all knew of his confrontations with Paley. We also knew he was ill and tired. But the sudden departure of Howard Smith was a shocker for all of us. The reason for CBS canceling his contract seemed too small for the enormity of the act, until we realized that, in this new era, the act of challenging management, however slightly, had become a cardinal sin that would not be tolerated. The era of Murrow and the Murrow boys, freewheeling, making all the decisions, had definitely come to a close in the savage sixties.

During the years from 1946 to 1957, when Howard did a weekly analysis feature for CBS from London, the editors did not worry much about his personal opinions. After all, he was talking about European politics and that was rarely a subject of heated discussion in New York or Washington. We knew that as foreign correspondents Paley's rules about fairness, balance, and objectivity, and his total injunction against editorializing or personal opinions, did not strictly apply to us.

Smith would discover that Washington was not London, that what you said in the nation's capital could bring powerful reactions, even recriminations. Editors and executives were highly sensitive to trouble lurking in a commentary. It would lead to Howard's downfall.

Although Howard Smith was a southerner, he was a liberal southerner, ashamed of the region's abysmal record on civil rights. Smith had also been a correspondent in Berlin, watching the Nazis beat, torture, and enslave Germans. He was traumatized by the memory of Storm Troopers beating Jews in the streets, and thus particularly sensitized to the beating of blacks in the South. Smith, in fact, was the one reporter CBS should have hesitated to send into a confrontation in Alabama. He was, however, the chief correspondent in Washington, assigned to major national developments.

Smith had already discovered what it was like to report in the United States. His first major story back home was the fight over desegregation of the schools in Little Rock, Arkansas. Bill Paley had watched his report and called Salant to complain that Smith had been editorializing and putting forth personal nonobjective opinions.

Salant informed Smith that the chairman had ordered him to check all Howard Smith scripts before they aired to make sure he conformed to CBS rules. Smith was shocked. Never had he been censored by the head of CBS News. This was a new era, a new ball game, and Smith did not like the rules of the game.

Inevitably, this would lead to the ultimate clash. Smith had gone to Birmingham, Alabama, to do a report on the Freedom Riders, a civil rights group trying to desegregate public places in the South. Smith went to the bus terminal where they were due to arrive. He noticed, uneasily, that the many police stationed there had suddenly disappeared. He had seen that happen in Berlin before a Nazi raid. There were bully boys in the terminal, like Storm Troopers to Smith. Some were carrying Ku Klux Klan banners.

When the Freedom Riders' bus arrived, Smith watched in horror as the Ku Kluxers charged into the bus and began to beat the riders with clubs and lead pipes. Blood spurted, men groaned. Smith was back in Berlin on Crystal Night. It did not last long. The Klansmen did their bloody work and then ran. The police suddenly reappeared and began interrogating the beaten Freedom Riders, as if they had been guilty of disturbing the peace.

Smith wrote a script that was factual, if emotional. He then wrote an endpiece, a "kicker" to the commentary. It was customary for us to write something profound or thought-provoking at the end of a report, a "thinkpiece," something to keep the audience thinking about what we had said after we had finished. For this Howard chose a famous quote by Edmund Burke, the British political philosopher: "The only thing necessary for the triumph of evil is for good men to do nothing." It was pungent, meaningful in the context of the report and not heavily editorial.

Salant, a lawyer, not a newsman, thought otherwise. He told Smith that the quote violated Paley's directives. It was not factual, it was opinionative. It raised controversial questions about who were the good men who did nothing and who were the evil ones. Smith was outraged, considered Salant to be pettifogging in the worst kind of lawyerish hairsplitting. In decades of broadcasting for CBS, Smith had never had a news director who censored his script. Everything was changing in the early sixties.

Smith had no choice but to drop the quote from his television script. Then he made a serious error. In his radio report on Birmingham, which Salant had not asked to see, Smith resurrected the Burke quote. There really was no excuse for what Smith did. He knew it had been forbidden on television and must therefore be forbidden on radio. It could be argued that it was not a grave breach, just an example of a deeply moved reporter, a good citizen, fearing that Nazis were emerging in our country. He could not resist a warning. What Smith had overlooked, however, was that management was completely fed up with freewheeling correspondents and would not tolerate another Murrow. Paley had already driven his long-time friend Murrow out of the company. He would not let Smith walk the same twisting path. That night, Smith's fate was determined. Paley, who had once admired Smith, was livid. He told Salant to fire him.

ABC jumped at the chance to get a CBS star and immediately gave Smith top assignments on the evening news, plus his own Sunday half-hour. Smith was never quite at home at ABC. No CBS man is ever at ease outside CBS, but he continued to have a career as a national headliner. I do not know if the Birmingham incident and the firing had a negative impact on Smith, but gradually, in the next few years, the once-fighting liberal became a true-blue conservative. It is hard for those who knew him at CBS and at the Labor Club in Oxford to believe that Howard Smith would become the one network partisan defending Nixon and Agnew, concurring with their vicious attacks on the media. Smith was Nixon's favorite Washington reporter and commentator, not the most brilliant epitaph to what had been a brilliant career.

Murrow and Smith were not by any means the only casualties in the upheavals of the sixties. Sig Mickelson was fired, as we have already noted, after NBC had beaten CBS at the 1960 conventions. Sig knew that the convention coverage would be crucial to him. He liked Cronkite but he was still being outrated by Huntley-Brinkley. Sig toyed with the idea of putting in co-anchors with Cronkite.

A young man with the most resonant, rich, warm bass voice, Charles Kuralt, was highly regarded at the moment. But Jungle Jim Aubrey stepped in and vetoed the idea. Kuralt was bald and heavy, not the right image for an anchorman, Aubrey decreed. Again, this was the first time that the head of the television network overruled the judgment of the director of News. All CBS traditions were crumbling and would never be restored.

Blair Clark, Salant's second in command of News, and my former colleague in Paris, called to tell me about the Smith dismissal. I was appalled when he defended the decision. I had originally hired Blair when he was taking courses at the Sorbonne to learn French. I had trained him and kept him on when Ted Church, the News director then, had wanted to fire him. Blair had not been a very successful reporter and he switched into an executive position. I did not like his view of the Smith case, but I was startled at his next observation. He suggested that I wind up whatever I was working on and fly back to New York for conferences about "the Smith Affair."

On arrival in New York, I first called my agent and business manager to tell him I was there and why. He told me that Howard was in New York at the Roosevelt Hotel. I called Howard and he asked me to come right over.

Howard told me in detail what had happened. He also guessed that I would be offered his job. I said that the way he had gone, and also Murrow, was not an auspicious augury for stepping into the same trouble. He told me I was wrong to think that way. "It's the top correspondent position in CBS, second only to Cronkite. CBS is still the best, so you'll be tops in the field," Howard said. He advised me to try it, to stick it as long as I could. His own case had set the rules and the new limits, so I was forewarned and could stay within the guidelines.

As soon as I saw Salant and Clark, they offered me the job in Washington, as Howard had predicted. I told them, truthfully, that I was honored and flattered but that it was a tough decision. I was deeply rooted in my Paris position, knew my beat there thoroughly, was three thousand miles away from home-office supervision, living well and happily. Salant smiled and said, "This is a new generation that has come to power, your generation. You don't want to miss an opportunity like this. Washington is the center of the world today and it's time for you to come home."

I said I needed some time to think it over and to consult my wife. "Sure," said Salant, "take as much time as you like. Say forty-eight hours?" He was always a considerate man.

I called my wife, discussed it only briefly. She agreed at once that this was a chance I should not pass up. It would be a wrench leaving Paris after seventeen wonderful years, but the French story was winding down. Due to de Gaulle's isolationism, Paris was less and less a world capital. Kennedy had drawn the world's attention to Washington. Why cling to an aging French general when I could cover a young, dynamic American president?

Despite my veteran status as a reporter, I came into Washington as a rookie. In Paris I had a big jump on my competitors because of having served with de Gaulle in Algiers, and having fought along with the French Army in the campaign of liberation. I spoke French more fluently than many other American correspondents and had studied the history and literature of which the French were so proud. In Washington I would be competing with some of the most able, intelligent, and experienced correspondents in the field. I had no advantages to exploit and would have to study hard to acquire the needed background. It was a challenge I accepted cheerfully. The only thing that worried me was CBS policy and how the company had changed.

Washington was splendid, a new Camelot—exciting people, big stories, a reporter's dream assignment. CBS was not. The men in my Washington bureau were nervous about what had happened to Howard, uneasy about what kind of a bureau chief I would be. There were outstanding reporters there and I made sure they knew I thought highly of them and that they needed no supervision from me. My job as bureau chief was to make sure that they had everything they needed to do their jobs and to shield them from New York management if they ran into difficulties. This did not cheer them up noticeably.

The climate inside the office did not match the glamour and excitement in the capital. But my colleagues were reporters who knew their job and did it superbly well. Roger Mudd covered Congress out of that bureau. Marvin Kalb was our man in the State Department, George Herman in the White House, all first-rate.

Despite my determination to be compliant, obedient, I did have trouble with New York from the start. I was the only bureau chief and chief correspondent in Washington who did not have a program or a column of his own. Washington is an elitist town and quickly rates the men and women who come there. Without my own byline, I was far down in the pecking order. It was also quite unfair, since Howard Smith had had his own program and I could not, at first, understand why Clark and Salant were resistant to giving me mine.

It soon became clear that it was a deliberate management decision in line with the developing policy of cutting newsmen down to size. They had had enough of independent, difficult stars like Murrow and Smith. Now they wanted hard-hitting reporters, not luminaries. They had picked me because of my record as a reporter in Paris. They told me that they wanted me to build my sources in Washington and to beat out NBC and Brinkley, who were still running ahead of Cronkite.

I gave it everything, working the beat day and night, building sources. I hit it off well from the start with Ted Sorensen, the president's right-hand man, and with Pierre Salinger, the press chief. I was invited to join a select bureau-chief group that met with top news sources, something like our Secret Six in Paris. We had a Saturday-night poker club going, a very important "in group" in Washington. Among the Saturday regulars were: the State Department's Soviet specialist, Ambassador Tommy Thompson, a genial gentleman but a frozen-faced poker player; David Brinkley; Pierre Salinger; Art Buchwald; Assistant Secretary of State Robert Manning; and a half-dozen others who would turn up on one Saturday or the other.

Meanwhile, I kept prodding Clark and Salant for a show of my own. They finally gave in, but grudgingly. They let me have a half-hour Sunday morning at noon, one of the worst time slots on the schedule, located in the "intellectual ghetto." Most Americans were either at church or having their first Bloody Mary of brunchtime. Management was taking little chance that I would become famous or powerful enough to challenge it.

They need not have worried. I already knew what had happened to Murrow and Smith. One would have to be blind and deaf not to know that CBS policy was based on management's complete control. Anyone who would challenge it would not be long with CBS. I had no desire to challenge management. I could live within the guidelines. All I had wanted was a chance to do my job as well as possible under my own name. That proved to be my undoing. There is more than one facet to management control or management's concept of what was best for CBS.

My main assignment was to do reporting and news analysis for the "Evening News with Walter Cronkite." That was all-important, for the Cronkite show was the standard bearer of CBS. As the evening news went, so did the reputation and income of the entire news division.

Cronkite and his director-producer Don Hewitt ran the show, decided which news stories to carry, and called in assignments to the correspondents. We were encouraged to work our own beats and dig up our own stories, but they had to be submitted first to Cronkite and Hewitt. They could overrule us and give us a different story to cover.

On my analyses, I would confer with Hewitt after he had made his lineup for the evening and had decided what kind of an analysis was needed. At times, I would work all day on a Supreme Court case, only to be told about an hour before air time that the Commerce Department had just released new figures on the nation's retail trade, sharply down, and they needed an analysis of the reasons and what it meant. At other times, I would be completing an exciting story on which I had worked for days only to be told by Don, "Sorry, no time for that tonight, there's a sensational fire raging among the movie stars' homes in Beverly Hills." He would chuckle and add, "A real hot story."

This was new and frustrating for a foreign correspondent who, for almost twenty years, had been solely responsible for covering his own beat, digging out his own stories, with no executive overseers. No one in New York knew much about what was happening in France and its disintegrating empire. They were not able to second-guess me. I was the acknowledged expert. Everyone was an expert on American affairs: the news executives in New York, 535 members of Congress, and all had sensitive toes and noses that would quickly snap out of joint. Even the elevator men and the cab drivers were Washington experts.

I was patient and well behaved, doing what I was told, determined to make it work on condition that they give me my own program where I would decide what to cover and carry, without instructions or orders from anyone else. I would do anything they asked me to do as chief correspondent just so long as they let me do my own thing, however modestly, in the worst time slot.

The program, titled "Washington Report with David Schoenbrun," was finally scheduled to air the first week in September. It began with a bang: President Kennedy granted me an exclusive interview. The program went well, week after week. Despite the bad time period, it built audience and there was a list of sponsors wanting to buy time on it. Although Sunday noon was low-level commercial time, we had enough sponsors and kept the budget down so that my program was showing a profit and the Smiling Cobra could not strike. Moreover, I was getting "picked up" (that is, quoted) almost every Monday in *The New York Times*, the ultimate accolade. The networks were still suffering an inferiority complex, although we were in the process of becoming the principal news source for the majority of Americans.

Upon occasion, despite my every effort to be cooperative and obedient, I would run into trouble with Cronkite or Hewitt. I do believe that it was their fault; or perhaps it is just the nature of the beast. They were so much in control, so much the shining stars of CBS, that they became arrogant. They failed to treat us with the minimum courtesy and respect that we needed to maintain any standing for ourselves in hard-nosed Washington society, which is always eager to gossip and pounce on anyone vulnerable.

One week there was a serious dispute between the State

Department and the French over some NATO policy plans. I had covered NATO in Paris since it was created. The French ambassador in Washington, Hervé Alphand, was a friend and a carefully cultivated news source for the past twenty years. Naturally I called him early in the story and booked him to appear in an interview for my Sunday show. Three days later I received a call from Hewitt. I admired Don, we were friendly and had always worked well together. He had been the producer of one of the most successful documentaries I had done in Europe, the wedding of Prince Rainier and Grace Kelly, so there was no personal hostility, no rivalry between us.

But trouble erupted that day. Don began by telling me that he had called Ambassador Alphand and had invited him to appear with Walter Cronkite in an interview for the evening news. The ambassador, a man of principle and an old friend, had said he was very sorry, he would have loved to be interviewed by Mr. Cronkite, but he had already promised the interview to David Schoenbrun. "So," said Don, "would you be good enough to call him, cancel your interview, and release him for Walter?"

Despite all my vows to behave, I blew up. This was simply too much, too high-handed and demeaning. If I did what was asked, Alphand would understand at once that I was a lackey of the Cronkite show, that I had no authority or standing of my own. Inevitably, he would feed the story to cocktail parties and I would have been severely downgraded. My own ego was not important to CBS, of course, but as chief correspondent I represented the network and it was foolish for them to knock down their own Washington chief. I told this to Don, adding, "Damn it, if you had called me first and asked me to get Alphand for you, I would have done so. That's part of my job here, to serve New York. But you just can't expect me, and should not ask me, to bow down and make a knave of myself."

Don, to his credit, did not argue the point. He agreed that it had been badly handled, but he said, ominously, "There's a problem with your Sunday show. You are competing with Cronkite and the evening news. Your program may be excellent, but it's once a week at Sunday noon and we are on every night from Monday through Friday at six-thirty. We are top priority."

I knew that, eventually, they would lower the boom on me. They wanted me to be the "scoop" reporter, the Hildy Johnson of the evening news. They cared nothing about, indeed resented, my program, for it led me to cover stories they would have liked. In all fairness, they were not altogether wrong. There was clearly a conflict of interest between my work as news analyst for Cronkite and anchorman of my own program.

There was nothing I could do to resolve the dilemma other than try to minimize the conflicts of interest. I would often call Hewitt and propose a story. If he turned it down, I was free to pursue it for myself. Often he would make it difficult by hesitating, then telling me to go ahead and do the story and he would see "if it played." That was one of his favorite expressions: "It doesn't play." He would use it to reject a report when he could not find specific reasons for the rejection. It used to irritate me until one day when I protested the killing of a piece and he took me to a screening room and showed it to me. When it ended he turned to me and said, "Well?" I shrugged and answered, "It doesn't play."

Most of the time, everything played well. I was getting on the Cronkite show three times a week, which was excellent exposure. My own program was making steady progress and I started to get little memos of congratulations or occasional phone calls from the CBS corporate president, Frank Stanton. News used to be the province of the chairman, but as Bill Paley devoted more time to building a conglomerate, keeping his distance from contentious newsmen, Stanton began to take a more active interest in news. He became our protector against James Aubrey.

My Sunday show hit a high point in October 1962, with a powerful national impact and an unprecedented break with television procedures, one that raised troubling ethical and political problems. It happened on Sunday, October 28, after two frightening weeks of the Cuban missile crisis.

U-2 spy planes flying over Cuba on October 14 had taken pictures that revealed that the Soviets had put nuclear missiles and delivery systems into Cuba and that the missiles were aimed at American cities. Day after day the tensions mounted, as the U.S. Navy blockaded and quarantined Cuba, stopped and searched Soviet ships at sea, while members of Congress and editorialists called for action against Cuba, including saturation bombing if the missiles were not promptly removed. By Sunday the twenty-eighth, the crisis had reached the boiling point. We would discover later that

President Kennedy had decided to send out the bombers that afternoon. The world teetered on the brink of Armageddon.

I was in my office, checking the script and the lineup for the noon newscast, when suddenly all the bells in the newsroom started to clang. Something very important had set off those emergency-bulletin calls. An office boy rushed in, carrying teleprinter copy from a news service and shouting, "He's pulled out, he's pulled out. We've won." I grabbed the copy. It was from the British world service, Reuters, reporting that Radio Moscow had announced a decision to dismantle the missiles in Cuba and return them to the Soviet Union. My office boy was right, we had won—or rather President Kennedy had won, for it had been his courage, determination, but flexibility that had saved the day.

I called Pierre Salinger, Kennedy's press chief, and woke him up. He had not slept much all week. I gave him the good news. He laughed and said that the president was at Sunday Mass and his prayers had been answered. Pierre promised to call me back if there were any major developments at the White House. I knew how important my broadcast would be that day, the end of the crisis, a step back from the brink at one minute to midnight. Further, I was the only network news show on the air, the only one with this dramatic story in my hands. My bad time slot had given me a tremendous break. The whole nation would be listening and watching. I would be able to make the first announcement and have an exclusive on the story all day long until the Sunday evening shows.

I tore up the prepared script. We would build a completely new show, getting expert opinion on the meaning of the event, retracing the days of crisis, looking ahead to the next steps. There would be no time for prepared interviews or film. We would have to call in our guests and go live in studio, building the show as we went along. I would have to ad-lib a half-hour program. There was no time to type and time a script or to structure it. I would have to wing it on the air, always a frightening challenge. It particularly drove editors mad, because there was nothing to edit.

I started to call all my sources high in the Kennedy administration. George Ball, under secretary of state, promised me a comment but said the White House had called him in and he would have very little time. Nick Katzenbach, number-two man to Bob Kennedy in the attorney general's office, said he would be in the studio at a quarter to twelve. I spoke with Senator Ken Keating, the Republican, who had first broken the story about Soviet missiles in Cuba. I then put in urgent calls to Paris, Bonn, and Moscow to alert correspondents there to be ready for a round-robin European reaction.

My producer, Bob Allison, and his assistants were in the film library, pulling out clips of people in the streets of Moscow, or outside the Kremlin, films of missiles displayed during the Red Army Day parades. Our show was still being hammered out as airtime approached. I would go on with only half the show sketched out. We would have to fill the time with the interviews and overseas reports. I would end up with a summary and concluding comment on this historic event.

The show began briskly and moved better than the most carefully scripted program. Everyone's adrenaline was flowing fast and we were flying on wings of relief and joy that the worst had been averted. Then came the climactic moment.

Our top-notch Moscow correspondent, Marvin Kalb, was standing by. We had no satellite then, so we ran his still photo as he talked to us on a radio circuit. Kalb, as requested by my earlier call, gave us a rundown on how the news had broken in Moscow. He went on to say that people were congregating in Red Square, talking in muted tones, with grim faces, digesting the Soviet defeat, the surrender to the American ultimatum to pull out of Cuba.

Within ten seconds of Marvin's comment, a bulb on my studio telephone began to flash red, blinking rapidly. It was an emergency signal usually because of some trouble in the control room or with the circuit. I cut in on Marvin and said that we had to take a break for about a minute, asking him to stand by until I came back to him.

I picked up the phone and heard Salinger's voice, crisp, urgent, emphatic. "David, I'm speaking from the Oval Office during an 'Ex-Comm' meeting. The president and top Cabinet members have broken off their meeting to watch your show. The president is standing right by me. He says that you must not let Kalb run on about a Soviet defeat. Do not play this up as a victory for us. There is a danger that Khrushchev will be so humiliated and angered that he will change his mind. Watch what you are saying. The Soviets are listening in, too. Don't mess this up for us."

Salinger hung up. For a few seconds I was numb, then my blood coursed. I was elated. My admiration for Kennedy soared.

His reaction was so sound, so exactly right, so generous. He would not try to crow over a defeated opponent and abrade the sores. What a man! It never occurred to me, not even for a microsecond, that a president ought not to be cutting into a live news program to tell a broadcaster what to say. It was a violation of every rule of the free press. I knew at once, however, that this was not the issue. The issue was war or peace in the atomic age. The stakes were beyond calculation. This was bigger than any TV program or any normal rules. He had done what was right for the nation and the world, and I jumped to comply.

Our commercial break ended and I called Kalb back. I said, "Marvin, I wonder if people in Moscow are thinking some of the thoughts that I'm hearing here in Washington? That this is not a victory or a defeat for any power, but rather a victory for peace and for all mankind."

Marvin Kalb, as bright a man and as fine a reporter as I have ever worked with, caught on at once. "Well, not generally, David, not yet, but there are a few people at the top who understand what a great moment this is for everyone. It will get through to the masses of the people very quickly. The Russians value peace as much as any people. They will rejoice when the realization sinks in that this is a great day for everyone."

I breathed a deep sigh of relief. I could just see in my mind President Kennedy, Secretary Rusk, Secretary McNamara, Secretary Dillon, Ted Sorensen, George Ball, McGeorge Bundy, all the big brass of the administration, glaring at the tube, their eyes bursting through and blazing at me, and then sitting back with a smile. I could imagine, too, the Soviets at their embassy, hastily translating the program and sending it off by teleprinter to the Kremlin. I just breezed through the rest of the show with a grin on my face as the tension receded. There is no doubt that the live, unrehearsed news broadcast can take unforeseen detours. This situation had become so explosive that instinctively I knew it had to be defused.

My red light flashed again. This time I knew who and what it signaled. I picked up the phone and heard Salinger say, "*Merci, mon brave.* Thanks, ol' buddy." I knew that we had served the cause of peace and the highest national interest. I knew, too, that I had scored heavily with the most powerful men in Washington and that there were favors I could call on in the weeks ahead.

It was a coup for television news and it proved that there was no such thing as a "ghetto show" or a bad time slot. Whenever you are on the air there is an audience, and anything can happen. I thought, mistakenly, that I had proven my point and that New York brass would not hassle me anymore about my Sunday program.

I was soon shorn of my illusions. None of my achievements or ambitions could be measured against what management wanted. CBS was no longer the CBS of the Murrow era, when correspondents reigned supreme. The boom that I thought had been lifted was about to be lowered on me. There is very little room at the top in any organization. The higher you get, the more people are trying to push you off the pinnacle. It happens in every human enterprise and, all evidence to the contrary, television is human. The more successful my Sunday show became, the more trouble I had with New York.

One fateful day Don Hewitt called to say that he, Cronkite, and producer Ernest Leiser, a former correspondent, would like to come to Washington to confer with me. "We've got great news for you." I suddenly recalled Ed Murrow telling me about Paley's "great news," which turned out to be the cancellation of his weekly "See It Now." I had a premonition that I would be the next victim of this kind of glad tidings.

I knew that good news is conveyed by phone or letter. If a delegation of three top men was coming to Washington, it was not to impart news but to confer with me. I knew just what they wanted to discuss. In fact, I knew there would be little discussion. A decision had been made, or Cronkite would not have flown to Washington.

I was right, although there *was* good news and I was delighted to hear it. It may seem incredible today to a new generation, but at that time, in 1963, the evening news was only a quarter of an hour long, even less when you deducted commercial time, barely twelve minutes. Twelve minutes to cover all important national and world news. We know now that even a half-hour is not enough and that local news stations generally add an hour of their own to the half-hour network news. Network news, if it is to survive in good shape, is going to have to expand in the 1990s.

The good news, as Walter told me, was that management had decided to expand the evening news to a half-hour. Then Don Hewitt took over to say that I would be the main Washington reporter and analyst on the new evening news. I would get a big national audience and a substantial raise in salary. It truly was very good news, although I wondered when the other shoe would drop. It did. They left that rude task to Ernest Leiser who, as a former competitor on the foreign staff, had no great love for me. Ernest informed me that James Aubrey had granted the extra time each night to news on condition that other time slots would be turned back to the television network to compensate for the evening loss. That other time, of course, was my Sunday show. It was being killed for its success, just as I had feared.

There is no reason to go into further details about that conference. My personal concerns are not relevant to this story of how TV operates. What is important is to demonstrate just how TV management functions and what its goals are. The biggest goal in those days was to subordinate everything to the evening news.

This is still the main goal, although, exceptionally, management has allowed Don Hewitt to carve out his own autonomous empire in his "60 Minutes" operation. Management permits it because it is the most prestigious, money-making show on the network. Don runs it with his hands firmly on the reins. When it was suggested about a year or two ago that Diane Sawyer, whom he had appointed as a "60 Minutes" reporter, might also be assigned to the "Evening News with Dan Rather," Don firmly said no. Diane could go to Rather, he said, but then she would have to leave "60 Minutes."

Dan Rather was relieved at Hewitt's stern rule and at Diane Sawyer's decision to stay on "60 Minutes," where she was quickly becoming a thoroughly accomplished reporter. Dan Rather wants no part of a co-anchor. He had no personal objection to Diane. She might be an ideal woman but ideal women are not necessarily ideal co-anchors.

Our meeting in Washington ended with my promise to Walter and Don to think over their new proposal and to get back to them. I was deeply distressed when they left. Friends told me that I was being foolish. What is there to be distressed about in being offered the top reporting job on the Cronkite show, making me the number-two man, right after Walter, in the CBS rankings? I understand their reasoning. From the outside it looks like one of the best jobs in journalism. In truth, it is. But I was tired of reporting to others, of being told what to do and when, of seeing my best pieces turn to ashes in the flames of Beverly Hills estates.

That was, perhaps, not the only or main reason. I have been accused of vanity, of being overly ambitious. This is a strange accusation in a world churning with ambitious men and women. Whatever the reason, right or wrong, I wanted no part of their deal. I was angry and hurt at the killing of a damn fine show that I had worked so hard to create. Pride goeth before a fall, I am told. Indeed.

My wife, Dorothy, wiser than I, made the final decision. She told me to turn it down. "You'll be swallowing bile every day. You'll be miserable and it will poison our lives. Don't do it, it isn't worth it." She added that I was not only a broadcaster, I was a writer, lecturer, and teacher. I had many arrows in my quiver and I would be happier after twenty years to go on my own.

I flew to New York to tell Clark and Salant my decision. They offered me the job of chief foreign correspondent, based again in Paris, and promised that they would get time from Aubrey for a half-hour European report. I did not believe them for a minute. If they really wanted to give me that show, which I doubted, I knew perfectly well that Aubrey, getting back the half-hour from my "Washington Report," would not graciously return it for a European report. They were just trying to shove me off to Europe with nothing much to do, to die on the vine there.

I went to see Frank Stanton. He said he was very unhappy with the way the whole affair had been handled, not only my clash but the conflict with Howard Smith. "We are losing our best men and I must stop this bleeding," he told me. Stanton went so far as to tell me confidentially that he was going to reorganize the News Division. He would pull Salant back to the corporate counsel position. Stanton said he was going to fire Blair Clark. He told me to go back to Paris on leave of absence at full pay. I could take a year, he suggested, to write the biography of Charles de Gaulle that I had been planning. CBS would underwrite it all and then, with new management, I could come back to a fresh start.

It was an astonishingly generous offer. I was ready to accept it, but my wife, knowing me better than I know myself, told me it would not work. "You can't sit in Paris, writing a book, while news is breaking all around you and then, after a year away, come back again." She was also weary of my globe-trotting and her own trips with me. They had been thrilling, but she had done it all; she felt it was time to stop. She wanted me to write more, to lecture at universities. She had also lost faith in CBS after what it had done to Murrow, Smith, and now me. She told me to "cut the cord and live your own life."

After much thought and soul-searching, I finally decided the time had come to leave CBS. The network had given me the most exciting, rewarding years of my life and I would always be grateful to Bill Paley. But nothing stays the same and I could see no future for me at CBS, or none that appealed to me. I did want to write, and began at once preparing my book on de Gaulle. I asked my agent to take steps to end my contract with CBS. Once again, Frank Stanton was generous. He expressed regrets at my decision and approved a severance pay almost double that which his News Division auditor had proposed.

This was not by any means the end of my career in broadcasting. I would continue doing news analyses and documentaries on radio and TV for ABC, Metromedia, and the Independent Network News (INN). I have been doing analyses on the average of three a week for INN for the past fifteen years and have learned a lot about the new development of rival networks to the Big Three. INN is a syndicate of local stations that carry a network program produced in New York by the news department of WPIX, channel 11. Its news director, John Corporon, is one of the most competent men in the field.

The decision to expand the CBS network evening news to a half-hour was carried out finally in September 1963. I was then doing commentary for ABC News. It seemed like a dream or nightmare when I tuned in to watch the first half-hour on CBS. I could not believe that I was no longer there.

Eric Sevareid, who had gone to London when Howard Smith came to Washington, had returned to Washington to replace me. However, my two titles had been eliminated. Eric was not chief correspondent or bureau chief; he was the analyst of the evening news. In keeping with the trend to take power away from the correspondents, CBS had simply not appointed a two-hatted chief to replace me. Eventually, they would name an administrative bureau chief and separate chief correspondents—Leslie Stahl, chief of national affairs, and Bruce Morton, chief political correspondent. When everyone is a chief, there is no chief.

As I watched that first half-hour news program, I was impressed by a report from Texas by a young unknown. His name was Dan Rather. He did an excellent report on a racial conflict in Texas. I thought he sounded good, crisp, authoritative. I wonder today how many people that night could possibly have guessed that the anchorman, Walter Cronkite, was on his way to fame and fortune as the "most trusted man in America," while the youngster in Texas, Dan Rather, would be his eventual successor.

Another headliner joined CBS in that turning-point year, 1963, and it was yet another indication of how CBS policy had changed. CBS News signed a big contract with Mike Wallace. Many at CBS were surprised. They did not consider Wallace to be a CBS-style class act. He was dynamic, had a following, but was more aggressive, brash, tough than CBS tradition. Most did not yet realize how CBS had changed. Wallace was the kind of newsman that Aubrey liked, a showman.

CBS then gave an important role to Harry Reasoner. Once again, it was a move toward another generation, a different one from the Murrow era. It looked as if Richard Salant was deliberately passing over all the Murrow men to bring in new faces with no built-in traditions or loyalties.

Reasoner was assigned as the anchor of a new CBS morning show. The mornings belonged to NBC. Their show "Today" was tops in the ratings. CBS could not compete. They thought Reasoner might do it, but he could not. No one ever could. NBC was finally matched in the mornings not by CBS, but by once lowly ABC. When ABC hired TV actor David Hartman to anchor their morning show, called "Good Morning America," they struck a lode of gold. It made no pretense of being a news program. The very name, "Good Morning America," had no hint of news in it. It was fashioned to catch the housewife at home, featuring "women's stories": birth control, pap smears, menopause, consumer advice, cake recipes, and interviews with Hollywood stars. It quickly became number one. "Today" would catch up, fall behind, and finally regain the lead. CBS got nowhere.

In 1987 CBS tried again after a long series of failures. They installed a co-anchor, now *de rigueur* on talk shows. A guy named

Harry Smith, bald, bespectacled, a Middle American middle brow by his own description. He was paired with Kathleen Sullivan, an attractive woman, with a youthful, pert face but long iron-gray hair and well-shaped thighs. Her thighs were prominent on camera, for she wore micro-mini skirts that did not reach within four inches of her knees. It was funny but sad to watch her, sitting down, her mini rising high, while she tugged futilely at it to bring it within modest range. As of this writing, neither Tom, Dick, nor Harry, nor Kathleen's mini skirts have been able to lift CBS out of the third-place cellar in the mornings.

Dan Rather, who had made a good debut on the new half-hour evening news in September 1963, became an overnight sensation in the middle of a national tragedy in November. On Friday, November 22, 1963, Rather was packing up, ready to move from Dallas to a new, bigger assignment as head of the New Orleans bureau. He stayed behind that day to help cover President Kennedy's visit to Dallas.

Rather, checking over the map of Kennedy's route, noticed an important "film drop" site that was uncovered. It was the last one on the route, near a railroad overpass, just beyond an ugly brick building called the Texas Book Depository. Rather felt that the area was also a good location to observe the motorcade. He chose a spot across the railroad tracks, behind a grassy knoll. He carried with him a bright yellow dispatch bag for the film that the camera crew would drop off to him.

Rather never saw his crew or the cans of film. Instead he saw a police car burn rubber, sirens screaming, as it turned full circle around. He caught sight of Texas Governor John Connally and Jackie Kennedy in an open limousine, but could not see the president. Dan heard no shots and did not at first know what was happening, but he guessed quickly when he saw hundreds of people throw themselves on the ground and begin screaming.

Dan raced to the CBS radio station, KRLD. He heard a police radio refer to Parkland Hospital. Rather quickly called the hospital and, astonishingly, the telephone operator, tears in her voice, shouted, "The President has been shot." Then a doctor picked up the phone and Dan asked him how the president was. The doctor replied, "I'm told he's dead."

Dan shouted out the news to the people in the newsroom. They told him to go on the air. He refused. He would not go out with the awful news that the president was killed on such scant, unconfirmed information. He called the hospital again and this time a priest told him, "Yes, the president was shot and killed."

Dan, still searching, unwilling to believe, afraid to go on with the news, called Eddie Barker, news director of KRLD, to tell him what he had heard. Barker said he had heard the same thing. Another voice cut in on their conversation. Dan thought it was a local editor talking to Barker. He did not know it was a CBS editor in New York. The voice asked Dan, "Did you say he was dead." "Right," said Dan, "he's dead." The next thing heard in the newsroom was a newscast from New York announcing a bulletin. "CBS correspondent Dan Rather reports from Dallas that the president is dead." Then CBS played the national anthem, while Dan Rather stood in the middle of the newsroom, clutching his heart and gasping for breath.

CBS and Dan Rather were "credited" with being the first to bring the terrible news to the American people. It took almost twenty minutes before any other network would confirm the report—twenty minutes in which Rather lived a nightmare of despair, grief, fury, unvoiced disavowal, fear for his country, certain of the ruin of his career. Dan knew he could never explain that he thought he was merely talking to a local colleague, that he had not offered the news for broadcast. He didn't even know who he was talking to, for the voice had cut in on Eddie Barker's line.

Producer Don Hewitt called Dan from New York. He would not use the news on the evening show, he told Dan, until it was officially confirmed by a government spokesman. Dan told him the whole story of what he had heard and how the story got out. A moment later, a vice-president ran into the New York newsroom, shouting that the president had been shot and was thought dead. Walter Cronkite, having his usual sandwich at his desk—he never went out to lunch—rushed into a studio and got a technician to cut into a soap opera, so that Walter could announce that the president had been shot in Dallas, that the wounds were grave, might be fatal. Cronkite just stopped short of saying the president was dead, although CBS news had already announced that a half-hour earlier with the so-called report from Dan Rather.

Finally, the official announcement was released. Walter Cronkite, always the calm, controlled voice, broke down. His voice cracked with emotion, tears filled his eyes as he read the dread announcement of President Kennedy's assassination. Even with the long delay after the earlier report, Cronkite's broadcast still beat the other networks by two to five minutes. A moment of national tragedy is no time to be thinking about "scoops" or beating the competition, but it was a cold, grim fact that everyone in the country began tuning in to CBS. People were frantically calling friends, asking what had happened, and were told "CBS has the story. They say he's dead."

For the next four days there was almost continuous round-the-clock coverage of the tragedy and its consequences. The nation saw Jackie Kennedy wearing her blood-stained suit, the funeral, the black horse with the saddle and stirrups reversed, and, over and over again, the heart-stopping moment when the president seemed to fall backward and then pitch forward. People sat and watched Lyndon Johnson, the new president, address a joint session of Congress. None of it seemed real, it was a national nonstop nightmare, the greatest tragedy of the television age, which brought the scene into every living room. It was the nation's blackest hour and television's finest.

The anchormen and reporters were magnificent. They worked without pause, without scripts, explaining everything, filling in what would have been a gaping void into which panic could have flooded. Television rose beyond a news service and became the glue that held the nation together, allowing Americans to share a common grief and a common resolve to carry on and keep the nation strong. In that tragedy, television became a permanent participant in and not just the mirror of American affairs.

Television news could do what the most brilliant drama or entertainment show could not do, touch a nerve in all the people, inform the population all together and all at once of a crucial national development. Television was ready, and so was fate, for the blackest series of heart-testing, brain-boggling events in our history: the Vietnam War, the assassinations of Robert Kennedy and Martin Luther King, race riots, burning cities, a president and his vice-president both kicked out of office in disgrace, the rise of terrorism around the world, the capture of hostages in Iran, the shooting of Ronald Reagan. There is no period of American history comparable to the sixties, seventies, and eighties. One can only pray that the black series will end in the last ten years of this incredible twentieth century.

8

THE
NOT-SO-FRIENDLY
YEARS

We could not know it then, but the sixties, first of the three terrible decades ahead, was the high point in the rise of CBS News. There would still be peak periods but, on the whole, the sixties historically marked the beginning of the fall from grace of CBS and network news. Not in terms of its power and influence, to be sure. On the contrary, TV network news would grow to giant size, blanketing the nation, dominating politics, far outpacing print journalism, so that today more than 55 percent of Americans get all or most of their news from television, which may well explain the present phenomenon of a nation that knows less about more things.

TV's fall from grace has been occasioned by a drop in standards, an emphasis on what is exciting rather than on what is significant, a virtual elimination of news analysis, and a dearth of thoughtful, in-depth documentaries that, alone, have the space to deal intelligently and thoroughly with the many complex issues of national and world affairs. With the retirement of Eric Sevareid and the departure of Bill Moyers, CBS News no longer has a news analyst on its programs. ABC never really had a designated analyst. The only survivor of the old analytical days is John Chancellor of NBC News and he does not appear often enough or with enough time to do what is needed.

TV is operating on a principle that was never valid: just tell the people factually what happened and let them reach their own conclusions. This cannot work. The complexities of national deficits, trade failures, budget gaps, negotiations to end the nuclear arms race, the crises of the Middle East, all these cannot be understood by giving the facts alone. The public needs appropriate historical background and clarification. People who are not taught much geography, history, economics, and physics simply cannot reach reasonable conclusions without help from specialists. This is not elitism, it is something far more important; it is called education.

No one believed more passionately in TV's educational obligations, and the ability to be interesting as well as informative, than Ed Murrow's producer Fred Friendly. Fred had proved in "See It Now" and "CBS Reports" that it was possible to win a big audience and make money, while digging deeply into a significant topic of national and world affairs. It was seemingly logical then for CBS President Frank Stanton to turn to Fred Friendly to head up the News Division and pull it out of the morass into which it had fallen in the first stewardship of Richard Salant as president of News.

Salant was Stanton's protégé. Paley did not like him, but Stanton admired his undoubted energy, brains, and dedication. Salant was a magna cum laude from Harvard Law. But he was inexperienced in news and in corporate management. Stanton told close associates that Salant had badly mangled the cases of Howard K. Smith and David Schoenbrun. "These men were two of our finest, most admired reporters, and we lost both of them in quarrels that could have been avoided," Stanton said.

His confidence in Salant's innate ability unshaken, however, Stanton did as he promised me he would when I left CBS. He pulled Salant back into the parent corporation and fired his vice-president, Blair Clark. To head up CBS News, he called in Fred Friendly. Logical though it seemed, it was a serious error. Stanton admitted this to me many years later. He said, "I should have remembered what happened when Bill Paley persuaded Ed Murrow to take over the News Division. It was a disaster." Creative reporters and broad-

casters are temperamental men; they are not executives or adminis-
trators. Writers almost never make great editors and great editors
rarely can write. They have qualities suited mainly to their own
talents and those qualities do not translate into different require-
ments.

Reporter Harry Reasoner knew that well. CBS thought it had
found a new Twinkly-Brinkley type in Harry Reasoner, a wry, sardonic quipster who had a gift for the pungent phrase. Reasoner told
Friendly, "You are an executive in the sense that Willy Sutton was a
banker." Reasoner, hearing about Friendly's appointment as president of CBS News, spread the word throughout the division that
"the inmates have taken over the asylum." There is no doubt that
Friendly was what the French called *une force de la nature,* an earth
power, a volcano waiting to erupt.

Fred faced serious competition from NBC News. Huntley-
Brinkley were still rating well above Walter Cronkite. It is forgotten
in the light of the Cronkite legend that he did not spring full-blown
on Mount Olympus but resided for a number of years down in the
valley in the underbrush of television. Bill Paley, who could not
tolerate being second, called Friendly in and asked what his plans
were to win back first place on the evening news.

Fred thought they ought to change the airtime from 6:30 to 7:30
P.M. Six-thirty was too early for many people still on their way home
from work. That was in the old days when people did not stop work
at 5:00 and chuck down a cocktail on the way home. Paley was not
impressed by so simplistic a proposal as a time change to win first
place. He told Fred to go back to the drawing board and do some
serious thinking.

Everyone knew that Fred was competent and creative as a
producer, but some cynics argued that what made Fred a great
producer was Ed Murrow. It is customary to throw stones at everyone at the top. French poet-philosopher Jean Cocteau once commented that "Statues to great men are made of the stones thrown at
them in their lifetime." In that sense, Fred ought to have a lot of
statues to his fame, for a great many stones were flung at him.

Fred was overflowing with energy, often misdirected. *Time*
magazine described Fred as the kind of man "who tosses in his
chair as though it were stuffed with thumbtacks." Fred's good
friend and admirer, poet-historian Carl Sandburg, a fan of CBS,

who used to call Ed Murrow after every year-end show and then talk in turn with each of us, once commented that "Fred always looks as if he had just dismounted from a foam-flecked horse." Bill Downs bellowed in his bull's voice: "Fred *is* a foam-flecked horse."

Fred was always ready, as Ed Murrow had been, to cut into any network program, no matter how popular and money-making, to put out an important news bulletin. Top management had clashed often with Murrow, who would cancel such major shows as Kate Smith and Bing Crosby because of some news development at the United Nations. Fred was warned not to follow in the footsteps of his mentor, Murrow. But that is exactly what he did.

NBC beat CBS by a long five minutes on a news bulletin. It was feared Fred had suffered heart failure. Fred heard the NBC bulletin in his office while his CBS monitor remained silent. He charged into the newsroom like a maddened grizzly, spraying everyone with saliva as he shouted out orders to get the bulletin on the air, while simultaneously firing the editor whom he had just ordered to put out the bulletin. He stood there, all six feet four inches of him, 220 pounds strong, and bellowed his rage, terrifying everyone in the newsroom. This is not considered to be proper executive behavior. Friendly was anything but cool, urbane, and tailored. Fred was always rumpled and looked as if he had just gotten out of bed after sleeping fully clothed.

Fred's troubles increased after the Republican convention of 1964 in San Francisco. Cronkite, the CBS standard bearer, was again trounced in the ratings by Huntley and Brinkley. Now it was Bill Paley, not Friendly, spraying CBS with saliva as he shouted his anger. I watched that disaster in the making as the anchorman for Metromedia. It was the first time I covered a major political event in competition with CBS instead of as a member of the team. I saw nothing wrong with Cronkite's coverage. It was just that the Huntley-Brinkley team had captured the public, who were amused by the contrast between serious Chet and Twinkly Brinkley. This was not acceptable to Paley, who called Friendly in for a roasting. I met my old friend Bob Trout in the corridors and he told me that morale had hit bottom and that Paley was threatening to fire everyone.

CBS's run of bad luck and bad decisions had not ended. The network ran into serious trouble with a report from its able, but overly ambitious and controversy-prone reporter in Germany, Dan

Schorr. Dan was one of America's best foreign correspondents, with a long string of exclusive stories to his credit. He was respected, even admired, if not well-liked by his colleagues and his peers. He tended to press just a little too hard and stretch just a little too far to get his story.

During the Republican convention, Dan sent in a dispatch asserting that as soon as Barry Goldwater was nominated he would fly to Germany to meet with military friends at Berchtesgaden, Hitler's Alpine eyrie. Goldwater, Schorr reported, would meet with Germany's controversial, extreme right-wing politician Franz-Josef Strauss. It all sounded like some kind of extreme right-wing conspiracy in Hitler's lair. It caused an uproar.

Goldwater was furious. He issued a flat, angry denial of Schorr's story, saying there was not a single word of truth in it—the worst kind of denial that can be thrown at a correspondent. Fred Friendly, buffeted by storms all around him, wanted to fire Dan Schorr at once, without even checking out the story, not one of Fred's wisest decisions. He was talked out of it by immediate, intense opposition from the entire corps of CBS correspondents. If a reporter could be fired on the basis of a denial by a politician, without even a hearing, then every correspondent was in serious danger and could not properly carry out reporting assignments.

Fred agreed not to fire Dan, but he did something almost as bad. He called him up and ordered him to do a broadcast retracting his story. Schorr, a fighter, angrily refused. He insisted his story was essentially correct. He did admit he had overreached himself by reporting that Goldwater was trying to arrange a meeting with extreme German right-wingers. The initiative had, in fact, come from the German side. They wanted to meet with Goldwater. But the rest of his story about Goldwater's trip to Berchtesgaden was correct, Dan insisted. He offered to clear up the one part of the report that was not completely accurate, but nothing else. Eventually the whole affair faded away, but it was harmful.

As soon as CBS's disastrous Republican convention coverage ended, new trouble broke out. To Bob Trout's astonishment and dismay, he was called in by Friendly, who informed him that Cronkite was going to be yanked out of the anchor seat for the Democratic convention scheduled to follow at Atlantic City in August. Cronkite had been the top CBS anchor since 1960, the acknowledged star. It was as if the heavens themselves had exploded, blowing up the CBS galaxy. Trout wanted no part of replacing Cronkite, but, a good soldier and the most experienced political reporter on the staff, going back thirty years to the Hoover-Roosevelt election, Trout had to accept.

Friendly, under heavy pressure from Paley, simply had to come up with something, no matter what. He devised the idea of a rival co-anchor duo to compete with Huntley-Brinkley. Trout would be the equivalent of the serious Chet, the elder steady man of the anchor team. And to oppose young David Brinkley, Fred chose one of the best political reporters in the field, Roger Mudd, who covered Congress out of the Washington bureau.

It was a good team, first-rate reporters, experience and youth. Only a year before, I had been Washington chief and Roger Mudd had been one of the best men in my bureau. He had come to me for advice on his career. CBS management thought well of him and wanted him to anchor a Saturday morning news program. Roger was torn between the bigger money and exposure and his concern about the nature of the program.

I told him to insist on being allowed to cover Congress in Washington, increasing his professional experience and prestige, but to state his willingness to accommodate management by doing the Saturday anchor stint, but only as an added chore, not a substitute for his Washington work. Mudd worked it out and eventually went on to be called in as a regular substitute for Cronkite on the evening news, a big step up in his career. Unfortunately, in 1964, Mudd's career was not helped by his anchor position in Atlantic City. Trout and Mudd did a competent job, for they are highly competent men, but they did not have the magic of Huntley and Brinkley, who again triumphed over CBS, sending Paley into fits of fury.

At the same time, Paley's anger at Cronkite's failure in the ratings was well-matched by the anger of Cronkite's fans. Thousands of them sent letters and cables to CBS denouncing the company for abandoning Walter Cronkite. These complaints came not only from the public but from peer reporters who admired Walter. One of the angriest and most vocal critics of CBS was one of the best, most respected Washington political columnists, Mary McGrory. When I met Mary on the boardwalk during a break in the proceedings, she, too, looked as though she had been riding a foam-flecked horse. She was almost spitting with rage, denouncing Friendly and CBS, defending Walter Cronkite with all the words in her extensive vocabulary, with all her emotions and brains working full speed.

The usual punsters and smart-asses who abound in the profession were having a field day with the names of poor old Trout and Mudd. "Here's Mudd in your eye," was the obvious and not brilliant greeting shouted at CBS executives. "Smoked Trout on the menu today," was another. Or, "Trout's hiding under a Mudd-bank." CBS, the proud leader of television news, had become the butt of bad jokes. It was unfair to both Trout and Mudd, two of the best political reporters, but fairness is not a notable quality in the ratings race.

It was also unfair to Fred Friendly. He had argued strongly with Paley against yanking Cronkite. He knew what a storm it would generate. But no one argues for long with the chairman. What Paley wants, Paley gets, even a disaster. As for Cronkite, it was, in some ways, despite his fall from power, his finest hour. He reacted in accord with the Hemingway formula so popular with President Kennedy, "grace under pressure." Walter never complained. He was a good soldier. He followed orders and let his fans fight for him. When questioned about the change, Walter quietly asserted that CBS had the right to assign whomever it chose to any position and that he would do whatever management asked him to do. In eclipse, Cronkite grew in stature, and when hundreds of people turned up on the convention floor wearing We Want Cronkite buttons, CBS knew it had made a serious error.

Cronkite had not failed at the Republican convention. He had done his usual top-notch job. It was unfortunate that his best at that time could not match the popularity and special chemistry of the Huntley-Brinkley duo. Their charm and top ratings would not, however, last. The television audience is fickle and tires of its own favorites.

Cronkite continued to anchor the evening news in his straightforward, competent style and began to increase his ratings, as the idea occurred to millions of Americans that here was a completely honest, trustworthy man who told them the news straight, without any twisting, without any wit or wisecracks. His evening ratings caught and then surpassed NBC. And when Huntley, tired and ill, quit broadcasting, Cronkite surged into the lead and was well on his way to becoming "the most trusted man in America." By the conventions of 1968, Cronkite was back in his anchor seat overlooking the floor and Bill Paley was smiling again, back in first place.

Roger Mudd was back where he should have been in the first place, down on the floor doing his job of gathering the news and relaying it up to Walter. And Walter, who liked his work, took Roger on as his permanent substitute on the evening news. This led Roger to believe that he had been anointed as the Crown Prince, the eventual successor to Walter when Cronkite reached retirement age. That was still more than a decade ahead, but Roger was young and he was not in a hurry. He loved what he was doing and was doing it supremely well.

CBS News was tall in the saddle again with a magnificent team: Cronkite; Mudd; Marvin Kalb at State; Mike Wallace, a new star in the firmament; and a most attractive young Texan making a name for himself as White House correspondent, Dan Rather.

While CBS News was in transition between the old Murrow team and the new Cronkite-Wallace-Rather era, challenging and tragic events were under way that would test the new men and the few women who were breaking through the gender barrier. The new killing fields of the world were located in Southeast Asia. It seems hardly credible that we would plunge first into the harsh, cold, mountainous country of Korea in the 1950s, fighting to a no-decision deadlock against North Koreans and the Chinese, led into disaster by one of our most illustrious soldiers, General Douglas MacArthur, who warned us never to fight a land war in Asia again, only to plunge once again, this time into the paddies and jungles of Vietnam.

Perhaps more than any other reporter in Washington in the early 1960s, I was acutely aware of the dangers of fighting in Vietnam. It was not due to any special perspicacity on my part, but rather that I was one of the few Washington reporters with long experience in Vietnam. As correspondent for France and the French empire, I had covered the murderous French-Indochinese War, which in eight years had all but destroyed France as a world power and had led directly to the disintegration of the entire French global empire. The equivalent of the graduating classes of St. Cyr, the French West Point, died in Indochina. Three countries existed under that umbrella title: Vietnam, Laos, and Cambodia.

The French conquered and annexed the three countries in the nineteenth century. They took over and exploited the rich rubber plantations, the rice fields, and the minerals of the area. But the Vietnamese, although conquered, were never completely subdued. They are a fighting people. They had fought for almost a thousand years against the Chinese, their giant neighbor to the north. And they had fought among themselves, Viets against Khmers of Cambodia and against the Laotians. They are a hardy, brave people able to live on a bowl of rice a day and the fish of their rivers and the South China Sea. They are small, rarely weigh much over a hundred pounds, but are wiry and astonishingly strong. On my reporting trips there, I would see teenage boys and girls who weighed under a hundred pounds balance a bamboo pole on their shoulders, hang baskets on the front and back of the poles, filled with materials weighing almost as much as they did, and lope across paddies, dikes, and jungle paths for five to six miles.

I watched them ambush the French, win total control of the country by night, so that the French soldiers did not dare venture out of their forts that, instead of strongholds, became prisons for the French troops. I was the only American inside the bastion of Dien Bien Phu, a strategic crossroads between Vietnam and Laos. The French, with powerful defenses there, dared the Viet Communists to come out and fight, instead of slinking in the dark jungle at night like leopards. They did. They carried mortars and artillery on their backs over mountains and installed them on the heights over Dien Bien Phu. They pounded the French in their exposed positions. Then they came down the mountains in a charge that overran the French defenses and captured ten thousand French troops.

For the first time in Asian history, a peasant people, in black pajamas, fought one of the great armed forces of the white, Western world and defeated them in a pitched battle. It was the end of white, Western domination of Asia. Indeed, it had already ended when giant China became Communist, but that was in a fight between Chinese. Vietnam was the historic battle between East and West. It brought to an end Western colonial power. I had witnessed it, lived through it and knew how correct was General MacArthur's warning to the West never to fight a land war in Asia.

I was naturally supersensitized to any signs of war in Vietnam and was dismayed, on arriving in Washington, to see too many signs that President Kennedy was beginning to undertake commitments in that region. I heard daily rumblings about "counterinsurgency," of the need to stop Communist subversion of all Southeast Asia, of the "domino theory" that would permit the Communists to knock over all the countries one by one. I was told by my sources that the Green Berets were being trained for jungle warfare and counterguerrilla action.

This talk, these plans, were, in my view, signposts to disaster, based on an almost total ignorance of the history of Vietnam or the nature of the terrain. American experts had never seen, as I had, Vietnamese soldiers submerged underwater in paddies, breathing through reeds, suddenly emerging, covered in weeds like sea monsters, to overwhelm a French patrol and wipe it out. The Kennedy advisers were unaware of supplies carried on bamboo poles or on bicycles, that could not be seen from the air and could not be bombed. Bombers could destroy a German six-lane highway but they could not wipe out jungle trails.

Our soldiers would not be able to match the lightly clad Viets, slinking silently through the jungle on rubber sandals, while we thrashed through in heavy boots, signaling our presence miles ahead of us. Our soldiers would not be able to live on a bowl of rice and a fish head a day. There were millions of Vietnamese prepared to fight the alien invaders of their land and they could live like leopards in the jungle, leaping out suddenly on the backs of Western soldiers unprepared for jungle warfare.

Whenever I had the chance to talk with President Kennedy, I kept pressing these arguments on him, until one day Pierre Salinger, escorting me to the Oval Office, said, "The President does not want to hear a word from you on Vietnam today. You've said your piece over again. Now knock it off." I knew that day that they were rushing into a tragic ambush in Vietnam and I feared for our country. I greatly admired Kennedy but he appalled me the day he said, "Schoenbrun, stop telling me about what the Viets did to the French. We are not the French. We are Americans, many times more

powerful, and they won't push us around." It was arrogance com-
pounded by ignorance, a deadly mix.

I was about the only reporter in Washington to express concern
of impending events and that did me great harm. There is nothing
more dangerous for a reporter's credibility than being prematurely
right. The American reporters in Saigon in those early days were all
gung ho. They considered themselves part of the team. Even David
Halberstam, who would later become a severe critic of the military
in Saigon, was one of the journalist-warriors in the early years. They
reported the American buildup with applause.

President Eisenhower had limited American military numbers
in Vietnam to the 750 to 800 observers permitted by the Geneva
Accords of 1954. But Kennedy broke through that barrier and began
sending "observers" by the thousands. They were not truly
observers, they were military men, although at first they went in
unarmed. Later they were authorized to carry arms and to shoot
only if shot at. Step by step we were walking into the jungle trap. By
1963 the American military in Vietnam had reached the total of
eleven thousand, far in excess of any observation mission. Even
then, no one in Washington took much notice and there were no
cries of alarm from the media or the Congress.

The events in Vietnam did finally get national attention in
September 1963, when CBS News finally inaugurated the long-
planned extension of the evening news from a quarter-hour to a
half-hour. To mark the occasion, Walter Cronkite interviewed President Kennedy. Walter asked the president to explain the big buildup
of American "observers" in Vietnam and asked about American
"involvement" there. The president side-stepped the questions. He
was good at that. There was no public reaction and Walter did not
press the issue. It made no headlines. Only one high official was
deeply concerned, Under Secretary of State George Ball.

Ball, one of the rare Kennedy officials with any knowledge of
the French-Indochinese experience, warned the president that any
commitment to defend South Vietnam against the Communist
North would require a minimum of 300,000 troops. Kennedy
laughed him off, saying, "George, you're crazier than hell." Well,
George was not crazy, although he was wrong. It would require
more than 500,000 men and some 55,000 deaths and hundreds of
thousands of casualties, wounded, shell-shocked, and drugged

before America—its pride humbled, its prestige crumbled, its finances in a mess, inflation rampant—finally staggered out of Vietnam after eight bloody, futile years.

The tragedy of the United States in Vietnam was a historic turning point for TV news. New technology brought the war into the living rooms every night. Vietnam became the first evening TV war in history. At first the TV reports from the battlefields did not provoke any public alarm or protests. People seemed numbed and glassy-eyed watching the "living-room war" on their tubes; it did not seem real. But suddenly it became very real when a young, relatively unknown television correspondent broke out of obscurity and became a national name, finding himself in the middle of a heated controversy and causing nerves to snap in the executive suites of CBS.

Morley Safer was a Canadian-born and -trained reporter, a newscaster for the Canadian Broadcasting Corporation (CBC). He had been hired by CBS News to work out of the London office and rapidly established a professional, if not yet a public, reputation as a highly competent foreign correspondent who sent through wide-ranging and thoughtful reports from Europe, Africa, and the Middle East. Safer achieved a high rank and respect from his peers and from the news executives in New York. They thought he was just the right man to cover the growing American involvement in Vietnam.

One day, on patrol with American forces, Morley saw a marine put the flame of his cigarette lighter to the dry, thatched roof of a Vietnamese hut. It caught on at once and spread from house to house, the whole village going up in flames. Vietnamese women and children ran screaming and crying out of their homes. Morley's camera team was shooting away. They caught the scene of an American atrocity against a defenseless village—not a combat action against enemy troops.

When Walter Cronkite and his producer, Ernest Leiser, viewed the film they were stunned. They conferred about it for hours, unable to decide whether to run it or not on the evening news. They asked themselves hard questions about whether this was just an isolated incident or whether this was the way American forces were conducting themselves in Vietnam. We Americans do not believe, do not want to believe that Americans can be guilty of atrocities against civilians. The Germans do that. The Japanese do that.

Americans do not. Unfortunately, CBS had proof in their viewing room, on film, and in a graphic description by Morley Safer that Americans do in fact do that.

They wondered whether the scene could somehow be "balanced" in a wider context. After long agonizing, they decided to "go with it," but not that night. They needed time to figure out just how to present it. They would have to confer with Fred Friendly. They knew that they would be plunged into controversy no matter how they handled it, and that they and CBS could be hurt.

They decided, in typical Cronkite style, to go with it "straight," as a hard-news item. With no moral, ethical, or philosophical commentary, or any consideration for the "balance" demanded by the fairness doctrine, for, they decided, there simply was no balance to the story. Let others debate it later, let editorialists, members of Congress, and the administration interpret and comment on it. It was the job of CBS News first to present the news as it happened and as it was caught on their cameras. Discussion could follow.

There was, however, a comment on the sound track that shook them up. They heard Safer's voice saying "This is what the war in Vietnam is all about." This was, without doubt, an editorial opinion, highly controversial, against CBS policy, but they decided to let it go. Safer was the man on the spot covering the war. Presumably he knew what it was all about and, at the risk of his life, had earned the right to say what he thought. Fred Friendly gave them his okay, knowing that he would pay a price for the decision. They all knew they were breaking the rules and provoking a serious controversy, but, as Cronkite would later admit (a highly controversial admission), "the filmed report was just too sensational to pass up."

Fred Friendly went to the office the morning after the Safer report to be bombarded with phone calls and telegrams denouncing CBS News and Safer, claiming the Marines would never do such a thing, that the Safer film was faked. These denunciations were based only on resentment and not relevant to the truth. There was no way that the film could have been faked or that a man of Safer's integrity would fake it. Later, someone discovered that Safer's cameraman was a Vietnamese, as though that were some kind of proof of fakery. TV news critics are often thoroughly irresponsible, responding according to their prejudices, totally uninterested in the truth.

A Defense Department official phoned Friendly and all but accused CBS News of treason, as though the Vietnamese cameraman were responsible for the Marine atrocity instead of the Marine who had torched the hut. CBS President Stanton was hit even harder on the highest level of government. Stanton was a close friend of President Lyndon Johnson. When Johnson was vice-president-elect, Stanton called me in Paris to say that Senator Johnson and his retinue would be coming there for a NATO meeting. Stanton asked me to do everything possible to host their visit, with an unlimited expense account. Johnson ran me ragged from early morning to dawn the next day. Johnson was larger than life, a Texas longhorn stampeding through Paris. The morning after the Safer report, President Johnson really went on a stampede.

Early in the morning Stanton's phone rang, waking him up. He heard a booming voice shout, "Frank, are you trying to fuck me?"

"Who is this," asked a shocked Stanton, still groggy from sleep.

"Frank, this is your president, and yesterday your boys shat on the American flag."

The president then went on from these auspicious opening remarks to denounce Safer as a foreign Communist, and asked Frank Stanton how he could broadcast an enemy film. Johnson never minced words and would occasionally use a four-letter word better to express his outrage. Frank Stanton told me some years later that he was both angry and frightened at the same time. The president had enormous power and Stanton knew that CBS was in grave danger. The power of the presidency is awesome. In the hands of a ruthless force like Johnson, it could be devastating.

An aroused public was equally to be feared. Protests poured in from advertisers, including one of the biggest sponsors of network programs, Procter and Gamble, the soap-opera sponsor. Americans often ask me in the question period of a lecture whether television "tells it straight." Well, those of us in television news know we are not beyond reproach. We try but we do make mistakes and are not always completely accurate. But television news journalists at least try to tell it straight and are far more accurate and reliable than presidents, government officials, members of Congress, or advertising sponsors. We serve the public perhaps imperfectly, but better than any other institution of public affairs.

Frank Stanton, despite his fears of President Johnson, stood strongly behind Friendly and the News Division. News waited nervously but breathed relief when no message came down from Olympus, the office of the chairman. Paley was silent and silence lends assent. Morley Safer survived angry attacks and went on for a quarter of a century to become one of the top stars of CBS News as a key reporter on "60 Minutes," the highest rated news program in television history.

If Morley Safer finally survived the fury of President Johnson, Fred Friendly, who had loyally backed him, ran into trouble. There is no more tension-ridden, controversy-prone post than president of a news network. Even before Spiro Agnew's intemperate condemnation of TV newscasters as "nattering nabobs of negativism," a phrase punched out on the typewriter of White House speechwriter William Safire, news was under heavy fire by many factions in the nation. Its power was feared and those who tried to control it seemed to believe that newsmen were prejudiced, partisan, subjective, harping critics of our society.

In fact, most newsmen were the most objective, most edited and supervised of all public spokesmen. They certainly were often critical of major American institutions, of big business and of labor, of Congress and the administration. That is truly their mission. Reporters are signalmen on the watchtowers of society. It is their job to look for potential enemies and dangers. Who else would do it? Could you conceive of a president or a secretary of state, or a labor leader or a corporate executive, calling a news conference to announce "a grave mistake I made today"? If newsmen do not dig out the facts of corruption in the Teamsters or the illegal sale of arms to Iran and diverting of funds, just who will? Sometimes members of Congress or other government agents will discover evidence of wrongdoing, but the media are the ones that bring it to the attention of the public.

We are, by the nature of our mission, almost always in an adversarial stance against the powers that be. It is not for us to be the cheerleaders of society. There are enough people in public affairs or private ventures to laud their own efforts and they do not fail to do so. It is for us to reveal their shortcomings and failures. But no one likes a critic, and newsmen are rarely liked. Walter Cronkite was a rare exception in his career. He was so highly regarded as a totally honest man that when Walter went to Vietnam, witnessed the Communist Tet offensive and began seriously, for the first time, to criticize the war there, President Johnson told his staff that it was all over. "If Walter has turned against us, it's a lost cause," Johnson concluded.

Fred Friendly's tenure as chief of CBS News was destined to be brief and stormy. Fred was a brilliant producer, one of the best in TV history, but his temperament was not suited to executive management. He was always convinced of his own wisdom and was often right. But management is concerned with more than being right. It worries about corporate "image" and the vulnerability of the corporation to pressures from government and advertisers. That is not a proper concern of a newsman. It certainly was not a priority concern for Friendly.

The inevitable, ultimate clash began in February 1966, when the chairman of the Foreign Relations Committee, Senator J. William Fulbright, whose own right-wing enemies dubbed him Senator "Halfbright," scheduled a series of hearings on the war in Vietnam. I was one of the many witnesses called by the senator, along with others from journalism, the military, the administration, and academia. I testified for hours, highly critical of the war, in its concept and its execution. Fulbright staffers kept me informed on the fighting in and about CBS News coverage of the war.

Friendly decided that the war was of immediate and historical importance and required the fullest coverage. He told management that he planned to cover the hearings from start to finish each day, in full and live on the air. CBS News was highly praised when it gave full time to a World War II hero, General James Gavin. Gavin was a tough, blunt-speaking witness. He clashed with several senators on the committee, as well as with his fellow officers. It was the first full airing of the issues of the war both by reporters and by some of the most illustrious leaders of our country.

Unfortunately, the full coverage necessitated the preemption of many profitable daytime programs. In one day, Friendly canceled some $250,000 of commercial programs. This loss was debited to the budget of the News Division, a management device to put tight reins on Friendly. President Frank Stanton, who had personally approved Friendly's decision to cover the Gavin testimony in full, became uneasy when it became apparent that Friendly intended to cover all the witnesses in full.

The day after the Gavin testimony, Fred told Stanton he was again going to preempt the daytime shows in order to cover the testimony of another famed witness, George Kennan, America's most respected expert on Soviet and Communist affairs, the architect of the Truman-Acheson policy of containment of Russia, a man whose patriotic credentials were beyond reproach. A professor at Princeton after having been a high-ranking State Department official, Kennan had a powerful voice and an influential following.

Friendly did not know the storm that was brewing on the thirty-fifth floor of Black Rock in the office of the all-high leader William S. Paley. Paley had just turned sixty-five, the official retirement age for CBS employees. But Paley was no simple employee. He was the chairman and the principal single stockholder, the father of the network that he had created. He had no intention of retiring. Rules were made for others, not for Bill Paley. And he would not let anyone take decisions that he felt were harmful or costly to his network.

Stanton, the heir apparent, knew he would have to be patient and wait until Paley himself decided to retire. Any attempt on Stanton's part to force the decision would end his hopes of succeeding Paley. A wily corporate politician, Stanton arranged to tell the board of directors that it was unwise to insist on the retirement of the brilliant chairman and principal single stockowner. He proposed that the age sixty-five retirement rule be waived in the case of Paley. It was speedily seconded and voted on unanimously.

Another board vote would bring on a crisis for Friendly that would end in his leaving CBS. It was a decision to promote John Schneider, from president of the TV network to group vice-president for all broadcasting. This would give him control of all broadcast divisions beyond the TV entertainment network. And that meant CBS News. Friendly, as president of CBS News, was used to reporting directly to Frank Stanton, the corporate president, even to the chairman himself. Now, a new layer of corporate management was being put into place, cutting off Friendly's access to top management. His foam-flecked horse was running head-on into a brick wall.

Friendly's decision to cover the testimony of George Kennan in full would cost CBS network another couple of hundred thousand dollars. What Schneider would do about that was a foregone conclusion. He simply overruled Friendly. Fred was furious. In all his years at CBS, the News Division only reported to the top. He told Frank Stanton that the new reorganization plan was a grave error. News could not function under a group vice-president who had no knowledge of the news and little interest in it, whose God was the bottom line and profit, without regard for the public trust and the public's right to know, particularly on as grave an issue as war.

Fred's outburst overlooked the fact that Stanton had approved the reorganization and that Fred was directly challenging the very man whose support he was seeking. This was, to say the least, an extremely unwise approach to Fred's problem. Instead of attacking the corporate reorganization, Fred could have challenged the wisdom of Schneider's decision and asked Stanton to rule for the News Division. By attacking Stanton himself, he was digging his own grave.

Fred would not back down. He persisted, reminding Stanton that when he had appointed Friendly head of News, Stanton had promised that he could report directly to him and to Paley. Now, Fred was not only criticizing Stanton's corporate decision but attacking his personal integrity. He told Stanton, "This will not do. Unless your order is rescinded, I will have to resign."

Stanton, his own deep reservoirs of patience drying up, quietly told Fred to "sleep on it and think it through." That was as close as Stanton would come at that point to telling Fred that, if he insisted, his resignation would be accepted. Fred probably understood this and had already made up his mind to quit and to go out riding a white horse as the noble fighter for news for the public. The Schneider decision had so cut his power that he knew he could not live with it and this was a splendid issue to quit over, making Fred the hero of his peers, the defender of the public trust.

Friendly shot off a memo to Schneider, insisting on approval of full airing of the Kennan testimony. Schneider may not have been a newsman but he knew that Kennan's testimony would be highly technical, dry, complex, and academic, without the drama of the Gavin testimony. It would have a small daytime audience and cost a fortune. Schneider offered Fred a reasonable compromise, to tape the Kennan testimony and present highlights on the evening news with a vast national audience. This was not illogical and it was not a hucksterish decision.

Friendly, riding his foam-flecked horse, would hear nothing of any compromise. He fired back another memo to Schneider telling him to approve his original plan or he would quit. When a man threatens to resign more than once, to two different top executives, you can be sure his offer will be accepted. Schneider simply told Fred he could not grant his request and he could do whatever he thought best.

Friendly's best thought was to take his case to his old friend Bill Paley, who had so often supported him in the past in even more difficult cases, such as the decision to do "See It Now" on Senator Joseph McCarthy. He went to see Paley over the heads of Schneider and Stanton. Don Quixote could not have done it better. He argued long, forcefully, and combatively. He told Paley that NBC was providing full coverage while Schneider was putting on reruns of "I Love Lucy," which would make CBS look ridiculous. The comparison was not well chosen. Paley was angered by being told CBS was ridiculous.

Paley had long felt that Friendly and other top News Division personnel had grown arrogant and undisciplined. He was no longer the Bill Paley who had approved the "See It Now" on McCarthy. He had already forced Ed Murrow, his greatest star and closest friend, out of CBS. Paley was not going to be pushed around by Fred Friendly. If he yielded to Fred, he would be disavowing both Stanton and Schneider and undermining his entire hierarchical corporate structure.

Paley explained this to Fred. He knew his fine qualities and did not want to lose him. But Fred, now a kamikaze, offered for the third time to resign. Paley told him he hoped Fred would not resign but that he was ready to work out a generous severance pay if Fred insisted. That was the kindest way to accept his resignation and to honor all the splendid work that Fred had performed over the years for CBS. Paley proposed that they both announce their regrets, mutual respects, and affection, no denunciations, just a friendly (no pun intended) separation.

CBS did give Fred a generous (for those times) severance of $400,000. Fred took the money but broke the agreement. He sent a scorching letter to *The New York Times* in violation of his pledge on no denunciations. Paley exploded. He called Fred and told him that he had broken his word and was seeking public vindication at the expense of the network that had made him famous and wealthy.

Fred had achieved his purpose. He did not want to stay on under John Schneider. His authority as the head of News had been undercut. He wanted to go out as the White Knight of News fighting a noble cause. He was the hero of all newsmen, fighting for George Kennan on the Vietnam War against old reruns of "I Love Lucy." Hundreds of thousands of Americans were fighting, falling wounded and dying in Vietnam. The good name and the prestige of the nation was at stake and CBS was rerunning a tired old comedy.

Fred made CBS look very bad. It was not fair. They had not refused to cover Kennan, they had only suggested that a much bigger, far more influential audience be given the most important remarks of Kennan. But it did not sound that way. Fred made CBS look like cheap hucksters interested only in commercial money and not in the greater good of the United States. After all, he was no Don Quixote. He knew exactly what real windmills he was tilting at and why.

The hero of news, some $400,000 richer, Friendly got two very good jobs at once: as full professor at the Columbia University Graduate School of Journalism and a highly paid consultant on public affairs to the prestigious Ford Foundation, then headed up by President Kennedy's former chief of national security, McGeorge Bundy. Bundy, coincidentally, was one of those best and brightest men guilty of plunging us into the Vietnam War. Strange that Friendly, who quit CBS over the issue of airing criticism of that war, should then become a consultant to one of the architects of that same war.

Fred became a much admired and popular professor at Columbia University and an increasingly valuable spokesman for the Ford Foundation on telecommunications and First Amendment challenges to the media. Friendly testified often and well before congressional committees and achieved the stature of an elder statesman of the communications industry. A good man cannot be held down, particularly one who rides a foam-flecked horse.

Fred calmed down somewhat in his elder-statesman years, but his energy still flowed unchecked. He could not be content merely to teach or to advise. He simply had to get back into active production. He did. On the occasion of the two-hundredth anniversary of the Constitution, Friendly persuaded the Public Broadcasting System (PBS), the educational network, to provide time for a series of documentaries on the Constitution.

Friendly produced, wrote, and narrated the scripts himself. At last he had realized his ultimate dream, a program with no correspondents, no executive overseers, no writers, no one but Fred Friendly himself. Fred did it all, à la Orson Welles. In all fairness, as one of the men who clashed often with Fred over his dictatorial behavior, let me say that he did it surpassingly well. His series on the Constitution was one of the very best of the bicentennial year. It was well-produced, well-written, and, if Fred is no Ed Murrow, he nonetheless did a creditable job as narrator. Fred Friendly is a towering figure of talent and brains, one of the greats of the greatest years of television history.

9

"60 MINUTES"
AND THE
SEVENTIES

In the closing years of the sixties, CBS News tried its luck with a new documentary program that would stumble off to an awkward start and then become the big surprise of the seventies and the national hit of the eighties. It was called "60 Minutes."

"60 Minutes" made its debut on September 24, 1968, in the same time slot that had earlier been given to "CBS Reports." "CBS Reports" had run its course and was no longer getting an audience. Producer Don Hewitt, who conceived "60 Minutes," felt he would get nowhere in that time slot, alternating with a fading "CBS Reports," and that proved to be the case at the start. "60 Minutes" got low ratings and was put down by the critics. *Time* magazine damned it with faint praise: "It's a good cub reporter's try." As a result, "60 Minutes" was often preempted by a special, and that generally signals the death of a series.

Producer Hewitt was in despair when, after futile years of his efforts, "60 Minutes" was moved to Sundays at 6:00 P.M. This meant it would be wiped out during the entire football season when games ran past 6:00 P.M. Don was certain he had failed. The show did poorly and was used as a kind of "filler" on the schedule. It staggered, always on the point of cancellation, from 1968 to 1975, seven years in purgatory, if not in the depths of hell.

After a brief trial run from July to September 1975 at 9:30 P.M. with no visible improvement in the ratings, management decided to move "60 Minutes" to 7:00 P.M. That was a time period that the FCC had set aside for public affairs or children's programs in the prime-time access period. ABC and NBC had already opted to run children's programs in that slot. So "60 Minutes" ended up there without any adult rival programs on a good listening hour on Sunday evenings. It was out from under football and other sports. This decision, taken routinely, with little discussion or thought about what it might produce, became a turning point.

In its very first year at 7:00 P.M., "60 Minutes" won first place for that hour. It also won a top management decision to exempt it from any football overruns. If a long, sudden-death game ran into the "60 Minutes" time slot, the program would nevertheless be shown in its entirety. All other programs following it would be bumped back, until "60 Minutes" ended. In its second year under this system, "60 Minutes," for the first time, shot up in the ratings to break into the top-ten shows of the nation. By the 1980s, it was in first place week after week. As we now approach the 1990s, "60 Minutes," with more than twenty years on the air, has become the all-time top-rated news show in television history. It has consistently beaten some of the most popular entertainment shows, at times outrating even the biggest hit, "The Cosby Show," and many others. It is now number three on the all-time list of programs in the top ten for twenty years, right after the number-one show, "I Love Lucy," which ran fifteen consecutive years in the top ten, and the number-two program, "Gunsmoke," thirteen consecutive years. Don Hewitt is now recognized as the greatest television news producer of all times, the resident genius of CBS News.

Hewitt did not, of course, manage all this by himself. He is, after all, only the producer, behind the cameras, and, like a football or baseball coach, he can't be any better than his players on the field. But he chose those players, guided them, gave them what they needed, made all the important decisions on stories to be covered, so Hewitt does deserve the credit for the success of "60 Minutes," the child he conceived and reared.

It was Don Hewitt who picked Mike Wallace and then talked him out of the absurd idea he had of accepting President Nixon's offer to be his press spokesman at the White House. Don told Mike that "a press spokesman is a nobody trying to become somebody. You're there already and there are no limits on how far you can go on this program." Mike took his advice, turned Nixon down, and went on to fame and fortune on "60 Minutes." Now press spokesmen bow to Mike Wallace.

Don then persuaded Morley Safer, who was happily ensconced as London bureau chief, into leaving London and coming home to report on "60 Minutes." Morley was resistant to the invitation, but finally agreed on the condition that if "60 Minutes" were canceled he could go back to his post in London. Twenty years later, Safer is now a fixture on "60 Minutes," a member of its "millionaire's club." (A million a year is the average salary on "60 Minutes.")

Don also recruited Harry Reasoner, who has had an astonishing career, in some ways beyond his talents. He is a very lucky man. Reasoner achieved national recognition on "60 Minutes." He had had instant name recognition on CBS. Because of that, he attracted the ABC news chief, Roone Arledge, who was starved for star quality at his network. Arledge made Reasoner an offer to co-anchor the ABC evening news with Howard K. Smith. He jumped at the chance, deserting CBS, which had made him a star, although he had no innate star qualities.

Reasoner was witty, sardonic, with a certain appeal and a lot of exposure. When he was later paired with Barbara Walters, their co-anchor performance was a disaster. Reasoner despised Walters, although she probably has more talent and audience appeal than he has. He simply ignored her, as though she were not sitting next to him. At lunch at the Café des Artistes, near the ABC studios, Harry would sit with his cronies and publicly bad-mouth Barbara. Arledge finally gave up on him and let him go when Reasoner asked to return to CBS. Arledge then gave Walters a program at which she could excel, her own interview specials with world celebrities, which have been successful money and ratings earners for ABC.

Astonishingly, CBS News did take Harry back. Normally, anyone who leaves CBS is considered a traitor. But what Don Hewitt wants, Don Hewitt gets. Harry did well until he almost lost his career and his life when he underwent lung surgery in 1987. Happily, he recovered and signed a new contract through 1989. Reasoner is a remarkable survivor in television and in life.

There was a strange, amusing incident that occurred when Harry left CBS to go to ABC. He had been the anchor on the Sunday evening news program. When he left, CBS correspondent Dan Rather went to management and asked to replace Harry as the Sunday anchor. He was turned down by Vice-President Gordon Manning who told him that he did not have the qualities to be a good anchorman on news, that he was a reporter, not an anchorman. This was not Gordon Manning's finest hour. Yet, he was usually one of the most astute editors in journalism.

Don Hewitt continued to have a magic managerial wand. Everyone he touched became a star. Hewitt was the first producer to give a black American, Ed Bradley, a starring role on a top-ten show. Ed, a fine reporter, has succeeded brilliantly. Perhaps the greatest Hewitt wizardry was his transformation of Diane Sawyer. It is hard for those who only know Diane today, the glamorous beauty and first-rate reporter of "60 Minutes," to imagine that she ever could have been a flop on the "CBS Morning News," that graveyard of the stars. She was so eager to make good as a news reporter and not a blonde beauty that she didn't care much about how she looked. She desperately wanted to be accepted as a professional journalist and also live down her background, which had brought her into CBS under clouds of suspicion and misgivings.

Diane had served Richard Nixon for four years in the White House as a researcher and writer. When Nixon was forced out in disgrace and went skulking off to San Clemente, Diane, loyal to him, went along with him. She stayed there with him another four years helping collate his voluminous papers. It is said that if you make a mistake once, that is forgivable, but if you make the same mistake twice, that is a sin. And CBS news people felt that Sawyer had sinned doing two four-year stints with Richard Nixon.

She gritted her teeth and just went on with her job as State Department reporter for CBS. She worked hard and did well and gradually the clouds began to fade away. Then they tried her out on the ill-starred morning news, where nothing ever succeeded, and she was down on the last rung of the ladder again.

Don Hewitt saw her raw talent and untouched beauty and knew how to make her come alive and radiant. To her credit, she took every tough assignment he threw at her to test her mettle, and her mettle turned out to be pure gold.

Diane walked among lepers in India and Africa, camped out in tents, sweltering by day, freezing at night, attacked by swarms of mosquitoes and chiggers and every kind of voracious insect and vermin. She gave Hewitt an exciting exclusive report when she went to the Philippines and, at a secret hideaway, interviewed rebel leader Colonel Gregorio Honasan, who was trying to overthrow President Corazón Aquino. Diane did this while Aquino's patrols were trying hard to find Honasan. They didn't, Diane did.

Diane Sawyer has more than earned her spurs as the equal of any man on "60 Minutes." At times, she seems to have learned some of their ways too well. She sometimes comes on as a female Mike Wallace, Ms. District Attorney, finger pointing, probing, and asking questions that are not only tough, which is legitimate, but often rude, which is in bad taste and not worthy of her. One such performance took place in an interview with Vice-President George Bush. Sawyer told him that a magazine writer had called him a wimp. She looked at him with beady eyes and snapped, "Are you a wimp?" Now, even if one is not an admirer of George Bush, he was the vice-president and his office demanded respect. In even worse taste was Diane's interview with John Connally after he had lost his fortune, auctioned off all his possessions, and was dead broke at age seventy-three. On camera, you could see Connally's ravaged, lined, defeated face. Then you could see the vibrant young beauty of Diane Sawyer. She looked at Connally and asked, "How could you come to this end?" He said sorrowfully, "Well, I made about four hundred millions in the oil boom, invested every cent of it, and then lost it all when oil went bust." Diane, radiantly young opposite this broken old man, then asked, "Were you stupid?"

As I watched and listened to that destructive sally, I felt as though I had been hit in the pit of my stomach. I admire Diane and I was ashamed for her. How could she possibly have said this to this utterly destroyed old man? Diane has tried too hard and succeeded too well to prove she is a top-flight journalist to risk her reputation that way.

"60 Minutes" was the great success of the seventies, which was an otherwise stormy period, with crisis following upon crisis at Black Rock and West 57th Street. John Schneider, the vice-president of the Broadcast Group, had been promoted to president of the network and had been promised he would move up even higher when Bill Paley finally retired. At that point, it was thought, Frank Stanton, the ever-patient corporation president, second in command to Paley, would finally realize his dream of becoming chairman. Schneider would then step into Stanton's office as corporate president. At age forty-three, Schneider was being readied for the biggest job in broadcasting.

Schneider walked into the climactic board meeting on a high, his feet barely touching the floor. Then his world came crashing down, as he sat and listened, not believing his ears, as board directors praised Paley, called him "the soul of CBS," and pleaded with him to stay on even though he was sixty-five and at the mandatory retirement age. There are no mandates on Bill Paley. He was the creator and single biggest individual stockholder, he was Mr. CBS. The board waived the retirement limit for him and he graciously agreed to stay on as chairman. Stanton's dream and Schneider's visions were crushed. Schneider later told associates that it was "the double cross of all times." Stanton, as ever, was stoic, the only sign of distress were his twitching jaw muscles. As a sop, he was "promoted" to vice-chairman. Still the bridesmaid, never the bride.

In a talk at his office, outside CBS, some years later, Stanton told me of another double cross. When he reached sixty-five, Paley asked him to stay on just a little longer, for they were having trouble finding his successor. Frank agreed but requested certain perks in return. He asked Paley to provide him with an outside office, a secretary, car and driver, modest perks for a man who, as much as Paley, had built CBS for some forty years. Paley agreed. But when the time came for Frank to leave, Paley reneged on the agreement. He told Stanton that CBS had made him a multimillionaire, and that should be enough. Stanton, outraged by this pettiness and bad faith, went to the chairman of the powerful Finance Committee of the Board of Directors and told him what happened. All the directors were angry. In a rare move they overruled Paley and Stanton got his office, secretary, and driver. On March 23, 1973, Frank Stanton left the company he had built. He turned down Paley's offer of a farewell party. He simply threw his keys on his desk and walked out, bitter and saddened by the experience.

Stanton was not the only old friend to be treated rudely by Paley. Paley's personal attorney and outside CBS counsel, Ralph Colin, a leader of New York society, famed art collector, with the world's most important collection of the works of Soutine, thought he was a close personal friend of Paley. He was to discover that he was not. Colin differed with Paley over procedures involving the forced resignation of Bates Lowry, director of the Museum of Modern Art. He opposed Paley at a museum board meeting. It was simply a difference of opinion on a matter of no earthshaking importance. Paley, however, did not easily brook opposition. He was so used to his word being law at CBS that he thought it was also law everywhere.

Paley felt that Colin had been disloyal to him, had contradicted and humiliated him publicly, although all Ralph Colin had done was to disagree with him. Paley called Colin into his office at CBS and summarily fired him as his personal attorney and as CBS counsel after forty-two years of service. Colin, shocked, attempted a personal reconciliation, quite apart from the job, which he no longer needed. He told Paley, "after all, Bill, we've been friends for forty-two years." Paley replied icily, "We were never friends. You were my attorney." Paley later denied that he had used those exact words, but Colin insisted that he had, and everyone knew that, whatever the words, Paley's meaning had been clear.

Paley, like other humans, also had his own favorite dream. Even a chairman could have greater visions. He wanted more than anything else to be the U.S. Ambassador to the Court of St. James' in London. Paley had been a friend and supporter of President Eisenhower but he was also high on President Nixon's paranoid "enemies list." President Nixon hated CBS, and his hatchet man, Spiro Agnew, viciously assailed CBS and all the media. Paley's dream was not to be realized.

Nixon and CBS were at swords' points all through the Nixon years. In June 1970, the FCC ruled that the networks be required to provide air time, under the Fairness Doctrine, to answer President Nixon's prime-time speeches defending his Vietnam policy. Paley had opposed the Fairness Doctrine as "government intrusion on a private network's decision on how to cover the news and make news policy." He was absolutely right. The FCC would not relax its rules and Paley was forced to comply with the decision.

Frank Stanton did not like the rule either but he went along with it and recommended that the air time be given to the opposition party, the Democratic National Committee. "Let the party choose the spokesman to answer Nixon," Stanton advised, "then the White House can't complain to us if it doesn't like the reply." It was so decided. The Democrats chose a veteran Kennedy New Frontiersman, one of the "Boston Irish Mafia," Larry O'Brien, to answer Nixon. O'Brien, a shrewd pol, was no orator. He gave a poor, rambling performance and even used the time to appeal for funds for the Democratic Party.

Stanton became convinced that CBS News had to answer government officials itself. CBS had a long, successful tradition of "instant analysis" following a presidential speech. Nixon and Agnew railed against this procedure, claiming that the people had the right to hear their president without immediate and confusing contradictions from the "nattering nabobs" of the media. It was Paley, weary of the constant struggle, who caved in and proposed that, instead of instant analysis by CBS News correspondents, the network provide time to an appropriate spokesman. Back to the Fairness Doctrine.

The public did not at all agree. It liked the lively, democratic opposition of the correspondents to the authorities. That is democracy's shield against dictatorship. The editorial writers across the country sided with the correspondents against Paley's decision to muzzle them. Letters poured in accusing CBS of knuckling down to White House pressures. Criticism of CBS was severe and widespread. It surprised Paley. He became convinced that he had erred when he dined with an old friend, Averell Harriman. Harriman was one of the nation's most dedicated, highest-ranking, and most admired public servants, one of the greatest diplomats in all American history, ambassador to London, to Moscow, to NATO, administrator of Lend-Lease during the war. He was also one of the wealthiest men in the world, far richer than his rich friend Bill Paley. He was everything that Paley aspired to be.

Paley knew he had been wrong when Harriman told him, "Bill, that was a damn foolish thing to do." Only a Harriman would dare tell Paley that. Instant analysis was immediately, albeit briefly, reinstated. White House pressures proved more powerful in the long run than the advice of an old, rich friend. After Stanton left CBS, Paley, without his strong right arm, surrendered again and instant analysis was silenced.

Nixon clashed again with CBS News with millions watching the exchange. It occurred at a Nixon news conference during the election campaign. When Dan Rather, the White House correspondent, arose to question him, boos and cheers rang through the hall. The boos came from Nixon acolytes spread through the room, the cheers from fellow correspondents expressing their support for Dan. As the noise erupted, Nixon, on the stage, looked down at Rather and asked with heavy sarcasm, "Are you running for something?" Dan, always impulsive, snapped right back, "No, sir, are you?" More boos, more cheers! Not the most dignified scene at a presidential news conference.

Dan was in trouble. It is one thing, perfectly legitimate, to challenge a president with tough questions. It is something quite different for a reporter to engage in a sassing contest with the nation's chief executive, no matter how obnoxious and wrong the president may be. CBS management was unhappy but felt obliged to support Dan. There were vehement denials of any planned punitive action against him. Nevertheless, when, some time later, Dan was transferred from his White House post to become anchorman for "CBS Reports," a lesser assignment, it was widely believed it was a delayed disciplinary action. Dan was depressed and feared that he had injured his career at CBS News. He had, but Rather is a fighter, a driven man of talent and forceful personality. He would rebound from a temporary setback.

Meanwhile, CBS was agonizing through a series of top management shifts and challenges to its programs. The most serious challenge came over the documentary program "The Selling of the Pentagon," in February 1971. Producers used Pentagon film clips and statements to explore controversial practices of the Pentagon in propagandizing the public in favor of its policies and procurements. It had thousands of public relations officers "selling" military views to the public, all at the taxpayers' expense. This took place during the already heated debates over the war in Vietnam. Pentagon analysts, examining the CBS program, charged a number of questionable practices by CBS News, such as slanted editing, splicing, and other editorial devices that made the Pentagon look bad.

A congressman from West Virginia, Harley Staggers, head of the Commerce Committee, with jurisdiction over the FCC, which regulates broadcasting, was outraged by the CBS News documentary. He subpoenaed CBS President Frank Stanton and ordered him to turn over all the "outtakes" of the report, that is films or tapes taken but not used, which might have affected the overall tone of the documentary. The congressman was, in effect, asking to edit CBS.

Stanton felt that freedom of the press was the issue. Dr. Stanton was an effective, determined champion of the First Amendment. He defied the House committee chairman and refused to supply the outtakes to the committee. Congressman Staggers was angered by Stanton's defiance and threatened to cite him for contempt of Congress. Stanton again refused. On June 30, 1971, the committee voted overwhelmingly to hold Stanton in contempt, making him liable to a jail sentence. The case was scheduled for debate and a final decision by the whole House. It was the gravest conflict ever between the Congress and a major national network, with unforeseen consequences for freedom of the press. A confirmed contempt charge, sending a network president to prison for many years, would have the most chilling effect on all reporters, editors, newscasters, and producers for years ahead.

Bill Paley, surprisingly, kept his distance from the conflict. Stanton might have expected full support from the chairman of his network, for the network itself had been cited along with Stanton. But Paley did nothing, leaving the fight in the hands of Stanton and CBS News President Richard Salant. Paley, in fact, was deeply disturbed about the techniques used on the documentary. He had heard, for the first time, about "reversals," that is the technique of shooting the interviewee on one camera, and then, when the interview ended, reversing the camera and shooting the reporter asking the questions he had posed in the interview. It was a handy and cheap technique to avoid the cost of a two-camera team shooting the interviewee and the interviewer simultaneously. It was legitimate in honest hands. But it could easily be misused by the correspondent asking his questions differently during the reversal shots. Paley, committed to total integrity of the news, felt uneasy about a technique so open to distortion. All the networks used it, but that was no excuse for Paley.

Finally, Paley called Stanton in to talk about the case. He agreed that CBS should not surrender to government demands to analyze and sit in judgment on their editorial procedures. The First Amendment was the heart of the case and on that there could be no compromise, whether CBS was at fault or not. As Louis Nizer once put it, "The First Amendment gives everyone the right to make a damn fool of himself, to distort, to lie, on conditions that they face the consequences under other laws, such as defamation, libel, or whatever." But under the freedom of the press law the media had to be free of government censorship or controls.

The case came to a conclusion in July, when the whole House rejected the Commerce Committee's citation by the margin of 226 to 181, a victory, but too close for comfort. It was deeply disturbing that 181 members had voted to cite the network for contempt. It was less a victory for Stanton than an escape from prison. The network's good name had been badly smeared.

A year later, CBS was again embroiled in a controversy. *The Washington Post* had broken the story of Watergate and had relentlessly explored a series of misdeeds day after day. Other papers got into the investigation but the networks were strangely silent. Friends at CBS told me that the story was too complicated to handle on the air, requiring a great deal of time to unravel all the threads, and that editors at the network did not know how to cope with Watergate. NBC and ABC sources confirmed this dilemma.

The day came when Walter Cronkite, who had been brooding about the lack of coverage, decided he would have to tackle Watergate. He prepared his report, only to discover, as his editors had warned, that a full airing was simply too long for his brief twenty-two minutes of airtime on the evening news. They could not cover Watergate and all the national and world news in that time bind.

Walter and his editors went over his report and broke it up into two segments to be aired on succeeding nights. The first report went on the air October 27, 1972. The White House point man, Charles Colson, called Frank Stanton at once and accused CBS of a vendetta against Nixon. Stanton told him, in effect, to go to the devil. Frank was fed up with all the pressures and threats against him and was tensed for a fight if that was what Nixon wanted. He let Colson know this.

What made this issue particularly sensitive is that it was very close to the presidential election. Nixon was running for a second term against George McGovern. Hardly anyone had any doubt that Nixon would crush McGovern, but Nixon and his men saw enemies everywhere. The principle of running a scandal story implicating the president just before an election was a valid question, whether Nixon was sure to win or not. Most of us newsmen agreed that the Cronkite piece was justified. After all, it was not CBS that had caused the scandal or chosen the timing of the affair; it was Nixon himself.

Paley watched the Cronkite report on Watergate, as did Stanton. They both thought the segment was much too long, more than half the entire news program. They also felt that Cronkite looked high-handed and unbalanced in his treatment of the story, a rare criticism of the most respected and trusted newscaster in the country. Paley asked Stanton to instruct CBS News President Richard Salant to keep a sharp eye and tight rein on Cronkite until after election day, indeed thereafter. Never before had top management ordered editorial supervision of Walter Cronkite. Yet, of course, management did have the right to supervise him.

Charles Colson once again called making threats. Paley finally was infuriated. He told Stanton that Colson was a "monster," that he was evil, and that Paley would not tolerate his threats. Paley was not alone in thinking that Colson was a monster. Reporters had all heard him say that he would run over his own grandmother in a car if that would help Nixon. Many journalists cheered when Colson finally ended up in prison, and they could not credit it when he came out to announce that he was henceforth going to be a crusader of Christ and help the oppressed and the downtrodden.

Cronkite planned his second Watergate report to air on October 30, right before the election. He paid little attention to Salant's attempts to tighten the reins on him. Paley then called in his top staff for an early-morning meeting on October 30th: Stanton, Salant, Jack Schneider, and the newly appointed president of CBS, Inc., Arthur Taylor.

Top executives were going in and out through revolving doors. Stanton had given up his portfolio as president and been moved up to vice-chairman. Stanton was approaching the retirement age and Paley was busy looking for his successor. Schneider, once the heir apparent, had been bypassed and moved back to being president of the Broadcast Group. He had eliminated himself by refusing to answer Paley's many memos, his "thunderbolts" from Olympus, airily dismissing them as "silly nonsense." Word got back to Paley, and Schneider lost his chance to go to the top.

Paley had called on an executive search agency, which had chosen Arthur Taylor, only thirty-seven, a vice-president of International Paper. He was famed for his energy and his scholarship, rivaling Dr. Stanton with his own Ph.D. earned in history at Brown. His record was impressive, but what pleased Paley most was that he had no previous experience in or knowledge of broadcasting. Paley felt he had no bad habits to unlearn. Taylor would come into broadcasting as a virgin, so to speak. Paley could seduce him and mold him into all the arts and skills of running a network.

Paley called in Taylor in 1972 and told him that Stanton would retire the next year. To tempt Taylor further, Paley hinted that he, too, having passed the retirement age, might finally decide to step down, leaving Taylor the number-one man in the most prestigious network in the nation. That was the way to dazzle and seduce a virgin broadcasting executive. In fact, Paley had no intention whatsoever of retiring. Taylor was truly dazzled by the offer and accepted the job. He would get on-the-job training of what it would be like to work under Bill Paley at that October 30 meeting in Paley's office.

The issue of Cronkite's reports on Watergate had been thoroughly thrashed out a week earlier. It had been agreed that Stanton would instruct Richard Salant to supervise Cronkite. Paley did not want the "monster" to call again with new complaints and threats. He had not forgotten the anguish over the sloppy job done on "The Selling of the Pentagon." He wanted the Watergate report to be absolutely unchallengeable, which is of course impossible. No news report can be beyond reproach. Paley found fault with the

Cronkite report: "Much too long," looks like a "hit job," "not objective." Paley claimed that Cronkite had mixed fact with unproven charges.

Arthur Taylor watched and listened as News chief Salant tried to defend Cronkite and rebut Paley's charges. Paley waved off Salant, as though he were a pesky fruit fly. Paley did not go so far as to cancel the segment, already publicly scheduled, but he let Salant know that he would not tolerate a repetition of the first report, which he condemned as falling far short of CBS standards of objectivity and fairness.

Salant paled. He simply would not pass this on to Cronkite, who, despite his loyalty and high boiling point, would have exploded and probably quit, causing CBS News irreparable injury. Taylor, bemused at Paley's power play, watched CBS News President Salant stagger out of the meeting, white-faced and sweating. Taylor was getting an idea of what it was like to work at the top for a power-boss like the chairman.

Salant left Black Rock and returned to his dungeon in West 57th Street, a sinister-looking, windowless fortress, more like a penitentiary than a broadcast-news headquarters. Paley had blasted Cronkite but had given Salant no specific guidance for that evening's report, other than "watch it," which was not helpful. Salant knew that if that evening's segment was judged by Paley as severely as he had judged the first segment, Salant's job was on the line. It is much easier to replace a news chief than the anchorman. Salant did not want the threat to his job to influence his opinion of the new report that Cronkite had lined up. He was in hot water, for if Paley could blast him so could Cronkite. He knew he could make suggestions to Walter but not order him to do anything Walter did not want to do.

Salant sat down with his top staff of producers and editors to review elements of the new scheduled segment. They all insisted it was a good and fair report. They were taken aback by Salant's sudden tough review of the plan. They all liked Salant but they did not hold him in awe. They fought him hard and hotly when he decided to cut the segment down to eight minutes. Cronkite did not attend the staff meeting with Salant. His spies had already told him that it was not Salant but the chairman himself who was turning the screws. You don't win fights with the chairman, not even the top anchorman. Cronkite said nothing when Salant decreed that additional editing was required and that the segment would not air that night.

The decision to cut the segment down did not mollify the chairman. Paley watched the program when it went on the air and was again severely critical. He felt it was still too long, showed anti-Nixon bias, although no one else at the network thought so. Paley counted other opinions the way President Lincoln did: when seven Cabinet members voted "Aye," and Lincoln voted "no," Lincoln would announce: "The Nays have it." So too did Paley's negative overrule all the positives. He called in Salant and severely criticized the program. Salant was not dismayed because he found that the chairman, while critical, was not angry or vindictive.

Ironically, Paley would discover that other top people in the media looked upon CBS as their champion because of the Cronkite report that he had so disliked. His close friend and peer, Kay Graham, owner of *The Washington Post*, which had broken the Watergate story and felt out on a limb with too few followers, thanked him warmly for backing her up. She said that CBS News, with its large and influential national audience, had confirmed her paper and shielded it from savage attacks by the Nixon administration. Paley did not confess that he had tried to emasculate the Cronkite report. He put his arms around Kay and said modestly that CBS had done nothing much, it was the *Post*'s own story, but he was glad to have been of help. Thus he had it both ways, chastising his own staff and being complimented by his peers.

Paley knew that his troubles had not ended. Nixon's triumphant reelection signaled a continuation of his vindictive, paranoid administration. Confirmed by the American people, Nixon and his bully boys were poised for new attacks. In December 1972, Colson was back on the phone to Paley to complain about Cronkite. Paley put him off by promising to stop by and discuss it on his next trip to Washington.

Paley first saw H. R. Haldeman, Nixon's chief of staff. Paley denied any partisan news coverage by CBS. He challenged Haldeman to submit specific examples of bias and promised he would personally review every case. As a result of this promise to Haldeman, Paley began applying even stricter controls over CBS News. He was no longer the Paley who had been proud of his News Division and had given it every leeway and backing. This change of climate has been overlooked by many television critics and writers who have almost deified Ed Murrow and the reporters of my day and tend to denigrate by contrast today's broadcast journalists. Of course, the Murrow team was very good, but we were not without fault. And our greatest strength was the enthusiastic support of Bill Paley.

The rosy lens of nostalgia has made us bigger and greater than we were. The abrasions of today, and the change of heart of Paley, make contemporary newscasters seem smaller and less able than they are. There are very good, first-rate men and women reporting and broadcasting today, most of them as able as our team, but this is a different America, a different climate, and the network reporters are no longer unique and "heroic" as we were coming out of World War II.

The new golden boy of CBS, Arthur Taylor, stepped into Stanton's office as soon as Frank left. To the astonishment of Paley and the delight of the News Division, Taylor, who had seen what Paley was doing, became the new champion of News, our gallant knight protector. Taylor told Salant that he was prepared to propose to the board an extension of the evening news to a full hour, a demand that had been on the table without action for five years. The proposal became, however, a nonstarter, not because of Paley but because of the affiliates who refused to turn over an extra lucrative half-hour of ad time to the network. But the offer from Taylor had boosted News morale, for it showed that they did have someone fighting for them on the thirty-fifth floor of Black Rock, someone they very much needed with Paley's change of policy.

Paley had chosen Taylor so that he could mold him to his own views, but life is filled with the unintended consequences of our acts. Taylor may have been a virgin broadcasting executive but he was no puppet. He was, at thirty-seven, a highly competent and self-confident executive. At First Boston and International Paper, Taylor had been a highly praised and pampered "whiz kid," wielding great authority. He would not kowtow before Paley. Indeed, he dared talk back to him. When an angry Paley shouted at him, he shouted back. He sometimes stormed out of Paley's office, slamming the door so hard behind him that the paintings on the wall would rattle.

To everyone's surprise on Olympus, Paley not only tolerated this *lèse-majesté*, he even seemed to admire Taylor's spirit of independence. He praised Taylor to his associates and in public interviews. This only encouraged Taylor to assert himself more vigorously. Paley had passed his seventieth birthday and seemed to look upon Taylor as a strong-willed, outspoken son who would take over and care for the network Paley had created and made into a multibillion-dollar conglomerate. No other executive had ever been given the authority and tolerance that Paley gave Taylor.

It could not last. Paley, in his seventies, still had plenty of fire burning within him. He was in good health and felt he was as good as ever. Most of us yield to that self-deception. Paley's short fuse burned quickly when he and his network were then hit by another black series of events. None of the trouble was of Taylor's doing, but when you are in charge you get undue credit for what you did not do and can be wrecked by it when you are not at fault.

The first lightning bolt came from a former CBS News president, Sig Mickelson, who had been so unfairly fired because Huntley and Brinkley were consistently beating out Cronkite in the ratings. In February 1976, Mickelson revealed that Paley had worked secretly with the CIA back in the 1950s, our so-called Golden Age. Mickelson said he had been present in Paley's office when he met with CIA representatives. They were discussing the case of an undercover CIA agent, Austin Goodrich, to whom Paley had given CBS credentials as a cover. This disclosure generated immediate, widespread media attention.

CBS News was embarrassed but was obliged to report the story, for it was big news everywhere. Chief Washington political reporter Bruce Morton was assigned to interview Mickelson, on tape, not live, for some protection. It proved to be good protection because the taped interview somehow never made it on the air. Someone killed it. It is not difficult to imagine who that someone was. Paley denied the story at first but then conceded that perhaps his memory was faulty after a quarter of a century.

It was during this period, in 1976, that Paley and Arthur Taylor, his outspoken "son," began to clash more frequently and more heatedly. Taylor was increasingly indiscreet and told several associates on the top floor that Paley was "a crazy old man." He should have known that such a juicy quote would make its way back into the inner sanctum of the chairman. Paley was equally indiscreet, although he could afford to be. He told CBS News president Bill Leonard (Salant had fallen victim to the sixty-five-year-old guillotine) that "Arthur Taylor was getting too big for his britches." Since Taylor was Leonard's immediate boss, Paley was breaking his own rules and undercutting his top management. It was the beginning of the end for the erstwhile "whiz kid." On October 13, 1976, Arthur Taylor was out and another "whiz kid," forty-four-year-old John Backe, president of a textbook firm, was in. He would not last either. Paley, in his dotage, had become a serial killer of top management.

These tempests on the thirty-fifth floor of Black Rock were clear signals of the coming decline of CBS and CBS News. The original strength of CBS had been based on Bill Paley's creative insights and dedication, buttressed by the solid organizational and administrative skills of Frank Stanton, and their combined readiness to give an almost free hand to a talented staff of reporters, editors, and producers. That was the true origin and nature of the Golden Age and CBS's preeminent leadership of network news. There was unity at the top and creative talent throughout the organization. When the top began to clash with its own corporate managers, when Paley turned on his once-favored newsmen from Ed Murrow to Howard K. Smith to Cronkite—while moving presidents in and out of revolving doors—that is when the crisis of CBS that we see today took root. It is that process which finally cast an overly ambitious, irresponsible egotist like Van Gordon Sauter into the top spot at CBS News and then up to the corporate level.

New York Times reporter Peter Boyer was quite correct in identifying Sauter as the gravedigger of CBS News, the villain who brought about its crises and decline. But Sauter was more the symptom of a wasting disease that had rotted CBS structures for years, at levels higher than Sauter. If there is a villain in the case, it is not Sauter, although he certainly mismanaged CBS News. There is a more important guilty party. Sadly, it is the man who, in his youthful genius, made CBS and then lost his judgment and became a cantankerous, willful old man, Bill Paley himself. The chaotic corporate turmoil of the seventies, the interference with CBS News operations, the attempts to censor Cronkite, all these were the seeds of destruction that produced the poisoned plants that would choke CBS News in the eighties.

Time and circumstances have changed the nature of newscasting. We used to deal in ideas, facts, substance, analysis. Today that has been largely thrust aside for sights and sounds. There is nothing wrong with great pictures. TV is after all a visual medium. This is what TV news does best. But it must be more than just a visual medium. It is not always true that a picture is worth a thousand words, perhaps it is not even often true. Ideas and understanding cannot be ignored. As Attorney General Robert Kennedy once told me: "You can't take a meaningful picture of a writ of mandamus or a Supreme Court decision. You need an articulate, well-informed specialist to explain it." Pictures enhance but cannot substitute for words. TV has gone too far away from ideas and intelligence, indulging too much in "human" stories, as though the issue of choosing a Supreme Court justice is not an interesting "human" story.

Television has gone as far as it can in sight, sound, glitter, and glitz. It is time to bring back what made it great, time to bring back substance, thought, analysis, urgently needed in an ever more complex world. TV news also needs more time to do its job. A half-hour program, cut down to some twenty-four minutes by commercials, is simply not long enough to cover national and world affairs. Anchormen are often obliged to switch every twenty seconds from news item to news item; that is no way to report important issues. There is not enough time to document or analyze news developments.

With all these handicaps, it is astonishing how well the networks do cover the news. It is clear that only the networks can do what the networks are doing. No one else has global correspondents, no local station or service has more than a thousand employees or the vast budgets of the networks. Even cutting CBS News down from $300 million news budgets to $270 million still leaves it far ahead of any possible non-network rivals. No one else even wants to try to do what the networks do.

TV news will not disappear, because it is vitally needed. Television network news unites the entire nation and creates the global village. Should the doomsayers be right, should network news die, a majority of the people of America would have no consistent, reliable view of the nation's and the world's affairs. We would all be even less informed than we are now. Such a development could lead not only to the decline of television news but to the decline of our civilization, for the two, television and society, have developed an inseparable symbiosis. Television not only reports the news, it participates in it. It is both the mirror of our society and its energizer.

POSTSCRIPT

David Schoenbrun was a member of the best team of foreign correspondents ever assembled. They were the best of the breed. Every time I think of them, I think of an incident years ago at the Vanderbilt mansion. Reporters for the New York dailies had descended on the house, and the butler told Mrs. Vanderbilt, "Madam, there are several reporters here and a gentleman from the *Herald Tribune*." That's how I always thought about David and his colleagues: there were the reporters from ABC and NBC, and the gentlemen from CBS. There were Schoenbrun and Murrow and Smith and Sevareid and Burdette and Kendrick and Hottelet. In those days there were two famous addresses in Paris. One was 21 rue de Berri, the headquarters of the *Herald Tribune*, and the other was 33 Champs d' Elysées, where David Schoenbrun hung his hat. Schoenbrun's apartment on avenue Bosquet at rue Cognac-Jay became a stopping-off place for everybody who was anybody who was coming to Paris. And I remember David looking wistfully out of the window in the front room, the one that looked out on the Eiffel Tower, and saying to me, "There's only one thing to do." "So, what's that, David?" I asked. He said, "The United States has got to buy Paris and make it into a national park because the goddamned French are going to ruin it."

Well, we didn't buy it, the French didn't ruin it, but one of its most famous landmarks is gone, and we're all the poorer because of it.

DON HEWITT